More praise for Nigeria: A New History of a Turbulent Century

'This book is a major achievement and I defy anyone who reads it not to learn from it and gain greater understanding of the nature and development of a major African nation.'

Lalage Bown, professor emeritus, Glasgow University

'Richard Bourne's meticulously researched book is a major addition to Nigerian history.'

Guy Arnold, author of Africa: A Modern History

'This is a charming read that will educate the general reader, while allowing specialists additional insights to build upon. It deserves an audience far beyond the confines of Nigerian studies.'

Toyin Falola, African Studies Association and the University of Texas at Austin

About the author

Richard Bourne is senior research fellow at the Institute of Commonwealth Studies, University of London and a trustee of the Ramphal Institute, London. He is a former journalist, active in Commonwealth affairs since 1982 when he became deputy director of the Commonwealth Institute, Kensington, and was the first director of the non-governmental Commonwealth Human Rights Initiative. He has written and edited eleven books and numerous reports. As a journalist he was education correspondent of *The Guardian*, assistant editor of *New Society*, and deputy editor of the *London Evening Standard*.

Also by Richard Bourne and available from Zed Books:

Catastrophe: What Went Wrong in Zimbabwe?
Lula of Brazil

Nigeria

A New History of a
Turbulent Century

Richard Bourne

Zed Books
LONDON

Nigeria: A New History of a Turbulent Century was first published in 2015 by Zed Books Ltd, The Foundry, 17 Oval Way, London SE11 5RR, UK

www.zedbooks.co.uk

Typeset by seagulls.net
Index: Terry Barringer
Cover design: www.burgessandbeech.co.uk

A catalogue record for this book is available from the British Library

ISBN 978-1-78032-907-9 hb
ISBN 978-1-78032-906-2 pb
ISBN 978-1-78032-908-6 pdf
ISBN 978-1-78032-909-3 epub
ISBN 978-1-78032-910-9 mobi

In memory of the late Beko Ransome-Kuti, human rights campaigner, and for my daughter Camilla, who met him, and my youngest grandchild, Ollie, who never had the chance.

Contents

Preface

Anyone who claims to understand Nigeria is either deluded, or a liar. It comprises so many ethnicities and perspectives, with a contested past and statistics to be taken with pinches of salt, that it is an act of immodesty to write a centenary history. My justification is that I like the country, have been befriended by many Nigerians, and want readers to appreciate the gigantic nature of Nigeria's challenges and achievements. To create a single state, to which all citizens can owe allegiance and in which all may prosper, is an ongoing struggle. The intention here is to elucidate, as fairly and readably as possible, a story that began with a colonial merger and bring it up to date. Nation-building is a requisite everywhere, and it was particularly difficult in newly independent states as the tide of European empires receded in the second half of the twentieth century. For Nigeria an existential question about the unity of this diverse polity has never quite disappeared. My purpose in tracing this story is to see how this manufactured state has, on the contrary, managed to survive.

My personal acquaintance began in 1981–2, when I was commissioned by Channel 4 – then an experimental TV station that went on the air in London at the end of 1982 – to see whether it was possible to run a weekly news-feature programme with the working title *Third World Week*. It would, for example, use material from African TV stations and African filmmakers, and I travelled round the continent over a month to report on the idea's viability. However, I had difficulty in getting a Nigerian visa because I was not long in any capital, and when I arrived in Lagos airport without one on a Bulgarian flight from Angola late on a Sunday night, the police asked me why they should not put me on the first plane to London.

I explained that I had a letter of introduction to Chief Ayo Adebanjo, then Presidential Adviser on Information, and said I did not need to stay for more than a day or two to see media persons like Mike Enahoro and key figures at the Nigerian Television Authority. With deft diplomacy, the immigration staff gave me a 72-hour transit visa, quite long enough to do my work. It was a positive moment, never to be forgotten. Earlier, as I waited unavailingly for a visa in a Fleet Street office, a middle-aged British salesman, brandishing his, told me, "Some of my greatest adventures in life have started here."

Researching this account I have been assisted by many persons, listed below, who share no responsibility for any errors of fact that have crept in. I would like to thank particularly my wife Juliet, who has patiently suffered once again from her husband's penchant for authorship. In the United Kingdom I am grateful to Professor Philip Murphy, director of the Institute of Commonwealth Studies, University of London, where I am a senior research fellow, and to Bryan Pearson, publisher of *Africa Confidential*, who facilitated my second research visit to Nigeria in 2014.

In Nigeria there are many to whom I owe thanks. They include the family of my late friend Beko Ransome-Kuti, with whom I worked closely in the Commonwealth Human Rights Initiative to campaign against the Abacha dictatorship; his daughter, Morenike, has been a constant source of encouragement. Over a decade ago I was interested in writing a book about the remarkable Kuti family, celebrated for nationalism, human rights and music and, in an earlier generation, Christian evangelism, but a prominent British publisher dismissed the proposal – I was too white, too old, and not sufficiently expert in pop music!

Chief Emeka Anyaoku, Secretary-General of the Commonwealth from 1990 to 2000, has been a friend and inspiration since the 1980s. Kayode Soyinka, publisher-editor of *Africa Today*, with whom I once found myself singing karaoke at a conference of the Commonwealth Journalists Association in Hong Kong in 1997, has also given continuing advice. I have been helped too by the family of the assassinated Prime Minister Sir Abubakar Tafawa Balewa; in 1983-4, when I was deputy director of the then Commonwealth Institute, Kensington, his son Sadik was a joint fellow there and with the British Film Institute, and we worked together on a film and TV element in a major cultural focus on Africa. In Lagos I would like to say a special thankyou to Ebun Ikenze, a former colleague in London at the Commonwealth Human Rights Initiative in the 1990s, who was kind enough to offer me a place to stay on Victoria Island during my research visits.

There are also institutions I have found especially valuable. In the United Kingdom they include the library of the School of Oriental and African Studies, the Imperial War Museum, London, and Rhodes House part of the Bodleian Library, Oxford. In Ibadan I was lucky to be able to use the Nigerian National Archives. *Africa Confidential*, edited by Patrick Smith, and the now discontinued *West Africa*, so long edited by the late Kaye Whiteman, provided helpful running commentaries on Nigerian affairs. I would like also to thank a foundation, which wishes to remain anonymous, for funding my valued publisher, Zed Books, to provide complimentary copies to a number of Commonwealth universities. Ken Barlow, my editor at Zed, has been encouraging throughout, and my friend Terry Barringer, deputy editor of *The Round Table*, has been kind enough to do the indexing.

Individuals who have assisted me are listed below and I would ask them to accept my thanks; if any have been overlooked, I ask their forgiveness: Femi Aborisade, Ade Adefuye, Adesoji Adeniyi, Jide Ajani, Sylvester Odion Akhaine, Babatunde Akinrin, Bola Akinterinwa,

Bajo and Chizor Akisanya, E.J. Alagoa, Shina Alege, Chief Emeka Anyaoku, Tarry Asoka, Senator John Azuta-Mbata, Mukhtar Tafawa Balewa, Sadik Tafawa Balewa, Adewale Balogun, Lalage Bown, Tim Daniel, General Idris Bello Dambezau, Prince Dateme, Ray Ekpu, Kayode Fayemi, Tam Fiofiori, Steve Fraser, Yakubu Gowon, Chuks Ihekaibeya, Ebun Ikenze, J.O. Irukwu, Jaafar Jaafar, Eric Jumbo, Martins Jumbo, Austin Kemie, Christopher Kolade, Akim Mogaji, Stuart Mole, Philip Murphy, Hafsat Mustafa, Wilf Mwamba, Matthew Neuhaus, Colin Nichols, Bethel Njoku, Eugene Nwala, Judith Nwondi, Chidi Odinkalu, Emmanuel Odoemene, Adrian Ogun, Joy Ogwu, Brian Oliver, Sola Olurunyomi, HE Ochie E.N.B. Opurum, Eghosa Osaghae, Bryan Pearson, HE Andrew Pocock, King Professor T.J.T Princewill, Morenike Ransome-Kuti, Inemo Samiama, Walter Schwarz, John Smith, Patrick Smith, Kayode Soyinka, Wole Soyinka, King Alfred Diete Spiff, Krishan Srinivasan, Maitama Sule, H.E. Dalhatu Sarki Tafida, Tekena Tamuno, Chuka Ufondo, Martin Uhomoibhi, Richard Uku, Pat Utomi, Michael Uwemedimo, Kaye Whiteman, Leo Zeilig.

Timeline

1914   Sir Frederick Lugard, as British governor, announces the creation of the new colony Nigeria, amalgamating the protectorates of Northern and Southern Nigeria and the colony Lagos and abolishing the independent Egba kingdom encircled by it; Nigerian troops in a joint Anglo-French force attack German Cameroon after the outbreak of the First World War.

1916   John Bright Davies, editor of the *Times of Nigeria* and critic of Lugard and British racism, is prosecuted for seditious libel; Germans surrender in German Cameroon.

1919   Lugard returns to the United Kingdom; subsequent governors are less committed to his theory of indirect rule.

1920   NCBWA is founded, representing Africans in four colonies, and sends a deputation to London calling for moves to self-determination, an African Appeal Court, and a West African university; Herbert Macaulay, hailed as the father of Nigerian nationalism, is a delegate.

1921   Katsina Training College starts training teachers in a centre of Islamic scholarship, the first impetus for western education in the north.

1922   The Clifford Constitution sets up a legislature in southern Nigeria with 46 people, four of whom are elected; the League of Nations mandates Northern and Southern Cameroons to be administered by Britain alongside Nigeria, with the bulk of the former German colony mandated to France.

1929–30 Aba women's riots in southeastern Nigeria shatter colonial complacency and lead to reform of native courts and an end to imposition of warrant chiefs

1934 Yoruba businessmen create the National Bank of Nigeria.

1936 National Youth Movement founded in Lagos.

1937 Nnamdi Azikiwe launches the *West African Pilot* in Lagos, campaigning against racism and for self-government.

1938 Southern Nigeria is split in two for administrative purposes, with the eastern capital in Enugu and the western in Ibadan; northern Nigeria remains a single region; cocoa growers boycott the Cocoa Pool of ten European firms which bought their product.

1939–45 Nigerian troops play an active part in the Second World War, in East Africa and Burma; Nigeria is a staging-post for supplies from North America for the war effort in the Middle East; Britain depends heavily on tin and other commodities; nationalists are angry that Churchill rules out independence for colonial peoples in Allied war aims.

1945 Labour unions, strengthened during the war, call a general strike that results in wage increases and a ten-year plan for economic development.

1946 Governor Richards imposes a constitution, criticised in south and north, which strengthens regionalism but does not promote elections.

1948 NPC is founded in a Zaria reading room and becomes the germ of a political party in the north; University College, Ibadan, is founded as an extension of the University of London.

1951   The Macpherson Constitution strengthens the regional system
and introduces elections; Obafemi Awolowo founds the
Action Group, on the basis of a Yoruba cultural association,
which threatens the dominance in southern nationalism of
Azikiwe's NCNC.

1954   The Lyttleton Constitution enables regional governments to
set their own dates for self-government; east and west become
self-governing in 1957, the north only in 1959.

1956   Oil found in Niger Delta; Shell-BP Petroleum Development
Company of Nigeria Limited has initial monopoly.

1958   The Willink Commission looks into the question of minorities
and human rights; it argues against creation of more states and
for an independent electoral commission, but is too close to
independence to have binding force.

1960   Nigeria becomes independent with much goodwill under a
government led by Tafawa Balewa and the NPC from the
north in alliance with Azikiwe's NCNC (now strongest in the
Igbo east); Azikiwe becomes ceremonial Governor-General of
the Federation of Nigeria.

1961   Southern Cameroons vote to join Cameroun, Northern
Cameroons vote to join Nigeria.

1962   A split in the Action Group forms between those who want
to work with the federal government and those opposed;
Awolowo is put on trial for treason.

1963   Nigeria becomes the Federal Republic of Nigeria; a preventive
detention act is passed and the federal government cracks
down on the press; turmoil grows in the Yoruba southwest.

1966 A military coup on 15 January brings down the First Republic, following elections largely boycotted in the east and growing public hostility to corruption; prime minister and prominent leaders murdered in coup which brings John Aguiyi-Ironsi to power as head of state; the perception of the military government as Igbo leads to anti-Igbo riots in north and an Igbo exodus; after a counter-coup on 29 July, Yakubu Gowon replaces him

1967 Emeka Ojukwu declares the eastern region an independent state, Biafra, after failed talks in Aburi, Ghana; Gowon creates twelve states out of existing regions (north, west, mid-west, east); civil war lasts three years, with major humanitarian tragedy among Igbos; Biafra is supported by France but gets little international recognition; the Soviet Union and Britain supply arms to the federal government.

1970 Biafra surrenders; Gowon promises 'No victor, no vanquished.' Increasing oil revenues aid reconstruction.

1971 Nigeria joins OPEC and becomes dependent on oil revenues, damaging agriculture and other industries while promoting corruption and inappropriate development projects.

1975 The unpopular Gowon regime is overthrown by Murtala Muhammed, a northerner, and others involved in 1966 conspiracies and civil war; the coup is welcomed by the public; Muhammed tackles corruption and the lazy and incompetent civil service, and he strikes a nationalist and anti-west position in international affairs.

1976 Muhammed is assassinated in failed coup, succeeded by his deputy Olusegun Obasanjo, a Yoruba; Obasanjo goes on to nationalise BP in protest at British failure to overcome white racists in Rhodesia (Zimbabwe) and moves rapidly to transfer power to elected civilian government.

1979   Shehu Shagari, a northerner, is elected president, with a civilian government comprising his larger National Party of Nigeria and its Igbo ally, the Nigerian People's Party; declining oil prices and increasing corruption lead to government unpopularity.

1983   The fifth military coup, following a dubious election won by Shagari, brings Muhammadu Buhari to power on austerity and anti-corruption platform.

1985   Buhari is overthrown by Babangida in the sixth coup, and a state of national economic emergency is announced; unsuccessful coup by Lt Col. Mamman Jiya Vatsa.

1986   Nigeria joins the Organisation of the Islamic Conference; the nationally devised structural adjustment programme hurts many Nigerians and causes widespread resentment; the date for return to civilian rule is first postponed.

1989   The new constitution is promulgated with only two government-created parties allowed, the NRC and SDP.

1991   States increase in number to 30; federal capital moves from Lagos to the more central location of Abuja.

1993   After a shift in election date and attempted injunction to delay presidential election on 12 June, the election is won by M.K.O. Abiola for the SDP; another injunction prevents official release of the results and Ernest Shonekan becomes head of state with an interim government. The public and international reactions are hostile; the High Court of Lagos State declares the interim government illegal. Abacha overthrows Shonekan, hints at deal with Abiola, and abolishes all democratic structures.

1995   The Abacha dictatorship claims Obasanjo and other
        military figures are involved in a plot; Ken Saro-Wiwa and
        eight other Ogoni are executed; Nigeria is suspended from
        the Commonwealth; the worldwide condemnation leads
        to pariah status for the regime, though Abacha becomes
        chair of ECOWAS in 1996 and Nigerian troops help restore
        Tejan Kabbah as president of Sierra Leone in 1998; Abacha
        increases the number of states to 36.

1998   Abacha dies unexpectedly after being nominated by five
        government-created parties to run as a civilian in new
        elections; Abdulsalami Abubakar, chief of defence staff,
        becomes president and releases Obasanjo and political
        prisoners; Abiola dies; the PDP is formed and wins local
        government elections.

1999   Obasanjo elected president as PDP candidate, dismisses
        defence chiefs and other senior officers, launches anti-
        corruption bill and inquiry into human rights abuses, seeks
        write-off of government debts and faces conflicts (including in
        Niger Delta, where the Army is accused of massacre in Odi).

2003   Obasanjo is re-elected for second term after failed attempt at
        impeachment; he becomes increasingly authoritarian.

2006   Senate votes against law to permit Obasanjo to run for third
        term after civil society mobilisation; PDP chooses Umaru
        Yar'Adua, governor of Katsina, as presidential candidate with
        Goodluck Jonathan, governor of Bayelsa, as running mate;
        Nigerian troops withdraw from Bakassi peninsula, which was
        awarded to Cameroun by International Court of Justice.

2007   Yar'Adua, in poor health, is elected president with claimed
        70% of vote in low-quality election, launches amnesty

programme to buy off delta militias and subsequently approves clean-up of banks following world financial crisis.

2010 Yar'Adua dies in Abuja after several months of illness in Jeddah and official secrecy; fears of a coup grow as his family seeks to retain power and Jonathan lobbies successfully to be Acting President and successor.

2011 Jonathan wins election for PDP, despite a north-south split in voting; he brings back Obasanjo's internationally regarded technocrat, Ngozi Okonjo-Iweala, to manage the economy.

2014 PDP crumbles; an alliance of regions and parties, the APC, is put together as a serious political opposition to Jonathan; the dramatic fall in oil prices threatens federal budgeting; Boko Haram, a ruthless Islamist insurgency in northeast, causes emergency rule in three states and becomes out of control; an international campaign is sparked after 276 secondary school girls are captured by Boko Haram in Chibok.

2015 Elections are postponed for six weeks as Nigeria and allies regain ground lost to Boko Haram; Muhammadu Buhari, for APC, defeats Jonathan by 15.4M votes to 12.8M in cleaner presidential elections in the first civilian alternation of power in Nigerian history; APC wins most states in elections for governors and assemblies.

Acronyms and abbreviations

ABN	Association for a Better Nigeria
ACN	Action Congress of Nigeria
ACP	Africa, Caribbean, and Pacific Group of States
AD	Alliance for Democracy
AG	Action Group
ALC	Abeokuta Ladies Club
ANC	African National Congress
ANPP	All Nigeria People's Party
APC	All Progressives Congress
APGA	All Progressives Grand Alliance
APP	All People's Party
AU	African Union
CARICOM	Caribbean Community and Common Market
CD	Campaign for Democracy
CDHR	Committee for the Defence of Human Rights
ECOMOG	ECOWAS Monitoring Group
ECOWAS	Economic Community of West African States
EFCC	Economic and Financial Crimes Commission
EPG	Eminent Persons Group
FEDECO	Federal Electoral Commission
FESTAC	Festival of World Black and African Arts and Culture (Festival Mondial des Arts Nègres)
FIFA	Fédération Internationale de Football Association

GNPP	Great Nigeria People's Party
HIPC	Highly Indebted Poor Country
HIV/AIDS	Human Immunodeficiency Virus/Acquired Immune Deficiency Syndrome
ICPC	Independent Corrupt Practices and Other Related Offences Commission
IMF	International Monetary Fund
INEC	Independent National Electoral Commission
ING	Interim National Government
ISIS	Islamic State of Iraq and Syria
MAMSER	Mass Mobilisation for Self-Reliance, Social Justice and Economic Recovery
MASSOB	Movement for the Actualisation of the Sovereign State of Biafra
MEND	Movement for the Emancipation of the Niger Delta
MOSOP	Movement for the Survival of the Ogoni People
MPLA	Movimento Popular de Libertação de Angola
NADECO	National Democratic Coalition
NATO	North Atlantic Treaty Organisation
NCBWA	National Congress of British West Africa
NCNC	National Council of Nigeria and the Cameroons (later: National Council of Nigerian Citizens)
NEEDS	National Economic Empowerment and Development Strategy
NEPA	Nigerian Electricity Power Agency
NEPU	Northern Elements Progressive Union
NLC	Nigerian Labour Congress

NNA	Nigerian National Alliance
NNDP	Nigerian National Democratic Party
NNOC	Nigerian National Oil Company
NNPC	Nigerian National Petroleum Corporation
NPC	Northern People's Congress
NPN	National Party of Nigeria
NPP	Nigerian People's Party
NRC	National Republican Convention
NYSC	National Youth Service Corps
OAU	Organization of African Unity
OIC	Organisation of Islamic Cooperation
OPC	O'odua People's Congress
OPEC	Organization of the Petroleum Exporting Countries
PDP	People's Democratic Party
PRP	People's Redemption Party
SDP	Social Democratic Party
UDI	Unilateral Declaration of Independence
UN	United Nations
UPGA	United Progressive Grand Alliance
UPN	Unity Party of Nigeria

Map of Nigeria today,
with its 36 states and their capitals

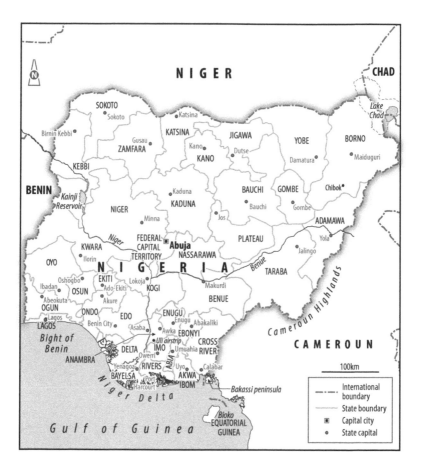

Section 1

1914–39: Invention of a country

Chapter 1
A merger makes a large possession for Britain

On 1 January 1914, the mix of peoples in a large part of west Africa became 'One Nigeria'. The announcement in the humid city of Lagos, which had been a British colony since the Treaty of Cession was agreed in 1861 between Great Britain and Oba Dosunmu,[1] King of Lagos, was made by Frederick Lugard, later Baron Lugard. He was now Governor-General of the Colony and Protectorate of Nigeria, and he never liked Lagos.[2] The name 'Nigeria' had been coined by his wife and admirer, Flora Shaw, colonial editor of *The Times*, in a letter she wrote to her paper in January 1897.[3] She used it to define the territories abutting the River Niger that were then being traded in or claimed by the Royal Niger Company.

In his speech, Lugard argued that the key reason for the amalgamation of the Southern and Northern Nigerian Protectorates with the Lagos Colony was to provide a unified railway policy. If this were really the case, it was as if British colonial policy had been hijacked by the heirs of George Bradshaw, publisher of the eponymous railway guides.[4] Lugard announced a new line from the head of the Bonny Estuary to join the Lagos–Kano railway, and claimed 'astonishing' progress in the fourteen years since the King's government – in fact it was Queen Victoria's at the time – had taken over from the Royal Niger Company trading monopoly. He concluded with the kind of grandiloquent guff that was expected at such a ceremony and echoed in later years as others came to power:

Today Nigeria enters on a new stage of its progress, and we all join in the earnest hope that the era now inaugurated will prove, not only a new departure in material prosperity, but also that the coming years will increase the individual happiness and freedom from oppression and raise the standard of civilisation and comfort of the many millions who inhabit this large country. To these sole ends the efforts of my colleagues and myself, with God's help, will be devoted.[5]

Lugard set himself and his successors an enormous challenge as rulers of this large space, which was British until 1960 and Nigerian from 1960 onwards. At 923,700 square kilometres, it remains roughly the same size today. How could they create a modern nation out of the 250 or so ethnicities in this region,[6] with three large cultural and religious blocs, and a major dysfunctionality between a numerous, poor and largely Muslim north, and an increasingly educated, Christian, and richer south? Lugard himself was sympathetic to the feudal, horse-loving north, which he had conquered in a series of military campaigns, concluding with the defeat of the Sokoto Caliphate in 1903. He never took to the advanced and critical citizens of Lagos and its Yoruba surroundings.

Without the British there would never have been a 'Nigeria'. For centuries, of course there had been peoples living in this huge region that now, in theory, belonged to King George V. It included kingdoms that had fought, made peace, captured slaves, traded with each other, risen and fallen. Speaking nearly a hundred years after the amalgamation, the diplomat and scholar Martin Uhomoibhi (b.1954) described this expanse as a kind of commonwealth, with peoples who were familiar with each other even if they were enemies.[7] Europeans – who had got to know the coastline in the sixteenth century, then traded slaves on a large scale and moved on to palm oil after the British ended that pernicious trade in 1807 – were frequently ignorant of this complex history. It was often Christian missionaries, learning and writing down local languages, and providing the first dictionaries for Igbo and Yoruba, who built cultural bridges.

The nineteenth century brought change, initially with the rise of larger states, then with an increasing European impact. In the north the Islamic jihad of Usman dan Fodio (1754–1817), a Muslim reformer whose followers became warriors, led to the formation of the Sokoto Caliphate in 1803. It brought not only the Hausa states under one government but also some provinces of Borno and lands that had formerly come under Oyo, a major state, and the Jukun territories. In the south the collapse in the 1830s of Oyo led to protracted wars in Yorubaland and a spread of refugees.

By the middle of the nineteenth century there was an acceleration of competitive European interest. The Portuguese had been overtaken. The competition was now between the British and the French, with late-starting Germany annexing the Cameroons in 1884 and encroaching on Calabar and Benue from the east. The Anglo-French contest was not only along the coast, but also inland, in the areas – desert, savannah and forest – served by the enormous Niger river and its tributaries. For reasons of trade, imperial rivalry, and 'civilisation', the British and French were moving inexorably, via protectorates, towards outright colonial control.

This process was uneven. The Lagos Colony was born when missionaries at Abeokuta, in Yorubaland, persuaded John Beecroft (1790–1854) – who was British Consul of the Bight [bay] of Benin and Biafra – to order the bombardment of Lagos in 1851 to expel its king, Oba Kosoko (reigned 1845–51). The excuse was that Kosoko would not sign a treaty to end the slave trade,[8] but in reality the missionaries were anxious about the safety of their new converts. However, the

British were not satisfied with Kosoko's successor, Akitoye (reigned 1841–45, 1851–53), and a decade after the bombardment Dosunmu signed the Treaty of Cession and a governor was appointed for the new colony. By 1872 the British had built a prison, and when it was rebuilt in 1885 with English bricks it cost £16,000 – at a time when the colony was spending only £700 on education.[9]

Christian missions in southern Nigeria were active quite early in the nineteenth century, assisted not only by traders, but also by the impact of the Royal Navy's West Africa Squadron, introduced to suppress the illegal slave trade. Liberated slaves frequently turned to Christianity and, even if they were brought to Freetown, Sierra Leone, the colony for freed slaves, Yorubas and others of the 'Nigerian' ethnicities would seek to go home. Samuel Ajayi Crowther (c.1809–91), the first indigenous bishop of the Anglican Church and someone who imagined a future Nigeria, was of Yoruba origin; he was baptised in Freetown in 1825 and became an active evangelist for the Church Missionary Society. Sarah Taiwo, who died in 1874 and was an ancestor of Olikoye, Fela and Beko Ransome-Kuti, was another of the so-called 'Saros',[10] freed slaves who eventually returned from Freetown to their Yoruba homeland. She returned with a second husband.

In the northern savannahs there was a kind of unity in the Sokoto Caliphate, with its Fulani emirs and Hausa populations and its Islamic primary schools, architecture and dress. Sharia law was not universal but there was an increase in Arabic literacy and Muslim awareness. Here, into its borders, the British were advancing by means of a trading monopoly granted to the United African Company in 1879, shortly called the National African Company in 1881 and then the Royal Niger Company in 1886. This was run by a buccaneering imperialist, Sir George Goldie (1846–1925). His ancestors had been smugglers in the Isle of Man, and he himself had had a raucous past. He got a royal charter in 1886 that gave him the right to trade on the

Niger between the Delta and Nupe and on the Benue, which joins the Niger at Lokoja, as far as Yola. Just as Cecil Rhodes (1853–1902), his contemporary, built his diamond monopoly by merging competitors to maintain prices, so Goldie merged first British and then French firms to monopolise the trade.

What was to become Nigeria was the product not only of events on the ground in west Africa, but of politics in Europe and London. In 1884–5 Otto von Bismarck, the power and brains behind the German Empire, masterminded a conference in Berlin designed to reconcile European rivalries in Africa. He himself wanted to open the continent to the traders and investors of the rising economy of imperial Germany. So Berlin was the scene of a major diplomatic victory by Britain over France, for the Niger territories were granted to Britain, even though neither state could be said to occupy them. This was a key moment in what was called 'the scramble for Africa' – an extraordinary late burst of European expansion – when even little Belgium came away with an enormous chunk of central Africa. King Leopold II's bogus 'International Association of the Congo' made off with a region of a million and a half square miles, stretching from the Atlantic to the Great Lakes, which he would rule with unprecedented cruelty until 1908.[11]

A growing spirit of imperial assertion led Britain to cast covetous eyes on the realms of the Ndebele and Boers in southern Africa. It was symbolised by Joseph Chamberlain (1836–1914), a Birmingham businessman who had made a fortune from manufacturing screws and who came to national attention as a radical and enterprising Liberal leader of his city. He split the Liberal Party with his opposition to Home Rule for Ireland and hostility to free trade, and he believed in extending the British Empire with the British government in control. In 1895, as a Liberal Unionist in coalition with the Conservatives, he became Colonial Secretary. In this capacity he was to support Cecil Rhodes' chartered company takeover of 'Rhodesia', victory in the Second Boer

War in 1902, an end to Goldie's charter with its multiplicity of treaties with local chiefs by the Niger in 1900, and the conquest of northern Nigeria in 1903.

Goldie's company had become unpopular with the palm oil traders and growers in the Niger – keeping out European competitors, ending profits for local African traders and middlemen and charging high prices for alcohol and guns. In December 1894 its headquarters at Akassa in the Delta were attacked by the Brass, a people who had been pushed to the edge of starvation by company exactions. There was looting and destruction, and some company employees were eaten in a ritual aimed at stopping smallpox. Nonetheless many in west Africa, and among the more knowledgeable in London, recognised that the way the company was run was at least partly to blame.

Chamberlain, then Secretary of State for the Colonies, decided that the forces of the Royal Niger Company were inadequate to control the region; they were also unlikely to deter the French who were trying to establish themselves on the upper Niger, threatening British suzerainty. He made the fateful decision to create the Royal West African Frontier Force, under Colonial Office orders, and gave the command to Lugard in 1897.

Lugard, who had played a key role in bringing Uganda under British authority, was a late Victorian figure not easily imaginable in any other era. He was convinced of British virtues, passionate for trade, a scourge of slavery, courageous, authoritarian and yet prepared to marry an equally strong-willed person in Flora Shaw. When he was older he mentored a young academic, Margery Perham, who repaid the compliment in two magisterial books of biography, which appeared when the empire was becoming an embarrassment and starting to fade into history.[12]

Hence, for Chamberlain, Lugard seemed ideal – a doer, a colonel with a brain, and with a strong imperial CV from east Africa where he had successfully ridden out controversy over harsh methods he had employed on behalf of the Imperial British East Africa Company. By 31 December 1899 the Royal Niger Company had been abolished, and Colonel Lugard was made High Commissioner of the Northern Nigeria Protectorate on 6 January 1900. He was given the Northern Nigerian Regiment – a force of 2,000–3,000 Africans and some 200 British officers from the West African Frontier Force that he had himself raised – with which to take control. He wrote that, for Europeans, the 'greater part' was 'quite unexplored' and that probably only a tenth was currently secured, and he doodled future provinces on a map.[13] In 1901 he decreed the abolition of slavery, and banned raiding and trading in slaves. He also appreciated the craziness of colonial expropriation:

> The vast majority of the inhabitants were not only completely unaware that they had been allocated to Britain but were ignorant of the very existence of such a country. Nor were the bulk of these peoples primitive and unorganised tribesmen whose subjection, when Britain was ready to claim it, could be taken for granted: the region contained some of the most highly developed and civilised Muslim states of tropical Africa, centred upon walled cities and defended by armies of horsemen.[14]

With little money, and in a situation where a third of his British officers and NCOs were either sick or on home leave, Lugard proceeded to build a civil administration and conquer the Fulani emirs. Kano was captured in 1903 and in 38 days, marching from Kano, he took Sokoto, Katsina and Zaria. The numbers were always adverse, but the British had discipline and Maxim machine guns on their side. It also seems likely that not all the Hausa soldiers were enamoured of the Fulani emirs who ruled them. At Sokoto, for instance, the commanding officer of the

West African Frontier Force, Thomas Morland, went ahead of Lugard with only 650 troops, 25 officers and two Maxim guns to face 15,000 horsemen and 3,000 foot soldiers. But in the battle only a hundred Sokoto men and one British carrier were killed: essentially the Sultan's forces ran away. When Lugard arrived five days later he accepted the surrender of the emirs and oversaw election of a new Sultan.

It was therefore with meagre resources of his own, and considerable respect for the societies he had captured, that Lugard set up and operated his administration. Maintenance of Islam, and therefore discouragement for Christian missionaries and their western-style education, were intrinsic elements of what he called 'indirect rule' in the north. Emirs were required to swear an oath of allegiance to the King. They said, 'I swear in the name of Allah, and of Mahomet his Prophet, to well and truly serve His Majesty King Edward VII and his Representative, the High Commissioner of Northern Nigeria, to obey the laws of the Protectorate, and the lawful commands of the High Commissioner and the Resident, provided that they are not contrary to my religion...'[15] Native courts were retained, but with a right of appeal to the High Commissioner.

But in 1906 Lugard was forced to resign as High Commissioner of the Northern Nigeria Protectorate and, shortly after, became Governor of Hong Kong, where he founded a university, in 1907. Lugard's forward policy in Nigeria and dismissal of Colonial Office concerns had hit a reef in a cruel punitive expedition against a peasant rising in the village of Satiru, only twelve miles from Sokoto, where his army killed some 2,000. Lugard ordered 'annihilation', and the young Winston Churchill, Under-Secretary of State for the Colonies 1905–08 in the Commons in the new Liberal administration, was deeply shocked.[16] Lugard had also failed to persuade officials of a scheme for 'continuous administration', under which he planned to spend six months of the year in England with his wife while refusing to allow anyone to deputise for him in Nigeria. For Lugard, Hong Kong seemed rather dull after the excitements, military action and empire-building of Africa. But west Africa had not seen the last of him.

In southern Nigeria there had been a confused picture: a colony and protectorate of Lagos, which surrounded an independent Egba state of Abeokuta, and an area round Calabar that an enterprising British consul had declared as the Oil Rivers Protectorate (for palm oil) in 1884 and then renamed the 'Niger Coast Protectorate' in 1893.[17] In 1906 this whole region was repackaged as the Colony and Protectorate of Southern Nigeria, although the city of Lagos remained a colony. It was a colony whose inhabitants were British citizens used to British courts and that was making progress in health and education, but the arrival of white officials with racist ideas was creating spatial and economic divisions.

Real British penetration in southern Nigeria, with its variety of petty chiefdoms and difficult geography, was slow and peppered with conflicts. In 1901–02 British troops occupied the centre of the Igbo areas in the east, by defeating the Aro, and they were fighting western Igbo communities until 1909. But across southern Nigeria there was a growth in western-type schools, a reduction in smallpox, and the introduction of a native court system, which allowed appeal from traditional courts to those chaired by the British, aspiring to British standards of evidence and assumptions of innocence before guilt.

Lugard finished his term in Hong Kong in March 1912 and, exploiting his status and contacts, successfully lobbied Lewis 'Loulou' Harcourt, Viscount Harcourt, Secretary of State for the Colonies in the Liberal government, to become Governor-General of Nigeria. In August 1913, as a gesture of thanks towards his patron, Lugard got his permission to name a newly built port on the Niger 'Port Harcourt'.[18]

Far from being just about railways, as he claimed the following January, this amalgamation had economic, political and ideological rationales. The economic rationale was simple. British colonial policy aimed to make the government of colonies financially self-sufficient, while opening territories to British trade and manufactures, and encouraging the export of products of use to the mother country. But the situation in Nigeria, prior to amalgamation, defied this aim. Administration in the north depended on subsidy from the Colonial Office and Treasury in London, while tax revenues were buoyant in the more prosperous, export-oriented economy of the south. An issue of economic inequality within the greater Nigeria, which would haunt the independent state throughout the twentieth century, was an obvious challenge to a tough-minded military administrator.

The nub of the case for merger, which Lugard put to Harcourt over a period of five months of persuasion in 1913, was about balancing the books. In 1912, Southern Nigeria had a revenue of £2.25M and its government was running a surplus. Northern Nigeria, with a possibly larger population and greater geographical extent, had only £500,000 of local revenue, which included a grant of £70,000 from customs income in the south.[19] Lugard did not argue that there would be enormous economies in the administration to follow. Nor, as will be seen, was he arguing to do away with the separate administrations and rather different colonial approaches to the north and south. It was essentially about making an unsatisfactory financial balance add up.

There were, however, wider political and ideological issues at stake. British control over both south and north could be regarded as still insecure, at a time when the balance of power within Europe was changing. Thanks in part to Lugard himself the French threat to British claims in west Africa had been thwarted, even if the Entente Cordiale was not always replicated in that sub-region. But, as the dreadnought naval race between the British and German empires expensively demonstrated, there was a growing German threat. The naval building competition was really caused by the Kaiser's ambition to create a worldwide presence for Germany.

Adjoining the Nigerias was German Cameroon. To the west, a short distance across the French colony of Dahomey, was Togo, a German protectorate since 1884. German merchants were already major players in trade with southern Nigeria. There was a strategic case for merging the two Nigerias, which would have military consequences less than a year after the Lagos ceremony in January 1914.

The ideological issues were different. Lugard sincerely believed in what he described as the 'dual mandate'.[20] He saw it as the duty of the United Kingdom, as a colonial power, to bring forward its native peoples to the kind of civilisation enjoyed by Europeans. At the same time, in the second part of the mandate, colonial administrators should assist British traders and investors to benefit from the enormous resources of the empire. In a refinement of this philosophy, Lugard also argued for and tried to practise a strategy of 'indirect rule'. By this he meant that administrators should not seek to abolish existing tribal or indigenous systems of government or law, but should use them. They would need to be tempered to match certain requirements, such as ending slavery, and there would be an overlay of British officials. But essentially the traditional systems would be preserved.

Because Lugard was an intelligent man, who wrote his own history and was married to a skilled journalist and propagandist, this ideology had immense influence on imperial thinking. Nigeria was to be its acme and advertisement. But the whole ideology, which Lugard had adopted in northern Nigeria and wished to extend to the south, was shot through with contradictions. For example, he did not much like educated Africans and 'indirect rule' was not going to help them. In a letter to Flora he wrote in Lagos in 1912, a year before being made Governor-General, he wrote, 'I am somewhat baffled as to how to get into touch with the educated native...to start with, I am not in sympathy with him. His loud and arrogant conceit are distasteful to me, the lack of natural dignity and courtesy antagonise me.'[21] As his biographer realised, the earliest attacks on indirect rule came from the first generation of western-educated Africans: they saw it as a ruse to ally conservative tribal leaders with imperial authority to restrain their advance.[22] At the same time his respect for the northern emirs and unwillingness to challenge Islam meant that he was slow to launch a drive for western-style education in the north; it had been Christian missionaries who had spread that kind of enlightenment in the south.

Further, indirect rule was an imposed system, backed by the Maxim gun, which did not leave traditional structures unchanged. In much of the south, especially in the southeast, there was nothing comparable to the feudal hierarchy of the north and British admin-istrators found that indirect rule required them to create one, building up the status of chiefs who were dependent on them. In his report to Parliament in 1919, when he left office, Lugard was dismissive of what he had found in the south: 'The Southern Provinces were populated by tribes in the lowest state of primitive savagery, without any central organisation, except in the West where the Yorubas, Egbas, Benis and some minor allied tribes had developed a social organisation under paramount chiefs but, in the early years, they were still addicted to many barbarous rites.'[23] He had also found British authority in the southern protectorate in a complete muddle, with the chief justice reporting 83 treaties and agreements of different kinds with local rulers.

But at the same time he strongly believed in what he was doing by ending slavery and curbing the tradition of murdering twins, fetish worship and even human sacrifice among 'pagans.'(Animists were often described as pagans by the British, at least until the 1930s.) In 1919 he told the British Parliament at the conclusion of his time as Governor-General:

The Fulani Emirates formed a series of separate despotisms, marked by the worst forms of wholesale slave-raiding, spoliation of the peasantry, inhuman cruelty and debased justice…The South was, for the most part, held in thrall by Fetish worship and the hideous ordeals of witchcraft, human sacrifice and twin murder. The great Ibo race to the East of the Niger, numbering some 3 millions, and their cognate tribes had not developed beyond the stage of primitive savagery.[24]

Chapter 2
First World War:
Nigeria on the front line

Throughout the empire, and to some extent in the self-governing dominions, politics, administration and economics were contingent on the needs and example of London. And in spite of its pride in a worldwide empire, with a navy to protect it, London remained fatally exposed to convulsions in its immediate neighbourhood. The murder of the Archduke Franz Ferdinand of Austro-Hungary in Sarajevo in June 1914 set off a diplomatic ricochet that became the First World War. In August 1914 the 20 million Nigerians found themselves, alongside other imperial subjects and 46 million in Britain and Ireland, lined up against Germany, Austro-Hungary and the Ottoman Empire. This was a war that Nigerians had not chosen, but that affected them profoundly. Because the merger of north and south was so new, the war had an impact in making some – especially the soldiers – see themselves for the first time as 'Nigerians'.

By the end of 1913 the local troops of northern and southern Nigeria had been merged into a single brigade of five battalions, around 5,000 troops in all, to be known as The Queen's Own Nigeria Regiment. But they had not practised joint manoeuvres and their ethnic makeup was unbalanced; the majority were Hausa and Yoruba, Hausa was the language of command, and some of the most educated people from the south were excluded because the authorities feared they might be politically unsound.[1] Nevertheless the war came quickly to west

Africa. By 25 August the French had occupied Germany's Togoland, destroying the transmission station at Kamina that was responsible for communications between Berlin and her African colonies. Britain and France rejected a German appeal, conveyed via the United States embassy in Berlin, to avoid hostilities in the greater Congo region, deemed to include both Cameroons and German East Africa.

The British in London had thought that the Germans might surrender German Cameroon, with its thousand-mile land frontier with Nigeria and useful port at Douala, without a fight. However, within two months of the declaration of war they were to be brutally surprised. Attacks by the Nigeria Regiment at three points across the border – on the hill fortress of Mora, on Garua on the Benue river and on Nsankang in the south – were successfully repelled by the Germans with the loss of Nigerian and British lives and valuable guns and ammunition. Colonel Charles Carter, the British commander, was withdrawn.

This embarrassed Frederick Lugard, who was Governor-General of the Colony and Protectorate of Nigeria 1913–18, and encouraged the British to work more closely with the French, who were still smarting from the cession of territory to German Cameroon in 1911. By the end of August 1914 it was agreed to organise an Anglo-French expeditionary force of 7,000 men under General Sir Charles Dobell (1869–1954); in addition there was another French force of 3,000 men, operating in southeastern Cameroons adjoining the Congo and Gabon. In October, three companies from the Belgian Congo's Force Publique joined this army. The German colony was surrounded, and on 27 September the port town of Douala surrendered to HMS *Challenger*, a battleship, even before Dobell's troops had landed. The British captured nine cargo vessels there and, by the end of 1914, had overrun cocoa, rubber and fruit plantations in nearby Buea-Victoria.

But the Germans were not an easy pushover, even though some of their subjects took the opportunity to rebel, and there was continuous friction between the British and the French at the command level. Although fewer in number than the Allies, the German-led African troops tended to withdraw inland rather than surrender. Ammunition was smuggled in to the Germans from the Spanish colony of Fernando Pó, which with Río Muni was blockaded by the British and French navies in late 1914. In April 1915 a German raiding party broke through the Nigerian lines and burnt government buildings in Mutum Biyu on the Benue river, inside Nigeria. The Emir of Yola and the British district officer fled. When the Anglo-French force captured the Benue port of Garua, the Emir of Yola, who was hoping to gain traditional Adamawa lands that were on the German side of the border, celebrated effusively. He presented a thousand head of cattle to the victors.

General Frederick Cunliffe (1861–1955), who was supposed to be in command of the Anglo-French force in the north, had difficulty in getting French acceptance. But by the end of 1915 he had cleared German forces from much of northern Cameroons, with the exception of the hill fortress of Mora. Lack of food, as well as lack of support from the fatherland and the superior numbers of the Allies, wore down the German-led forces. The bulk of the British forces were Nigerian but some came from other west African colonies, the Gambia, Sierra Leone and the Gold Coast. In July 1915 Dobell was reinforced by the 5th Light Indian infantry battalion, brought over from the Straits Settlements in Malaya.

With the French coming up from the south, and Cunliffe advancing from the north, the German defenders were caught in a pincer. By February 1916 the war was virtually over. The Germans withdrew from Yaoundé, their capital, in a fighting retreat to the Spanish border of Río Muni. From there Ángel Barrera, Governor of Fernando Pó[2] – who did not hide his sympathy for Germany – requested Dobell to forward a message to Berlin from General Carl

Zimmermann reporting his surrender and evacuation. There was only one footnote. The German garrison in the far north at Mora, half starved but difficult to storm, was still holding out. Lugard and Cunliffe decided to offer them terms; the officers could keep their swords, the African soldiers could return home, the Europeans would go to Britain as prisoners of war. Captain Ernst von Raben, knowing that his military situation was hopeless, accepted with the proviso that £2,000 be lent to him to pay his African soldiers. Lugard found the money from the credits of liquidated German firms in Nigeria, for which von Raben took responsibility.

The Nigeria Regiment and the other African soldiers fighting for the British in the Cameroons were generally admired by their white officers. They fought barefoot. They put up with hardships that would have daunted Europeans. Even the porters, carrying food and ammunition for the troops, were heroes in their way. It was inevitable therefore that, after victory in the Cameroons, the War Office in London would consider the use of Nigerian troops in the unsatisfactory campaign in Tanganyika, German East Africa. This was the 'ice cream war'[3] in which the brilliant German general Paul von Lettow-Vorbeck, commanding his skilled askaris, locally raised African troops, outfoxed the imperial forces led by General Jan Smuts until the 1918 armistice.

Lugard was not best pleased when, in April 1916, the War Office asked him to find a battalion of around 40 Europeans and 740 Nigerians to send to east Africa. He wanted to rest troops after the Cameroons; his existing European officers wished to get to the more exciting war on the western front, which meant he would have to conscript civilians; and he had the underlying worry of what large numbers of trained African soldiers might get up to when they were eventually demobilised.

As an old Africa hand he was aware that it took time for African troops to get used to a new set of white officers. He wrote:

In these circumstances it would be unwise to force the men to embark for East Africa. It was precisely in similar circumstances that the Sudanese mutiny arose in 1896… After a short period of rest with their women and, when their sore feet had had time to heal, when their tattered rags had been replaced and their arms and accoutrements overhauled they would respond to any call if led by officers who were not strangers to them.[4]

But the problem that the British faced was that white troops were suffering big casualties from disease in east Africa, South Africa was unwilling to recruit 'native troops' and von Lettow-Vorbeck was obstinately refusing to surrender.[5] A battalion of the Gold Coast Regiment sailed for east Africa in June 1916 and the first Nigerians – effectively volunteers given a bonus of £3 each – went in November. Once again they were commanded by Cunliffe, and once again they gave a good account of themselves in spite of hunger in the Rufiji Valley, in the first half of 1917, when flooding disrupted their food supplies. After von Lettow-Vorbeck had retreated into Portuguese East Africa (now Mozambique) in late 1917, the British decided that they had won in Tanganyika. The Nigerian troops were sent home in February 1918, although their carriers had to wait until the armistice. Plans to send another Nigerian force to the Middle East were overtaken by a flu outbreak and the collapse of the Ottoman Empire in October 1918, but not before Lugard had had to deal with desertions and a near mutiny in Zaria in September. The men were complaining about poor pay and their hardships in the Rufiji, and Lugard was conciliatory.

The shooting war was arguably less important outside the pre-1914 boundaries of Nigeria than inside the just-created state, where its impact was both political and economic. Politically the war laid bare the colonial government's anxieties about disaffection, especially with a risk of pro-Turkish 'Mahdism' in northern Nigeria. Economically the war disrupted trade patterns and saw American businessmen replacing German ones in the Nigerian economy.

The first political crisis, at the beginning of August 1914, precipitated the end of the independent Egba state in Yorubaland. A village leader aged about 90, Shobiyi Ponlade, and his cousin were arrested, beaten and tied to a tree because he had failed to get his people to build and repair roads in his area without pay. Although the Alake, head of a state that had enjoyed theoretical independence since a treaty of 1893, had ordered his arrest, it was a British Commissioner, Mr P. V. Young who was responsible for the cruel punishment of Ponlade. The situation rapidly worsened as Ponlade's Ijemo people rioted and a British officer sent to put down the demonstrations opened fire, killing 7 chiefs and 29 others in what Sir John Anderson, later Lord Waverley, Permanent Under-Secretary of the State for the Colonies, described as a massacre.[6] The soldiers went on to loot and destroy houses in the town of Abeokuta, centre of the disturbances, and the population fled into the surrounding countryside. The 1893 treaty was annulled, and the internal customs on the road to Lagos, which had been a source of income for the Egba government, were abolished.

Lugard had always been cynical about the Egba state. He thought the illiterate Alake was manipulated by 'an educated native':

> Side by side with a Secretariat, and minute papers which only the Secretary and a few clerks could read, with Estimates prepared on the Colonial model, and Orders in Council and Regulations passed by an illiterate body of conservative Chiefs, practically all of whom were very old men, who looked on these proceedings probably with amused indifference, there existed the ancient regime with all its abuses – extortionate demands from the peasantry, corruption and bribery in the

Courts, arbitrary imprisonment and forced labour. By such methods a large number of Chiefs of various grades – there were over 2,000 in Abeokuta, I believe – lived a life of idleness and sensuous indulgence.[7]

There were other revolts in the south, though these were more against colonialism – corruption in the native court system introduced by Lugard and imposed taxation – than in favour of Germany or the Central Powers. Nonetheless the German merchants had been popular because they extended more credit than the British, and there were periodic rumours that they were winning the war. There was a rising in Kwale district, part of Warri province, in 1914, and between 1914 and 1916 there were also revolts in Owerri and Calabar provinces. In October 1916 there was a serious rebellion at Okeogun, in Oyo province. Some of these revolts were put down with hundreds of casualties, with temporary European-led forces put together as the Nigeria Regiment was fighting in the Cameroons.

The reasons were often local and involved hostility to outside tribes as well as to the British-backed native courts. But an underlying issue was the inappropriate nature of Lugard's philosophy of indirect rule in the south. Yoruba obas had never collected taxes, and they ruled by an intricate system of consensus. In the north, the Muslim emirs had been taxing their peoples for hundreds of years, in a not always benevolent despotism. The colonial authorities were nervous about pro-Germanism at a time when most of their trained troops were outside Nigeria. The reality was that the country was still unsettled and not accepting of external British rule.

This was illustrated in the last year of the war when direct taxation was imposed on Egbas, the most independently minded Yoruba group, at the start of January 1918. Every adult was to pay not less than five shillings to replace compulsory unpaid labour. At the same time Egbaland was divided into seven districts, and their obas were required to leave Abeokuta and live in their villages. By May an agitation against these changes had become a revolt; rebels were supported by friends from French Dahomey and nearly captured Abeokuta. The government had no shortage of troops after seizure of the Cameroons, and around 2,600 soldiers put down the rebels; the government soldiers suffered a hundred casualties and about a thousand rebels were killed. A commission of inquiry, which included Eric Olawolu Moore, an Egba lawyer, put much of the blame on Lugard for introducing direct taxation and constitutional changes in a hurry. In fact the forced labour, compulsory and unpaid, had continued. But the commission's report strengthened the hand of the incoming Governor-General of Nigeria, Sir Hugh Clifford (in office 1919–25), to ease up on the ideology of indirect rule.

In the north the question was whether Islam, in the form of support for the Turkish Caliphate, would lead to a jihad against the colonial authorities. In fact the emirs and Muslim hierarchy, who had been privileged ever since Lugard conquered the north, stayed loyal even though there were signs of opposition beneath them. Lugard took active propaganda measures to firm up support for the British, calling a meeting of Muslims in Lagos, translating into Arabic an appeal for Muslim loyalty by the Aga Khan, and encouraging the emirs to donate to the war effort. By the end of the first year a sum of £38,000 had been given to the governor, with a promise of £45,000 a year for the duration.[8] For the Emir of Kano and the Shehu of Borno the war in Cameroons seemed close at hand. For Lugard these 'voluntary contributions' made up for wartime revenue losses.

The Shehu of Borno and the Lamido of Yola, whose territories ran along the Cameroons border, offered transport, remounts and other help to the Nigerian troops. The Lamido was hoping that a British victory would allow him to regain lands that had fallen on the German side of the boundary in the colonial carve-up. Nonetheless, there were sporadic revolts in the Nassarawa and Niger provinces in 1914 and in the emirates of Kano and Borno in 1915. German propaganda had little impact, the authorities' worries about 'Mahdism' reduced,[9] and an important turning point occurred in 1916 when Ali Haidar Pasha, Grand Sharif of Mecca, declared that he was the guardian of the holy places of Islam and the Turks no longer ruled Arabia. In fact Nigerian pilgrims continued to make the Haj to Mecca throughout the war.[10] The loyalty of the emirs was underpinned by an ordinance of 1916 that prohibited any Christian missionary activity in their territories.

The worst crisis in the north took place late in the war. It was caused by a large-scale revolt by Senussi in the French Sahara from Timbuktu to Lake Chad and threatened an invasion of northern Nigeria. Two British columns from the Nigeria Regiment marched into French territory in January 1917, responding to a plea for help from the French, and stayed until June. They relieved pressure on the French garrisons and the French brought the situation under control, but not without friction with the British authorities, similar to the Anglo-French frictions in the Cameroons.

The war not only opened the eyes of some Nigerians to their significance in the British Empire and west Africa, it also had important economic impacts. One of these saw the replacement of Germany by the United States as Nigeria's second trading partner after Britain. Nigerian exports steadily grew, with vegetable oils essential for margarine and glycerine for munitions. Lugard, against fierce opposition from producers in Nigeria and free traders in the United Kingdom, introduced export taxes on palm kernels, palm oil and cocoa in August 1916. Trade was in the hands of a Liverpool-based combine, which saw firms like the Niger Company enjoy a huge rise in profits.

Imports were cut back – there was a 25% surtax on all imports – and some encouragement was given to local import substitution. Tin mining on the Jos plateau saw a steady increase in employment, and a railway between Port Harcourt and Enugu was opened during the war to facilitate coal traffic. Inflation, labour shortages and the exactions of taxation were all features of a colonial economy affected by war. Male participation in the war, followed by the deadly flu pandemic after it ended, gave new opportunities to women. In the southeast it was women who grew cassava, and in the southwest many women extended their commercial skills as traders.

The end of the war in Europe coincided with the departure of Lugard. As a result of the successful campaign in the Cameroons the British were to administer only a small sliver adjoining Nigeria, but not the port of Douala, with the bulk of the former German colony going to France. Only a fifth of German Cameroon came under British administration. France also picked up the League of Nations mandate for most of the German colony of Togo, adjoining the Gold Coast to its west, with only a sliver going with the Gold Coast. London had little ambition for further imperial expansion in west Africa.

Nigerian emirs who had eyed their traditional lands across the German Cameroon border, lost by the Anglo-German agreement of 1890, were largely disappointed. Some parts of the old Bornu Empire and Adamawa Emirate were retrieved, and some valuable plantations fell on the British side of the line. But when the Foreign Office talked to the French it was clear that Whitehall cared much less for the Cameroons than did Lugard or Dobell; officials were prepared to swap their interest in more territory in west Africa for Djibouti, or the French share in the Pacific condominium of the New Hebrides (today's Vanuatu). They were conscious that the Union of South Africa had swallowed up German South-West Africa (today's Namibia) so France deserved a recompense.

Chapter 3

Lugard struggles with opponents

What had Frederick Lugard achieved? He retired as the first Governor-General of the Colony and Protectorate of Nigeria in January 1919, two months after the First World War had ended. He always had his critics in London, but the widespread British view that he was a great proconsul, the empire-builder of west Africa, looked rather different on the ground. He had made Nigeria a fact, but it was still really at least two Nigerias, north and south. He had rejected the advice of administrators such as Charles Temple, lieutenant governor in northern Nigeria from 1914 to 1917, to break up the whole of Nigeria into four or seven provinces. By prohibiting Christian missionaries in the north and not doing much else to promote modern education in that large region, he had disadvantaged northerners. Their culture and religion led them to look northwards across the Sahara, along the old trading routes, and east via Cairo and Khartoum towards Mecca. They shared little with their neighbours to the south. Apart from tackling slavery and sending punitive expeditions when required, Lugard did little to challenge the autocracies of the north: he was an autocrat himself.

One of the most serious deficiencies in the north was educational, which meant that the region was to be a brake on southern enthusiasm for independence some 40 years later. In the south the Christian missions had invested in schooling in English, and parents had contributed fees. King's College, Lagos, was set up in 1909 as a model secondary school. But in the north, where Islam and Arabic were cherished, 'Nassarwan schools' for the children of rulers were established following the model of the Gordon Memorial College,

Khartoum which had opened in 1902, and modern education was for the elite, not the masses.

There was also a question as to how good an administrator Lugard really was. He was not good at delegating or following regular procedures. He insisted on retaining executive and judicial powers for most of Nigeria – though there was still a legislative council for the former Lagos Colony – but he was in England for part of each year under his scheme for 'continuous administration'. This was largely because his wife, Lady Flora Shaw, was unwilling to join him in Nigeria. By 'continuous administration' he meant that he would remain in charge, whether he was in Nigeria or in England. He was overloaded with trivia. Hence the colonial regime he commanded was not as efficient, prompt or flexible as the uncertainties of a diverse, recently occupied territory required, especially in wartime. In the course of 1917 the scheme for continuous administration was abandoned.[1]

Also, the southerners resented the bogus structures imposed on them by indirect rule. Families from the old Lagos colony had been Christian for three generations when the colony was abolished; some had good English and a western education, and enjoyed their status as British colonial citizens. The independent-minded Egba, dismissed as living in a corrupt little statelet by Lugard, resented the condescension and bullying of the colonial authorities. Igbos and those in the Niger Delta were not persuaded by Lugard's warrant chiefs, a system of tax-collecting noblemen invented by the authorities. There was a paradox between Lugard's claims to be assisting Nigerians to acquire a higher civilisation and his actual, frankly racist, disparagement of the rising professional class in Lagos. He justified his hostility by a fear that concessions to such professionals would be at the expense of the less educated majority. But Lagosians saw this as self-serving colonialism, and the appointed Nigeria Council, created by Lugard to give an appearance of popular consultation, as a sham.

Criticism of Lugard was a regular feature in the Lagos press, and James Bright Davies (1848–1920), editor of the *Times of Nigeria*, was prosecuted for seditious libel by the Attorney-General of Nigeria in February 1916. He had written a series of articles about the cruel rule of the colonial authority, its iniquitous measures and laws, but the article said to bring the government into hatred and contempt related to a Lugardian proposal to move the capital from Lagos to Kaduna:

> [It] threatens with ruin the progress and prosperity of the only town of importance in the Colony and Protectorate of Nigeria and which…by austerities and severities of a continuous series of measures and enactments which could only have been dictated by a rancorous negrophobism and which apart from German rule could only flourish under the British Crown Colony system of government or under a constituted or authorised autocracy.[2]

Davies had run articles raising funds for wounded Nigerian soldiers and attacking the monopolistic British firms that had benefited from the departure of the German merchants. But he was fined a hundred pounds for his criticism of the possible removal of the capital from Lagos, and sentenced to six months in prison for suggesting that people angry at the British firms would actually like to see Germany win the war.

Nonetheless, Davies did have one clear victory to his credit, in addition to rallying the small but growing class of educated professionals against the colonial regime. In July 1917 Lugard asked the Colonial Office for permission to impose permanent press censorship. Davies then wrote to the Office to point out that in Britain the wartime censorship was a temporary regulation, under the 1914 Defence of the Realm Act, which would cease when the war was over. The Colonial

Office turned down Lugard's request, pointing out that he had adequate provisions under a British Protectorate Order in Council, and there was no cause for permanent controls on the press.

A key figure opposing Lugard, Herbert Macaulay (1864–1946) – now regarded in retrospect as a father of Nigerian nationalism – was a product of the emergent professional class. He was frustrated by what he saw as racism and imperial exploitation at the end of the nineteenth century and start of the twentieth. His grandfather was Bishop Samuel Ajayi Crowther, the Christian evangelist who had been subsequently deprived of his bishopric by the Church Missionary Society because he wanted to make compromises with prevailing African traditions. His father, Thomas Babington Macaulay, ran the Church Missionary School in Lagos and married Samuel Ajayi Crowther's daughter Abigail in 1854. Hence Herbert came from a privileged background, and he studied civil engineering in Plymouth and worked as a land inspector in Lagos before resigning in 1898 to take up private practice.

Macaulay was a cultural nationalist and gifted musician, and he helped design buildings in Lagos. But he became prominent in the Lugard era as violently hostile to the administration and white racism. Lugard dismissed him as a 'convict' because he had had a run-in with the courts and was twice in prison. Macaulay attacked corruption in the railways in 1909, agitated with local chiefs against Lagos water rates and, as a leader of the Lagos affiliate of Britain's Anti-Slavery Society, led a campaign against colonial attempts to change land tenure arrangements in Lagos and Yorubaland. Throughout the 1920s and 1930s he would front continuous attacks on the government, especially after he became proprietor of the *Lagos Daily News* in 1927. He memorably stated that 'The dimensions of "the true interests of the natives at heart" are algebraically equal to the length, breadth and depth of the white man's pocket.'[3]

While he came to have a 'Nigerian' viewpoint later in his life – he died in 1946 – his concerns initially were those of a Lagosian, and at its foundation his Nigerian National Democratic Party did not seek independence. Its aim was 'To ensure the safety or welfare of the people of the Colony and Protectorate of Nigeria as an integral part of the British Imperial Commonwealth and to carry the banner of "Right, Truth, Liberty and Justice", to the empyrean heights of democracy until the realisation of its ambitious goal of a Government of the People by the People for the People.'[4]

Although the different factions in Lagos society could support him he was not precisely a democrat, supporting the hereditary Eleko of Lagos in his opposition to water rates. Invited to visit him at the end of 1931, the 36-year-old Margery Perham (1895–1982) was struck by the contradictions in his way of life. Perham, a feisty Oxford academic, was just starting her career of research on colonial administration. The self-described 'Gandhi of Nigeria' lived in a house that seemed strange to her: 'all antimacassars and shell-covered boxes, reflecting a bygone England'. She thought he had a number of personal obsessions, yet she remarked, 'But he is one of the ablest Africans I have met and at once a potentially dangerous yet rather pathetic figure.'[5] She wondered whether this was the beginning of an African rerun of the Indian independence struggle.

Colonial society was fractured, and in Lagos there were the hereditary authorities, different Muslim groups, the Christians, the 'Brazilians'[6] and the Saros, those from elsewhere who had arrived because Lagos was the capital; and of course the majority were Yoruba, some of whom were still animists or retained animist beliefs with a Christian overlay, who retained links with their own districts. The small educated elite, represented by Macaulay, had little in common with the emirs and peasantry of the north, or indeed some of the hereditary leaders in the south, such as the Alafin of Oyo, who was said to have

500 wives.[7] This elite was subject to conflicting emotions. On the one hand it sought the full rights of British citizens and valued positive aspects of British civilisation in contrast to German *Kultur*. On the other it hated the snobbery, authoritarianism and covert racism that were intrinsic to the colonial system.

Chapter 4
Between the wars:
Nigeria is not a single state

Between Frederick Lugard's departure as Governor-General in 1919 and the outbreak of the Second World War in September 1939, Nigeria went through significant change without becoming a single country. What had been northern and southern protectorates retained largely separate identities, and by the 1930s some British officials were worrying about the backwardness of the north, where a third of the population was not Muslim. Constitutional changes brought more Nigerians closer to the administration, without the colonial government ceding real power. The depression in global trade in the 1920s and 1930s hurt economic growth while leaving power in the hands of British and European firms and shipping lines. The exactions of tax-gatherers, pushing people into the cash economy of the pound sterling, created strong resentment; in the southeast, for instance, tax started to be collected only in 1926. Campaigns by nascent nationalist, producer and union groups gave notice that the colonial status quo was not eternal. West African students in Britain exchanged ideas on political advance and watched as the India National Congress Party pushed reluctant imperial governments to acknowledge its claims to self-rule in the subcontinent.

There was a sense, too, that Nigeria was not entirely conquered and that resistance was not just a matter of civil disobedience. In the 1920s there was a Mahdist protest in Borno, led by Sa'id, son of the 19th-century Mahdist leader in the Sokoto Emirate.[1] There were serious disturbances in Tivland in 1929 and 1939, and women's riots in the east in 1929 and 1930 were put down with violence. The Igbo women were angry that direct taxation might be extended from men to women and were protesting at a collapse in the price of their palm produce when import costs were rising. Factories were looted. Native court buildings and property were trashed. Some 55 women died.

The unexpected outbreak, starting in Owerri province, shattered the complacency of the colonial government and led to reform of the native courts and an end to the imposition of warrant chiefs. The government then sought to base its native authorities on Igbo clans, but the clan unit was too small to be viable and each village was autonomous; in moving away later from traditional headship towards a leadership based on merit and public acceptance, the British gave a fillip to more democratic approaches in the east.

Lugard was succeeded by Sir Hugh Clifford, who was Governor-General from 1919 to 1925. He had already been governor of the Gold Coast since 1912; his career as a colonial administrator had started in Malaya and Borneo in 1896, and he had come to the Gold Coast from Trinidad. He went on from Nigeria to be Governor of British Ceylon. The globetrotting of British officials reflected a view in London that what really mattered was expertise in managing the imperial machine, rather than in particular regions or societies; such knowledge could be suspect if the official had 'gone native'. On arrival in Lagos, Clifford had to cope with an anti-Lugard backlash from administrators in the east, who told him that the native authority system there was not working. He procrastinated, calling for two reports, but eventually authorised a system of direct taxation that led to trouble after he had moved on.

Clifford, like Lugard, was not an instinctive democrat, but he was surprisingly willing to give Nigerians a larger say in their own affairs. With other west African governors he had advised the new Secretary of State for the Colonies, Alfred Milner, Viscount Milner, who held the post from 1919 to 1921, not to see or make concessions to a deputation from the National Congress of British West Africa. This went to London in 1920 to press for an African Appeal Court and moves towards self-determination. The congress was the brainchild of a Gold Coast lawyer, J. Casely Hayford, and was representative of an interwar sentiment among educated Africans that the British colonies in west Africa should advance together.[2] It was founded in Accra and influenced by the ideas of Marcus Garvey and W.E.B. DuBois. The delegation included representatives from the Gold Coast, Sierra Leone and the Gambia, as well as three, among them Herbert Macaulay, from Nigeria.

The NCBWA had six demands. It wanted a legislative council for each of the west African colonies, with half its members elected and half nominated. It wanted the appointment and deposition of chiefs to be in the hands of their peoples, not the colonial governors. It wanted separation of the executive from the judiciary (a rather blurred area under Lugard). It sought the abolition of racial discrimination in the civil service and in social life (for with vaccinations and improved health for Europeans in west Africa there had been a growth in expatriate numbers and racism). It asked for an appeal court for British West Africa and the establishment of a university for west Africa. Some of these demands – such as the call for university education – would take more than two decades to achieve, and the Colonial Office fell back on its paternalist line that they had to defend the west African population as a whole from the ambitions of a small educated elite.

But in 1922, rather against the opposition of the Colonial Office, the governor of Nigeria appeared to change his mind. Clifford produced a new constitution for southern Nigeria, which set up a Legislative Council of 46 members with a small elective element. Winston Churchill, the new Secretary of State for the Colonies, reluctantly agreed.[3] There were to be 27 official members, 15 appointed unofficial members and 4 members elected by adult males with an annual income of £100 or more – three from Lagos and one from Calabar, which was seen as a key commercial centre in eastern Nigeria. Although the elected members were few, this opening gave an enormous stimulus to political organisation, especially in Lagos, where Macaulay founded the Nigerian National Democratic Party to contest elections the following year. From 1923 until 1934 the NNDP dominated the political life of the capital, winning all three Lagos seats in three elections, though its attempt to become a nationwide party was not successful. Furthermore, while the 1922 Clifford Constitution was the first to permit African elections in the sub-Saharan British Empire, the governor was still ruling the north by proclamation, with sensitivity to the views of the emirs.

Significantly, Clifford did not entirely believe in 'Nigeria'. Speaking to the Nigeria Council on 29 December 1920, he said that there could be neither a west African nor a Nigerian nation. He thought such a concept was 'as manifest an absurdity as that there is, or can be, a "European nation" at all events until the Millennium'.[4]

Nonetheless the pressures to make a reality of 'Nigeria' grew in the 1920s. In 1929–30 the education departments of north and south were united, and in 1930 the southern and northern police forces were amalgamated: '85 European gazetted officers, with some African chief inspectors, superintended the whole country's law and order in uniform, backed by the various native authority forces, court messengers and *dogaris* in the bush overseen by the provincial administration.'[5] European education still met a measure of suspicion in the north, where craft schools were merged with primary schools and some chiefs withheld their children. The object in the north was to educate artisans and junior officials and prevent these occupations being colonised by better-educated southerners. Many clerking and junior technical positions were being filled by Yorubas and Igbos because northerners lacked literacy in English. Katsina Training

College was opened in 1921 to train teachers in the north, and when the education departments were unified in 1929 it was renamed the Higher College, Katsina, in imitation of the stronger Yaba Higher College in the south.

When Margery Perham visited Katsina in early 1932, she found that it had become a significant educational centre. Building on a much older tradition of Islamic scholarship in the town, it now boasted a middle school, an elementary teachers' centre[6] and, like Kano, a girls' school. Many of the students were the children of the emir and his wives and concubines, and of his privy councillors. At this period the feudal and polygamous traditions of the north were hardly touched. In Katsina, for instance, Perham found that the emir had four wives and 60 concubines and was happy for them to spend four hours a day drawing water; he did not want to install pumps because he worried about what they would get up to if they had more free time. Visiting a middle school in Katsina she was struck by the difference between north and south: she had never before visited a school where almost none of the pupils wanted to learn or the teachers to teach.[7]

The Higher College, which was residential, was to prove important in training a generation of male northern leaders, notably Abubakar Tafawa Balewa from Bauchi and Ahmadu Bello (to be Sardauna of Sokoto), who were contemporaries. Tafawa Balewa, the man who was to be the first Federal Prime Minister at independence, joined in 1928 and left in 1933, aged 21. Schooling was through the medium of Hausa, but key staff were British. Students had to sign a contract with their Native Authority to serve as a teacher for five years following graduation. Tafawa Balewa got a third-class certificate, but his best subject was English and he had been a prefect. His biographer, writing about a group who were to fill the public life of northern Nigeria in the 1950s, commented:

What they were all to claim, in their years of fully matured nostalgia, was to have arrived at college unable to string a sentence together and, in the care of teachers who did not think of themselves as unusually gifted or clever, to have acquired discipline, a work ethic and leadership – with no promise of material reward for the duty that must be done.[8]

Awareness was growing among administrators that there were serious risks in permitting two such different societies, in the north and south, to continue to diverge. Sir Donald Cameron, Governor from 1931 to 1935, tried to pull Nigeria together at a time when the world was beginning to recover from the slump and austerity was the watchword of colonial administration. Born in British Guiana and married to the daughter of a Barbados planter, he, too, had toured the empire. He had worked in Mauritius and southern Nigeria, he had been a secretary in Lugard's central secretariat, and he arrived back in Lagos from a stint as governor of the League of Nations mandated territory of Tanganyika.

What he found when he got back to the vantage point of Lagos was that indirect rule had led to a loosening of imperial control in the north. The success of the emirs in raising their own funds had led them, and the British Residents who advised them, to excessive independence. Cameron shared the Lugardian view that the emirs should not have the de facto independence of the princely states of India. He successfully challenged the British administrators in the north who had wanted the Colonial Office to extend the powers of Muslim sharia courts; a proposal to enable Muslim courts to rule on cases involving southerners living in townships adjoining northern cities had gone as far as a parliamentary bill in London, which Cameron got withdrawn. He agreed a compromise with the Residents under which, even though the townships would be partly under native administration, tribal assessors who were not Hausa-Fulani would be employed to try cases.

When Perham visited Kano, she saw the Emir overruled by the Resident in a case in which the Emir wanted to let boys off schooling because they were fasting during Ramadan. She said that although in theory the Emir had almost total autocratic power 'in practice, behind the curtain, he is checked and propelled not by a ministry, still less by a democracy, but by an unobtrusive, kindly, middle-aged Englishman who derives his authority from the military power and wealth of Great Britain'.[9] In reality the British could always depose an unsatisfactory emir and had troops stationed in every capital.

Cameron also challenged European prejudice. Going to the horse races with him in Lagos, Perham was impressed by the absence of a colour bar and the fact that the governor-general would invite Africans to his private pavilion. She had travelled in east and southern Africa and seen nothing like this. She reported him as saying, 'Africans – I never think of people by race. To me they are just individuals.' She commented, 'What a contrast, this! But of course the reasons lie deep in history, the absence of settlers and the length of the culture contact, as well as in Cameron's temperament.'[10]

Chapter 5
Between the wars:
the economy in a world depression

The interwar years were rocky for the economy, and opposition to taxation and to the continuing grip of British and European companies fed a growing nationalist feeling. In 1919–20 there was optimism that a boom was coming, with shipping released at the end of the war and competition to buy the cash crops of cocoa, palm oil and groundnuts. But it turned out that the European economies could not afford to buy, and there was a wave of bankruptcies among Nigerian firms in Lagos, which only the big European combines were unaffected by. During the short era of optimism there was a burst of strikes, as workers tried to make up for the compression of wages they had suffered during the war. Tin miners, miners at the Udi coalfield near Enugu, railwaymen and civil servants all agitated for better wages.

Prices for primary products gradually recovered, hitting a peak in 1926–7, before the onset of the depression. They were then held back throughout the 1930s, a period of severe deflation in Nigeria. Between 1929 and 1940, for example, the export of cocoa grew only from 55,000 tons to 90,000 tons, but the price per ton dropped from £72 to £28; the quantity of palm oil was the same, but the price fell by 75%, from £48 a ton to £12; and although the export volume of groundnuts rose from 147,000 tons to 169,000 tons, the price more than halved to £10 a ton.[1] The overall value of Nigerian exports almost halved from over £17M in 1929 to £9.7M in 1938.[2]

Transport in Nigeria, away from the rivers, had always been a challenge, depending on donkeys and horsepower. In the 1920s there was investment in rail lines, with the eastern line extended from Udi with its coalfields to Jos and Zaria on the plateau; the line from Lagos to Kano was improved. But the arrival of lorry transport, often owned by aspirant African entrepreneurs like Obafemi Awolowo (see below), led to complaints from the government-owned railways. Although roads were still poor the lorries could provide an end-to-end service. The railway department started demanding protection from 1926, and in 1933 there was an arbitration that forced the railway to reduce its freight rates yet gave it some help. But the African lorries could still compete at a profit.

The world depression saw some strengthening of economic links between north and south, as southern producers of palm oil and other products looked for national markets when international ones shrivelled. This trade was not all one-way. Perham noted in Kano that the town was exporting 20 tons of dried mudfish a month to markets in the port of Lagos. Cotton, which the British could not afford to buy, strengthened a traditional textile industry. Good harvests in the north in the early 1930s meant that farmers there had surplus incomes, and food prices came down.

But taxes for the emirs and the colonial regime and retrenchment in the administration led not only to reductions in capital investment and impositions on the populace, but also to relative hardship for colonial officials. There was at this time around one British official per 100,000 native people in the more extensive north, compared with one per 70,000 in the south, some 200 bureaucrats in all. Along with their fellows in the other west African colonies and British traders, they described themselves as 'coasters'. Writing in early 1932 about the poor quality of European housing in Katsina, Margery Perham noted, 'In the present economic crisis there is no hope of new buildings or even adequate grants for maintenance, while the "bush-allowance" which this suffering northern service was granted has been cut by fifty per cent.'[3]

A certain confidence and aggression in indigenous Nigerian enterprise was reflected in the setting up of a National Bank by Yoruba businessmen in 1934 and an attempt to challenge control of the export business in cocoa by international firms, the so-called 'Cocoa Pool'. Cocoa growers, especially in the southwest who had been building solid houses with tin roofs from their profits, decided in 1938 to boycott the ten European firms responsible for buying nearly all their beans. The firms had set up a cartel and jointly agreed to reduce the price they paid. This struggle raised awareness and saw the dynamic Nigerian Youth Movement, which had overtaken the NNDP of Macaulay in Lagos, winning the support of Sir Bernard Bourdillon, Governor of Nigeria from 1935 to 1943. Bourdillon was friendlier to the class of western-educated professionals than his predecessors, and he persuaded the Colonial Office to set up an inquiry. This led to a commission to oversee the cocoa trade. Nevertheless, while the British share of imports to Nigeria was falling from up to 80% in the three decades to 1930 to only 54% in 1939,[4] two-thirds of exports remained in the hands of only seven European firms of which the largest was the Anglo-Dutch firm Unilever.

Economic differences between the north and south, which had existed in Lugard's day, became more pronounced in the 1930s. The motor transport revolution rippled out from Lagos and the southern cities, but vehicle ownership in the north was tiny. Demand for trained persons, although they might hit the glass ceilings of a stratified colonial society, advantaged southerners even in the businesses and administrations of the north. The growth of unions tended to be southern-based, and significantly the Nigerian Union of Teachers, which was founded in 1931 and of which the Reverend Israel Oludotun Ransome-Kuti was to be a leading light, became the biggest union in that decade. Taxes bore down harder on northerners. It was impossible to seal off the north totally, with its Koranic schools and aristocratic controls, but the region lacked the burgeoning, critical press of the south. The first Hausa paper, *Gaskiya Ta Fi Kwabo* (literally, 'Truth is worth more than a penny'), was not set up until 1939. It was founded by Rupert East, who had married a Fulani and was running a literature bureau in Zaria on behalf of the education department in the north. A growing nationalistic ferment in the south was, for both economic and cultural reasons, not truly about 'one Nigeria.'

Chapter 6
Between the wars:
a new assertive nationalism

The sense of anti-colonialism in the south was fostered by a small elite, some of whom had gone to universities in Britain and helped found the West African Students Union there in 1925,[1] and by a wider group that was frustrated by the racism, exploitation and limited opportunities of colonial society. There were different currents. In western Nigeria, for instance, there was an effort to bring the different Yoruba sub-groups and clans together into a modern pan-Yoruba awareness, which had both cultural and political aspects. But there was also a nascent attempt to build a Nigerian nationalism, associated with Nnamdi Azikiwe and his first newspaper in what became a chain, the *West African Pilot*, in 1937. It was emblematic that the Lagos Youth Movement, started by students who thought the Higher College in Yaba should be a university, changed its name in 1936 to the Nigerian Youth Movement.

For the late 1930s saw powerful stirrings, and the first prominence of two men, both initially inspired by Herbert Macaulay, who would play leading roles in the tortuous story of Nigeria over the next 30 years. They were Nnamdi (originally Benjamin) Azikiwe (1904–96) and Obafemi Awolowo (1909–87). Neither fully enjoyed the political authority to which they aspired, though Azikiwe was to be Governor-General of Nigeria (1960–63) and then the first President of Nigeria (1963–66), and Awolowo was to be Premier of Western Nigeria (1954–60) and then federal Commissioner of Finance during the civil war. Both died when their country was ruled by generals, and both were part of a civilian political establishment that was to be blamed for Nigeria's collapse into military dictatorships.

Azikiwe, nicknamed Zik, was born in a grass hut in Zungeru in the Niger province in the north. His father, who was an Igbo and directly descended from the first King of Onitsha, was an administrator attached to the Nigeria Regiment; he had been born 25 years earlier, on the day Onitsha was bombarded by a British gunboat, HMS Pioneer. For the first eight years of his life, the young Zik lived in the north, speaking Hausa fluently, but after his father moved to Lagos he was sent to the Wesleyan Boys' High School there at the age of ten,[2] where he learnt Yoruba. He was therefore trilingual, well placed to think in 'Nigerian' terms as he entered adulthood. This formative experience was strengthened by spells in the Gold Coast and the United States, which gave him a sense of perspective.

Showing the enterprise that was one of his hallmarks as a young man, Zik got to the Gold Coast as a stowaway, where he joined the Gold Coast police in Accra. Then, persuaded by his mother and with £300 from his father's early retirement pension through ill-health, he crossed to the United States to study. He moved through Howard University and Lincoln University to Columbia University, where he took a journalism degree, which included the study of international law and labour problems. Graduating at the age of 29, he was full of ambition. He wanted to raise funds either to start a paper or found a university. He also wrote unsuccessfully to Herbert Macaulay to see if there was a job going either at his *Lagos Daily News* or in the Nigerian National Democratic Party.[3]

In the end it was one of his Accra contacts who came good. A Mr O.J. Ocansey was the owner of a store, cinemas and a press in the Gold Coast. Zik persuaded him to start up a new Accra paper in 1934, with himself as editor.[4] He called it the *African Morning Post* – borrowing a title from an old and recently expired paper in London, the *Morning Post*.[5] Starting a paper is a high-risk enterprise, but, even though he was not himself from the Gold Coast, the *African Morning Post* was a roaring success. In two years the circulation had shot up from 2,000 in 1934 to 10,000 in 1936.

Zik edited with brio, taking sides in Gold Coast politics to such effect that a new Mambii Party, which his paper backed, rapidly overtook the Ratepayers Association in elections. The philosophy was pan-African, calling for a new nationalist spirit in the continent, and inspired by the ideas of Marcus Garvey and Gandhi. He was sympathetic to younger Gold Coast nationalists, writing to Lincoln University in 1935 to recommend Kwame Nkrumah for a place. However, Zik came up against the colonial regime when he was put on trial for seditious libel in 1936. His proprietor had asked him to publish an article by a contributor entitled 'Has the African a God?' The writer, Wallace Johnson, attacked Europeans for believing in a deceitful god who sought to 'civilise' the 'barbarous' Africans with the aid of machine guns. In fact Zik had not wanted to print the article, and he was released on a technicality – he was not actually editing the paper that day.

But whether this disenchanted him with the Gold Coast, or his growing reputation now made possible a return to Nigeria, he was able to move to Lagos the following year as an editor-proprietor. He founded the *West African Pilot*, launched on 22 November 1937 with a motto he said was derived from Dante: 'Show the light, and the people will find the way.' A fifth of the staff came with him from the *Morning Post* in Accra. In due course Zik's campaigning journalism made the paper into a profitable enterprise with linked media in other Nigerian cities.

Zik attacked racism and colonialism, subsequently stimulating 'extreme Zikists' who wanted direct action, as part of a ferment of proto-Nigerian nationalism, which also swept up local clan and improvement associations, unions, and students coming back from Britain and the United States. He pushed the Nigerian Youth Movement. But there were strong elements of west African solidarity and nascent pan-Africanism in his approach. The Italian invasion of Abyssinia (Ethiopia) in 1935 had created a profound impression, and a mass meeting in Lagos expressed anger that a European dictator had attacked the oldest independent African state on the continent.

Although Lagos was a Yoruba city it was also the capital, drawing in Igbos and other ethnicities (though not many northerners) in the 1930s. Muslims outnumbered Christians until 1950, thanks to a substantial number of Yoruba Muslims. Its population roughly tripled in the three decades to 1931, with public health standards rising after a serious bubonic plague. Zik was not running a Yoruba paper, but one with a wider vision, and indeed in criticising earlier activists like Macaulay, who was then seen as compromising and conservative, he could be critical of Yorubas. Younger people like him were increasingly fed up with European-only hotels, the European-only Ikoyi Club, and the lack of African promotion to the higher levels of the administration. Cameron had been unusual in having easy intercourse with the educated elite.

But if Zik had come to the fore as a journalist, his great rival, Obafemi Awolowo, had a different background. Although he, too, had briefly tried journalism, he came out of a background of business – including failed businesses – and quasi-political organisation. Awo, as he was later known, was born in 1906 in Ikenne, in Ijebu Remo in what is now Ogun state. This was a Yoruba area, and his father David, a yam farmer and lumber merchant, was the first Christian convert in the family. But a happy childhood was abruptly ended when he was a young teenager. First his father took another wife, and he rapidly died of smallpox in 1920. Then Awo's beloved grandmother moved away to Abeokuta. Finally, his own mother moved back to her parents and remarried.

The result was that Obafemi was destitute, had to withdraw from school because there was no one to pay fees, and had to earn his own living. But in 1921 he moved to Abeokuta to seek his fortune, and things looked up. He managed to get back into education, studying at the Wesleyan School in Imo, and passed the exam to enter a four-year teacher training establishment, the Wesley College, Ibadan. He joined it in January 1927, where he hated the obsequious attitude that African teachers had to whites, and for a couple of years he also worked as a teacher at a Wesley School in Abeokuta. He said that he and a group of friends vowed never to dine, or associate socially, with white people, a vow he claimed to have kept until 1953.[6]

Awo was college clerk at Wesley College, Ibadan in 1932–34, a period in which he also learnt shorthand and typing and read widely. He spent three months as a trainee reporter at the *Nigerian Daily Times* in 1934 but then sought to make money in business. He tried several enterprises: money lending, lorry transport, and buying and selling produce. Bankrupt at one point, he was rescued by a freight contract to deliver yam flour between Lagos, Abeokuta, Ibadan and Kaduna.

As a lorry owner he proved his organisational mettle, becoming Secretary to the Nigerian Motor Transport Union. He also became heavily involved in the struggles against the attempt to maintain a rail monopoly and against the European buyers in the 'cocoa pool'. His strike by the lorry owners against the imposition of a licence fee to protect the railways was at least partly successful. Unfortunately for the cocoa campaign, the subsequent Cocoa Marketing Law ended up by keeping most of the export business for the European firms. At this stage Awo, while a nationalist, was not yet a democratic socialist, and he was particularly concerned about building Yoruba cooperation and identity. Indeed his entrepreneurial struggles typified the efforts of Yoruba traders, often trained in European firms and with interests stretching to Kano and the north, to build indigenous capitalism.

By the end of the 1930s there were signs that the administration and traditional authorities were also smiling on moves to build a pan-Yoruba identity. Young men from four sections in Abeokuta, who were working in Lagos, got together to create a social centre and association called the Lisabi Club. Both the governor and the Alake of Abeokuta turned out for the laying of the foundation stone in 1939. Editorialising, *West Africa*, the journal that still represented the interests of British merchants and colonial officers, commented that this showed the governor wants to 'encourage Africans to the great goal of unity.'[7]

Both Zik and Awo, along with other younger intellectuals and activists, belonged to the Nigerian Youth Movement, which defeated Macaulay's NNDP for the three elected seats in Lagos in 1938. In February that year Sir Bernard Bourdillon, subsequently criticised for lacking sympathy with the nationalists, thought it politic to meet the NYM leadership. In retrospect this party could have been the core of a unified independence movement for Nigeria, comparable to the Congress Party of India or the later Tanganyika African National Union, founded by Julius Nyerere in 1954. Its collapse was a setback to the always difficult project to make a single nation.

The NYM's charter set out genuinely national and Nigerian objectives. It wanted to develop a united nation out of the different ethnicities in the country, aiming for autonomy within the British Empire. It proposed mass compulsory and free education, universal adult suffrage, separation of the judiciary from the executive, protection of Nigerians against unequal economic competition, better pay and promotion prospects for Africans in the civil service and an end to unequal pay as between Europeans and Africans who were doing the same work.[8]

But conservatism by the feudal emirs, abetted by their British advisers and the colonial administration, prevented the NYM from building a substantial membership in the north. Southern migrants and traders had been kept to townships outside the main cities of the north, known as *Sabon Gari,* in a parallel to European-enforced segregation in southern Africa. The colonial regime simply did not wish to see a modern politics developing there, although there were NYM branches in Jos, Kaduna, Zaria and Kano, and there were individual members elsewhere who joined. One northern teacher who signed up was sacked for belonging and had to be found a post in the NYM secretariat in Lagos. The net result was that the north came to view the NYM as a southern party, which was not its intention, and southern suspicion of British tactics of divide-and-rule, protecting undemocratic societies in the north, would grow over the next decades.

This defect would also play into friction between the southern groups, stimulating competition between Yoruba and Igbo and leading to the party's break-up in 1941. The scope for friction increased because of an important administrative decision of 1938. In that year the British decided to split what had been the southern protectorate into two – the West, and the East; there was to be an additional commissioner and secretariat in Ibadan, as well as in Enugu. There was a manifest disparity between the large size of the north, although it was not a politically or culturally monolithic region, and the now divided south.

The 1920s and 1930s saw an expansion of Nigerian-owned business, in spite of the difficult economic circumstances and the continuing grip of British and European firms. But in terms of regional or national awareness the expansion of education was equally crucial. In part this was because it promoted the spread of the English language, the bridge language not only between Hausa, Yoruba and Igbo, but also a medium of exchange for up to 300 other ethnicities. By the outbreak of war in 1939, however, only 12% of Nigerian children were in school.[9] Yet even in the north, where the British prevented students from going to Al-Azhar University in Cairo,

:ause it had been contaminated by anti-European and ιary sentiment, there was some need for western education. British officials and some emirs wanted *Malams* (teachers) who could write in roman rather than Arabic script to keep the minutes of the Native Authorities, and to provide a small educated cadre for financial and other purposes. British Residents and officials in Nigeria were unlikely to read Arabic themselves, and they had done little to stimulate a modernised Islamic schooling.

British fear of possible disaffection in the north linked with most emirs' dislike of un-Islamic ideas at a time when they had many wives and concubines, and the difference between ex-slaves and slaves was not obvious.[10] As one author comments, seeing the 1930s as a period of conservatism, 'The system of providing Western education to the Northern peoples had, right from its inception, been decidedly guarded in order to maintain the status quo, to ensure development on 'native lines' and to prevent the bringing up of a generation of rebels as in the South.'[11]

Hence the handful of northerners who obtained a western education and then passed it on to others as teachers was precious and influential. Sir Abubakar Tafawa Balewa, the future federal Prime Minister, had left school in Bauchi in 1933 to become a *Malam*. He taught at Bauchi Middle School, where he was to become a housemaster who was relatively strict, quite academic and deeply religious. This was a Native Authority school operating at a time of gradual reform, promoted by Donald Cameron, when pre-adolescent girls started attending elementary schools alongside boys.

Abubakar Tafewa's biographer described how all was not well in the Bauchi Native Authority in these years. 'While modernity was reflected in the planning of a new 'aeroplane ground' with drains and hard strips to facilitate the weekly airmail delivery from Kano, Yakubu II reigned approvingly over peculation in the native treasury, and most officials in the native administration were in debt to moneylenders. Some owed up to two years' salaries because they had accepted grossly overvalued cloths and other articles from shysters. The chief moneylender, Kwara, had so much influence that the emir wanted to make him his *waziri,* or chief adviser and senior council member. The British administration frustrated this and planned with the chief *alkali* to have any disputed goods truly valued and fair periodic repayments of the loans organised from salary deductions, but they could not stop Kwara from driving round in the emir's car (for which the Native Authority paid) and only with difficulty discouraged the emir from taking Kwara with him to chiefs' conferences in Kaduna.'[12]

Sir Ahmadu Bello, who was Abubakar's contemporary at the Katsina Training College, did not stay in teaching for long. He was of aristocratic birth. His great-grandfather had been Sultan Bello, founder of Sokoto and son of the famous Islamic leader, Usman Dan Fodio. Although Ahmadu Bello taught for a while at Sokoto Middle School, he soon went into administration in the Native Authority, becoming divisional head at Gusau in 1938 and in that year tried unsuccessfully to become Sultan of Sokoto. However his victorious rival, recognising his talent, gave him the traditional title of Sardauna and brought him onto the Native Authority Council.

The significance of education for political development in the southwest has already been alluded to, and this western-style education was on a totally different scale from the north, started much earlier, was linked to Christianity and helped girls as well as boys. The remarkable Ransome-Kuti family showed its power and range. The Reverend Josiah Jesse Ransome-Kuti (1855–1930), father of the Reverend Israel Oludotun Ransome-Kuti and grandfather of the musician Fela, was the son of Anne, who had converted to Christianity around 1848. Her husband Kuti was hostile to Christianity, but, after his death, the mother and son joined the Church Missionary Society, and Josiah became a minister at the CMS Training Institute in Lagos and then a music teacher at the CMS School in Ake, Abokuta. Josiah Jesse was a driving force, allegedly founding 16 churches in and around Abeokuta and becoming well known for setting Christian hymns in the Yoruba language. He had six children, and Israel Oludotun, born in 1891, started his education at the CMS Grammar School in Lagos but completed it as the first pupil of the Abeokuta Grammar School.[13]

Israel Oludotun was a junior assistant teacher at the same school until 1912, then going to Fourah Bay College in Sierra Leone to get a degree and teaching qualification. In 1916 he was an assistant master at the CMS Grammar School in Lagos, and in 1919 he was made principal of the Ijebu-Ode Grammar School, near Abeokuta. In 1925 he married the feisty Funmilayo Thomas, who had been one of the first girls to go to Abeokuta Grammar School in 1914 when it became coeducational. She came from a farming family that was aspirational for daughters and had been sent to an English girls' school in Cheshire. In England she learnt to ride a bike – it was said later that she would be the first black woman in sub-Saharan Africa to drive a car – and on her return she became head teacher of the girls' section of the Abeokuta Grammar School.[14]

She also ran a succession of 'ladies clubs', initially concerned with middle class housewifely skills but subsequently bringing her into contact with wider and poorer sections of society. Her sense of community awareness, which led her to a radical, feminist nationalism in the 1940s, chimed with a strong sense of professional dedication in her husband, Oludotun. He was a driving force in the creation of the Nigeria Union of Teachers out of separate associations in the towns of Lagos, Agege, Ibadan, Abeokuta, Ijebu-Ode and the non-Yoruba Calabar; in July 1931 he was elected the first president. Like the National Union of Teachers in England and Wales this union was interested in the content of education, as well as pay and conditions, though it was a struggle to maintain salaries during the depression. He happened to be in England on an educational course when the Second World War broke out and was chief speaker at anniversary celebrations for the West African Students Union.

This was a family with Christian parents that was ambitious for Nigeria, socially minded, and disciplined in its approach. Israel Oludoton was of the view that to spare the cane was to spoil a child.[15] It was an example of a more assertive middleclass, aware of what was going on in the rest of the world – especially the campaign for Indian independence – which was becoming increasingly impatient with colonial status.

Yet when Nigeria was once more brought into a European war, in 1939 by virtue of Nazi Germany's invasion of Poland, it was as part of the British Empire. Unlike South Africa, whose white parliament only narrowly voted to join an imperilled mother country that not all Afrikaners saw in that light, it had no choice in the matter. Furthermore, in important respects it was not 'one Nigeria' but two distinct countries, or possibly three now that the west had been separated administratively from the east. One of the main issues over the six years of the Second World War was whether the experience would add to a sense of unity or division.

In the Secretary of State's message to the colonies on 9 September 1939, Malcolm MacDonald, Secretary of State for the Colonies[16] wrote:

> Our knowledge of the feelings of 60 millions of our fellow citizens in Colonial territory has sustained us in Great Britain in our efforts for peace and steeled us in our own preparations for war. We, in the United Kingdom, are prepared to make whatever sacrifices may be necessary in the course of this struggle. We shall be ever mindful that you, in Colonial territory, are sharing our task and our

burden, and our sympathy and sense of comradeship with you will be constant. In the words of his Majesty the King, let us stand calm, firmly united in this time of trial. The long and happy association of so many peoples of different races and creeds under the British Crown is itself the best proof that the idea of peaceful and fruitful cooperation between diverse peoples, who are willing to understand and respect each other, is attainable; and that knowledge will fortify us in our fight to secure the establishment of that ideal in the wider world.[17]

Politically aware Nigerians will have wondered how far they were truly fellow-citizens with the people of the United Kingdom, while noting that they were as many as a third of the population of the colonies, excluding India. It had not always been such a happy association. The concepts of liberty and democracy, for which the British were fighting, meant rather less in the colonies, and the 'idea of peaceful and fruitful cooperation between diverse peoples' was a less attractive slogan to die for. Only the vicious, deadly racism of the Nazis, some of whom referred to Africans as 'semi-apes', struck a chord. In 1938, when a rumour spread that Nigeria might be handed to Germany as part of an appeasement deal, there was a strongly hostile reaction among Nigerians. Colonial Office planning assumed that the war would last only three years, and when the four west African governors met in September 1939, just as it started, their agenda of oil palms, aerial surveying and the need for a west African university seemed remarkably untroubled.

Section 2

1939–64: Rocky road to freedom

Chapter 7
Another world war
and strategic importance

In retrospect it is easy to see most of Nigeria's second quarter-century, starting in 1939, as merely a prologue to an inevitable independence. It did not seem so at the time. Winston Churchill, who had come of age under Queen Victoria and taken part in a cavalry charge at Omdurman against the Mahdist army in 1898, was a dyed-in-the-wool imperialist. The politician who had spoken out against the rise of Hitler in the 1930s had simultaneously attacked the idea of independence for India and denigrated Mahatma Gandhi. Yet from 1940 on he was the British Prime Minister in the Second World War, from whom the governor and authorities in Nigeria took their orders.[1] It was not until 1947 that the Indian Empire was dissolved, and it took a further decade before Ghana became the first British colony in sub-Saharan Africa to gain its independence. Independence for Nigerians was for some years a distant and divisive prospect, and, until 1945, the existential struggle against Nazism had more immediate consequences.

As in the First World War, the Second saw Nigeria acquire a new importance. This was partly strategic because the country was surrounded by French colonies, some of which owed allegiance to Vichy. In fact Nigeria was not attacked, but the French colonies of Dahomey (Benin) and Niger were with Vichy while the governors of Chad and French Cameroons backed Charles de Gaulle. Significantly, Chad, which had one of France's first black colonial governors in Félix Éboué, declared for the Allies in August 1940. More positively, Nigeria lay along the supply route by which munitions and equipment from the United States were flown to Allied armies in the Middle East. Its commodities and minerals became more valuable. With the Japanese occupation of Malaya, for example, the output of tin from the mines on the Jos plateau became the main supply for the British Empire. Nigeria's importance was also as a source of troops and porters. The reputation won in the Cameroons and east African campaigns in 1914–18 meant that there was an instant call for Nigerians to join the war against the Italians in Somalia and Ethiopia, followed soon by a request from General Archibald Wavell, that Nigerians should join the struggle in Burma.

For most Nigerians the impact of the war was economic and negative. As before, the traditional rulers made financial contributions. Responding to an appeal from the Sultan of Sokoto, the chiefs in the north contributed 5% of their salaries to the war effort.[2] Governor Bourdillon authorised the Native Administrations to draw on their reserve funds to pay for their expenses. By the middle of 1940 there was an element of conscription in all four west African colonies for men aged 18 to 48.

The worst part was the rising cost of living and shortages of essentials, especially of salt in 1943. Prices of staple foods, such as yams and *gari*, soared, and in the north the government's ill-conceived policies, diverting labour from the land and imposing price controls, led to famine.[3] At the same time the British firms, led by Unilever's United Africa Company, were making substantial profits from exported commodities, which were seen as exploitative by nationalists. A West African Produce Control Board, working with the Ministry of Food in London, bought oilseeds, palm kernels and cocoa at fixed and ungenerous prices.

Zik's *West Africa Pilot* focused its ire on the price controls on foodstuffs and produce. For instance, the paper pointed out that the price paid for palm kernels had been £10 a ton in 1908, but was only

£5.10s a ton in 1941.[4] By 1942 the cost of living had risen by 46.89% compared with 1939 and the government appointed a Cost of Living Committee. In the markets there were complaints about rising prices of basics. Captain A.P. Pullen, the Controller of Native Foodstuffs, introduced a system designed to fix prices on a small number of basic foods, but it was too easily evaded and unpopular with traders. In Lagos 8,000 market women signed a petition against it, and it became a factor in the wartime unpopularity of the colonial regime. A minimum wage and Labour Welfare Board seemed inadequate to curb continuing price inflation as the war continued.

Britain's demand for tin led to abuses at Jos. In 1942 it was agreed that forced labour could be used to conscript up to 100,000 peasant miners, aiming to produce 20,000 tons of tin a year. The target was not hit. Labourers unused to the conditions suffered from poor health and poor housing and deserted, and questions were asked in the House of Commons. It was a scandal, and two years later the forced labour was abandoned.

At the same time some workers benefited from wartime needs, and unionisation spread rapidly. The most spectacular building boom was created by the air bridge to carry aircraft and supplies between the United States and the armies in the Middle East. The route went from Takoradi in the Gold Coast to Apapa/Lagos, then Kano and Maiduguri in Nigeria, then across to El Geneina, El Fasher and Khartoum in Sudan, ending in Cairo. Well over 10,000 Nigerian men were employed in building not only the aerodromes but all the ancillary facilities, including roads, hospitals and camps.[5]

One benefit for Nigerian workers of the wartime coalition in London was the arrival of the Labour Party in government. Labour ministers in Britain inserted a clause in the Colonial Welfare and Development Act, 1940, by which no grant could be made to a territory unless there were proper facilities for trade unions. An order in 1942 under Defence Regulations made strikes and lockouts illegal. The reality of rising prices and the diversion of labour into the army and priority occupations gave a huge incentive to unionise. Whereas there had only been three unions in 1938, 82 were registered by 1945.

While for many Nigerians the war, and the reasons for it, seemed remote, there was a gradual shift in elite opinion as it dragged on. As already noted, initially there was strong support for Britain, based on the racist attitudes of the Nazis. A rumour at the time of the Munich agreement already mentioned that Nigeria might be handed to Germany led to demonstrations. In September 1939 a mass meeting of 10,000 in Lagos was addressed by the Oba, offering full support for the Allies. The *West African Pilot* attacked German racism and quoted the appeasement policy as showing that democracies had tried everything to avoid war. This attitude was buttressed in 1940 when Italy, the colonial power that had occupied the oldest independent black state in Africa, joined Germany in the Axis. Propaganda reached down to the primary schools, with children involved in collecting rubber and palm kernels. While British soldiers were singing 'Hang out the washing on the Siegfried Line', Nigerian children were singing, 'Hitler that is throwing the world into confusion/Push him with a shovel into the grave.'[6]

But this mood of wholehearted backing for the war did not last, particularly among the southern nationalists. This was not only due to the economic burden. Two other factors were the foggy war aims of the colonial regime with regard to Nigeria and irritation at contemporary British racism as more Nigerians saw their contribution undervalued or disparaged in spite of claims that colonial peoples were equals in the struggle. Governor Bourdillon's statement that the only war aim that mattered was survival seemed inadequate, and Churchill's gloss on the Anglo-American Atlantic Charter of August 1941 was infuriating. Point three of the charter, subsequently adopted the following year by all the 'United Nations' fighting the Axis, stated clearly that all people have a right to self-government. But Churchill, still a man of empire, stated that this did not apply to the colonies of the European protagonists.

Zik's *Pilot* commented angrily:

> Day by day I become embittered when I ponder the fate of Africans who had no choice but to become colonial peoples and to experience what it means to live in a colony. Day by day as I taste the bitter pill of being a member of a subject race, I become sceptical and laugh at the effusions of those who proclaim to the world how paradisial is the lot of colonial peoples in the present scheme of things in the world.[7]

Particular incidents added to this anger, as did the overly white appearance of the Allies from a Nigerian perspective. Far from getting more opportunities, black Nigerians saw white wives of colonial officers getting jobs ahead of them, and the Yaba Higher College was closed with students transferred to Achimota in the Gold Coast. Higher posts were still a European preserve, with only four Africans in the Administrative Department in 1940, compared with 361 Europeans. In 1944 the administration commandeered the King's College building in Lagos and transferred students of this prestigious secondary school to the Bonanza Hotel, next to a noisy cinema, and they found it was infested by rats. There was a strike, but when eight boys were expelled they were forced to join the army. Youngsters taken to court for unruly conduct were defended by some of the best barristers. They were found not guilty.

Closer to the war itself there were more frustrations. As in other colonies, funds were raised to buy Spitfires and other aircraft for a threatened mother country. But whereas Caribbean airmen played a significant role in the Royal Air Force, few Nigerians had this chance.[8] In east Africa, where Nigerian troops fought in the successful early campaigns in Somalia and Ethiopia (Abyssinia), they had to watch as white South African soldiers were preferred to black Africans to march in at the liberation of Addis Ababa. In the war in Burma, largely fought by Indian troops, they saw many Indian commissioned officers. But Major Seth Anthony of the Gold Coast, who went to Sandhurst in 1942 and fought with the 81st division of the Royal West African Frontier Force in Burma, was the first west African officer.

The war saw a huge expansion in the number of Nigerian troops. There had only been six battalions of the Nigerian regiment in 1935. By July 1945 there were 92,000 Nigerian soldiers.[9] The great majority were illiterate, with young men joining up for adventure and travel, not from ideological conviction. While Hausas were predominant, other ethnicities were represented and the RWAFF, which also included volunteers from the Gold Coast, Sierra Leone and the Gambia, trained in Nigeria before going overseas. English replaced Hausa as the lingua franca in the west African divisions. In addition to the combatants the authorities also relied heavily on west African carriers, porters who could carry food and equipment on their heads over difficult terrain. Young men preferred soldiering to these non-combatant roles.

The Nigerian regiment, fighting as a distinct part of the RWAFF, saw service in east Africa where the Italians were poor fighters and their colonial troops, unlike von Lettow-Vorbeck's askaris in the First World War, showed little loyalty. Two divisions were involved in the attack on Ethiopia, each containing one west African and one east African brigade. The war in east Africa required improvisation and the Allied troops were not well equipped, but after taking Mogadishu they got to Addis in only three months. The commander of one of the Nigerian brigades wrote from Harar in 1941 to General Sir Alan Cunningham, overall commander of British forces in east Africa, in the most glowing terms: 'I think I may be permitted to take this opportunity to tell you how completely the Nigerian soldier has falsified all doubts as regards his reactions to the conditions of these operations…He is magnificent.'[10]

There were of course exceptions, and in wartime not all soldiers are angels. One example was recalled by Brigadier Gerald Cree, interviewed much later for the Imperial War Museum's sound archive. He remembered an occasion when a Nigerian soldier shot dead an 'Abyssinian' soldier because he wanted his watch. The higher command decided that looting was getting out of hand and an example had to be made. The man was tried by court martial and executed by military police. Normally a firing party was recruited from a man's own regiment, but as the Nigerians were about to go into action they were excused from this unpleasant duty.[11]

In Burma there were two west African divisions, the 81st and 82nd, and some Nigerians fought with General Orde Wingate's Chindits, guerrillas infiltrated deep behind Japanese lines. Conditions, especially in the monsoon, were difficult. The Japanese were tough and willing to fight to the last man. The Burmese jungle, with steep hills and watercourses, was hard to penetrate. Nigerian troops had to learn to swim and work boats, and their first contribution was to build an 80-mile 'West African Way' to the Kaladan river. Battle casualties in the North Arakan fighting, between March and July 1944, included 431 from the 81st West African division.[12] As in east Africa, and in the First World War, the Nigerians generally impressed their officers.[13]

To the Japanese, the Africans looked strange, tall and physically strong. But in the tough Burma campaign, remote from awareness in Britain, west African height, stamina and familiarity with tropical conditions were precious assets. The Africans knew the Japanese were ruthless and disinclined to take prisoners. One man who was lucky to survive was Isaac Fadoyebo, caught in a 1944 ambush with comrades, severely injured and expected to die by the Japanese who bayoneted others around him. But he was fed by Bengali-speaking peasants and then hidden by them and given the name 'Suleman'.[14] When the Japanese retreated he was rescued and taken home to Nigeria. In November 2011, when he was too frail to travel, an al-Jazeera journalist took a message of thanks to the family in Burma.[15]

Troops who went to Burma had seen Indian troops fighting on both sides, and British men as ordinary Tommies as well as the white officers who commanded them. There were Poles among the officers of the 81st division, which had Ananse, the cunning spider, as its symbol.[16] The state of Indian nationalism had an impact on thinking Nigerians, for while Indian soldiers were dying for the empire, Gandhi's 'Quit India' movement convulsed the subcontinent and Subhas Chandra Bose recruited an Indian National Army from captured prisoners to fight alongside the Japanese. Some of the European mystique of race was peeled away. In Gold Coast the ex-soldiers became a key part of the movement that led to independence. In Nigeria, with ethnic divisions that became more profound in the 1940s, this was less true.

For while soldiers from different parts of Nigeria might fight together in Burma, the Second World War saw a fragmentation of the nascent nationalist movement at home. Some of this was due to the ambition of Zik, the dominant figure among southerners, because of his effective, campaigning journalism. Some of it was due to the inherent caution of northerners, worried that clever, better-educated southerners might end up ruling over them.

A key moment in aborting a potential pan-Nigerian nationalism came in 1941, when the Nigerian Youth Movement was split in a dispute between Zik and Ernest Ikoli, its leaders. The NYM had won the three elected Lagos seats on the Legislative Council in 1938, and Zik supported Samuel Akisanya, a Yoruba from Ijebu, to stand to replace Dr Kofi Abayomi, who resigned to pursue his studies in the UK. Zik's man was defeated within the NYM executive, and Ikoli, an Ijo and president of the NYM, got the nomination. Zik then pulled out of the NYM, taking with him most of the Igbo and Ijebu Yoruba membership.

This was not the only hint that ethnicity was a growing factor. The war years saw the creation of a number of local, tribal and cultural associations that became the seeds of political activism. In 1945, when in London, Awolowo helped found a Yoruba cultural body, Egbe Omo Oduduwa (the society of the sons of Oduduwa, mythical progenitor of the Yoruba). These sentiments affected the north too, though to a lesser extent, so that in 1943 in Bauchi the future prime minister Abubakar Tafawa Balewa was one of the founders of a Bauchi Improvement Association. In July of the same year the British Council invited seven editors of west African papers, including Zik, to come to Britain. Zik was secretary of the group.

This was a public relations exercise for the war effort, but five of the seven journalists decided to take advantage of their visit by presenting a memo to the Colonial Office calling for independence. They wanted the move to independence in the four colonies to take place in two stages, starting immediately, or after the war ended, and leading to full independence in 15 years.[17] Significantly, Malam Abubakar Imam, editor of the Hausa paper *Gaskiya Ta Fi Kwabo*, refused to sign the memo; he feared that early moves to independence risked handing power over the north to the westernised elite in Lagos. One of the demands was that the UK should provide 200 scholarships for Nigerians to study abroad, but he feared that these would all go to southerners. The northern peasantry was hostile to western modernity, unwilling to send children to schools even if they were free, or to use modern hospitals.

The year after the trip to England, Zik founded the National Council of Nigeria and the Cameroons. Some of the impetus for this came from the Nigerian Union of Students, representing the young, ambitious and potentially educated, who were determined to keep pressing forward in spite of the break-up of the NYM. The NCNC, which became Zik's vehicle, was a kind of national front, built on unions, literary groups, tribal and local improvement organisations; initially it was not a political party in a modern sense, not having an individual membership. It not only galvanised Nigerians as the war came to an end, but also persuaded the colonial authorities that political development was imperative. The wider context was of impending victory for the Allies, whose main players were the United States and the Soviet Union. Neither of these were fond of colonial empires, and in December 1944 the new Governor of Nigeria Arthur Richards, Baron Milverton (in office 1943–48) proposed constitutional changes.

Within Nigeria there was an upsurge of militancy in the strengthened labour movement, fanned into flame by Zik and the *West African Pilot*. This coincided with their wider criticisms of the colonial regime. Writing later, Zik stated, 'Towards the end of World War Two, the civilian population in Nigeria was restive as a result of various hardships created by the war. At that time the Nigerian worker was one of the lowest paid wage-earners on the face of the earth.'[18] What became a general strike, lasting for 44 days in 1945, started with the Railway Workers' Union, which wanted a wage rise to match the rise in the cost of living. On 21 May, after the end of the war in Europe but when Nigerian troops were still in combat in the Far East, the African Civil Service Technical Workers' Union demanded a 50% wage increase. The colonial regime rejected these claims, precipitating the strike by 17 unions, involving some 30,000 members. Other African colonies were affected by labour unrest caused by wartime privations and inflation; in Southern Rhodesia, for instance, 2,000 black railwaymen in a new union went on strike, paralysing the Copperbelt in Northern Rhodesia. In Nigeria the authorities were forced to look into the strikers' complaints and concede pay increases. A commission of inquiry was set up under a British barrister, Tudor Davies, which recommended a 50% pay increase from the day the strikers returned to work.

The new assertiveness was illustrated at a more local level by the Abeokuta Ladies Club of Funmilayo Ransome-Kuti, which in 1944 had opened its membership to market women in the town. These women complained that the administration was confiscating their rice. The following year the ALC sent deputations to the assistant district officer and the Egba Native Administration Council, to no avail. It then held a press conference, reported by the *Daily Service*, and within a week the confiscations had stopped. Wole Soyinka, a relative of the Rev. Israel Oludotun Ransome-Kuti, commented in a memoir, 'The movement...begun over cups of tea and sandwiches to resolve the problem of the newlyweds who lacked the necessary social graces was becoming popular...It became tangled up in the move to put an end to the role of white men in the country.'[19]

At the centre of the campaign for a general strike, in the excitement of the end of the war, were Zik and his newspapers, the *Pilot* and *Daily Comet*.[20] There were many grievances, including the cost of living, compression of wages, problems of food supply, and the unemployment of returned soldiers. In 1943, in a series of articles collected in a book on economic reconstruction, Zik had advocated the nationalisation of tin and other mines. A British visitor, representing the Conservative Kemsley group of newspapers, reported that there was 'a revolutionary native press that quite seriously threatens the stability of this part of the Empire'.[21] Governor Richards, who was to describe this press bitterly as 'free to do the Devil's work', decided to crack down.[22] Using wartime defence orders he closed Azikiwe's papers on the grounds that they were misrepresenting the facts. Zik then founded a substitute, *The Public Defender*, and, claiming that his life was threatened by a colonial assassination plot, retreated to his home town of Onitsha.

The 'plot' against Zik was dismissed by the governor as rubbish and regarded as self-aggrandisement by a number of Yoruba intellectuals. In fact Zik milked the alleged plot for all it was worth, writing appeals to world leaders such as Harry S. Truman, Joseph Stalin and Charles de Gaulle saying that his life was in danger. Those who were his fans became even more dedicated, and a group of younger, more radical supporters became known as Zikists. They were looking to a more socialist, independent Nigeria and willing to use force to achieve their ends. Azikiwe in due course disowned them. Whether there was really a plot to murder him is hard to verify. Although it would seem an extreme reaction by the colonial authorities, they were certainly afraid of his rabble-rousing journalism. There may yet be revelations from intelligence files in Britain that settle this matter.

But the general strike looked different from the more conservative north. The biographer of Malam Abubakar Tafawa Balewa, then on an educational stint in Britain at the London Institute of Education, described the Malam's reaction as one of 'strong disapproval': 'Radical action that drew no moral or economic distinction between industrial strikes against a private employer, and political sabotage against a government responsible for the welfare of every sector of the community and for supplying almost every public utility, seemed to him [Tafawa Balewa] contemptible.'[23] He was uninterested in an NCNC delegation that came to Britain to try and win support, which suffered some criticism at home over its finances.

The *Pilot*, which had been fighting for the democratisation of the Legislative Council since the outbreak of war, recognised that it could not count on the north in its campaigns. In an editorial of 19 April 1943 it had asked rhetorically whether 'we can honestly say that the North, as it stands at the present is with us?' It answered, 'we rather doubt it'.

Chapter 8
Political change
and divisive regionalism

While Arthur Richards was Governor of Nigeria in 1943–48, he wanted to get ahead of, and pre-empt, what he saw as inevitable: the pressure for political change and 'Nigerianisation'. But he was also a colonial administrator of his time. Although his predecessor Bernard Bourdillon had promised reforms in the late 1930s and early 1940s, it was Richards who put forward proposals for constitutional change. He sent these to the Colonial Office on his own initiative, without advance consultation with the Legislative Council in Lagos. The only comment he requested the Colonial Office to obtain was from the now rather elderly Lord Lugard; this the Office stamped on huffily, on the grounds that it would encourage other previous governors to put in their penny's worth.

The Richards proposals did little for democratisation[1] and provided for consultation with, rather than real legislative or financial powers for, Nigerians in new regional assemblies. But they did draw north and south together; they did strengthen the regional system; they did link the Native Authorities, a key plank in indirect rule, with the old Crown Colony heritage of Lagos and Calabar with their four elected members still part of the Legislative Council; and they did involve more Nigerians as 'nominated unofficials' in the administration of their country. Taken together, they pointed the way to a federal future for a country of such diversity, in which Lagos would have to take more account of opinions elsewhere. For all that, this constitution was roundly abused by the National Council of Nigerian Citizens, which sent a delegation to the UK before it was due to take effect to try and change it. It was approved late in 1945 by an indifferent House of Commons, which by then had a large Labour majority supporting a government keen to withdraw from India.

What did the constitution contain, and why were the NCNC and the Lagos press so strongly opposed? The new Legislative Council was to have 41 members and cover the whole country in its ambit; 28 of these were 'unofficials', not employed by the administration, and most of these were selected by the new regional councils. Members of the three regional councils, in each of which the 'unofficials' had a majority of one, were selected by the Native Authorities. But in the north a house of chiefs was set up alongside the regional council, which all first-class chiefs were entitled to attend. Richards had wanted a house of chiefs in the west also, but was advised against it by his senior administrators on the grounds that the Yoruba chiefs did not have the semi-feudal authority of the emirs. The Executive Council remained wholly European.

There was also an anti-Lagos bias in the constitution. Speaking to the Members Estimate Committee of the House of Commons just after he had retired, the now Lord Milverton, as Richards had become, said frankly that its object was to 'end the absurdly predominant influence of Lagos on Nigeria'. To that end he had insisted that the annual meetings of the Legislative Council should rotate around the regional capitals of Lagos, Kaduna, Ibadan and Enugu. He claimed to the MPs that Zik's constitutional proposals would have meant that one vote in Lagos would have been worth 3,000 in the North.[2]

Many obas, emirs and chiefs thought that the 1946 Richards Constitution was an advance. Yet there were two main reasons why the southern nationalists were so hostile. They did not want more discussion fora and an imposed constitution; they wanted genuine participation both in making and operating a constitution. Secondly, they thought the Native Authorities were themselves undemocratic and therefore the expanded Legislative Council rested on the bogus indigeneity of indirect rule.[3] Below the surface, too, lay the suspicion that, by hardening regional divisions, the British were playing a game of divide and rule.

The critique in the north was different. As set out by Abubakar Imam, editor of *Gaskiya*, the problem was that with around 60 Native Authority areas it would be impossible to represent their views fairly; there were considerable cultural and ethnic differences in the Muslim areas, and around a third of the region was animist or Christian. Further, the habits of respect for the emirs and traditional authorities meant that the voices of younger, better-educated northerners might not get heard.[4]

For all these reasons, at a time of galloping change in the rest of the world, the Richards Constitution had a short shelf life. A new governor, Sir John Macpherson, arrived in April 1948; he brought with him Hugh Foot, from a celebrated family of Cornish radicals, as a young Chief Secretary.[5] Together they realised that political progress had to accelerate and that it was essential that this be done in genuine consultation with Nigerians.

But this was not an easy task. The divergences among politically conscious Nigerians were growing. Following the failed NCNC delegation to London to try and stop the Richards constitution, the NCNC itself lost momentum. With criticism at home of the financing of the trip and lack of more constitutional progress, it began to shed support, not least to a youth wing, the Zikist Vanguard movement. The Zikists sprang into existence as a result of the 'assassination plot' and got initial support from the Azikiwe press. The government brought sedition charges against Anthony Enaharo, editor of Zik's *Daily Comet*, and Assistant Editor Christopher Agwuna, who had given a public lecture entitled 'Call to Revolution' at a meeting chaired by Enaharo.[6]

The Zikists were determined to protect their leader's life. Starting by celebrating Zik's birthdays, they took on a revolutionary flavour in the late 1940s, inflaming disturbances. They organised strikes, encouraged the non-payment of taxes and the boycott of colonial Empire Days, and were accused of training militias and bringing explosives into the country.[7] In April 1950, after the shooting of unarmed miners in Enugu, an attempt on Hugh Foot's life and the declaration of a state of emergency, the Zikists were declared illegal. Foot's attacker was an ex-serviceman named Heelas Chukuwenka who stabbed him in the back and was alleged to have told an inspector that he was looking for the governor but decided to kill the chief secretary instead.[8]

The Zikists were disowned by Azikiwe, and what might have turned into an armed struggle for independence was snuffed out. But their action had been stimulated by frustration. In neighbouring Gold Coast, nationalists had managed to defeat a first post-war constitution. In Nigeria, in 1947, Awolowo, the up-and-coming Yoruba leader, was dismissing the idea of Nigeria as 'a geographical expression',[9] and the following year he launched the Egbe Omo Oduduwa organisation inside Nigeria to foster 'a single nationalism throughout Yorubaland' and build 'a virile modernised and efficient Yoruba state' within a federal polity.[10] Northerners, still worried about the risk of southern domination, were in no mood to join an armed rebellion. In a Legislative Council debate in April 1947 Abubakar Tafawa Balewa said, 'Since the amalgamation of the Southern and Northern Provinces in 1914, Nigeria has existed as one country only on paper. It is still far from being united.'

In retrospect the defeat of the Zikists was a turning point for modern Nigeria, though sadly it did not banish forever the threat of warfare inside the country. Just as the NCNC did not become a country-wide national movement, so the defeat of the Zikists and the conciliatory approach of Macpherson and Foot headed off the kind of armed, revolutionary anti-colonial struggles that started in Algeria in

1954 and broke out in the Portuguese empire and southern Africa later.

In 1951, the Nigeria (Constitution) Order in Council laid the framework for a strengthened regional system, buttressed by elections, which set the pattern for independence nine years later. This, the Macpherson constitution, provided for a central council of ministers presided over by the governor. It contained four ministers from each of the three regions – one from the east had to represent the Cameroons – which would be elected by the three regional houses of assembly. In addition to these ministers there were six ex-officio members – a Chief Secretary, three Lieutenant Governors, the Attorney-General and the Financial Secretary. But Alan Lennox-Boyd, Colonial Secretary in the new Conservative government, elected in 1951, subsequently assured Nigerian politicians that the role of these ex-officio members was advisory; the governor had to act on the views of the Nigerian elected ministers and was not expected to use the veto powers in the Macpherson constitution.

Backing up the council of ministers was a central House of Representatives with 136 persons, as well as up to six 'special members' chosen by the Governor to represent communities or interests he thought were overlooked. The elected members exactly balanced. There were 68 from the north, chosen by a joint council of the two northern houses, with 34 from the west, chosen from their membership by the two western houses (there was now a house of chiefs there) and 34 chosen by the house of assembly in the east. The regional legislatures had considerable powers. They could make laws covering, for example: agriculture, animal health, fisheries, forestry, local industries, cooperative societies, education, social welfare, customary land tenures and town and country planning. They could also make financial provision for policing and public relations.

Elections under the new constitution took place in late 1951. They revealed that the new system was cumbersome and liable to create internal conflicts; that the era of Azikiwe's dominance of southern nationalism was over, as it has been successfully challenged in the west by Awolowo's Action Group, which had emerged as the political wing of the Egbe; and that although the north lacked the more democratic character of the other regions, its emirs and traditional native authorities were quite capable of mobilising to defend their interests.

The sheer complexity of the new system was described by Funmilayo Ransome-Kuti in an article in *West Africa* on 3 November 1951. Both she and her husband, the Rev. Israel Oludotun Ransome-Kuti, were now well known and linked with Zik's NCNC but had failed to get elected. She had led a successful campaign against the unfair taxation of women, accompanied by mass demonstrations, which had led to the abdication of the Alake of Abeokuta. In this article she explained that, in Abeokuta and her part of Western Yorubaland, 3,500 villages and 143 townships had to elect five members of the Western House of Assembly via 96 primary colleges and 16 intermediate colleges; the intermediate colleges had to choose 169 representatives to make a final choice of the five members.

She wrote that, as soon as it was announced that successful candidates would get £300 a year in allowances[11], a number of voters said 'those who were nominated must pay for our votes.' However only those who could prove they had paid their taxes could get a vote, which ruled out most women. And the 'whispering vote', which allowed an illiterate to whisper the name of a preferred candidate to the returning officer, was open to abuse. She added that the public was against the new system because of its glaring defects. In the north it was even more open to manipulation at the hands of the native authorities.

There was considerable excitement over these elections, with traditional hornblowing in western villages and a bellman announcing them in some of those in the east. But they discouraged the growth of simple party politics for it was confusing that it was only late on in this electoral process that a candidate had to declare support for a party. The way that the council of ministers was structured, representing regions but not the balance within the central house of representatives, meant that there were Federal ministers from the NCNC elected by the east, even though the NCNC was in opposition in that house.

Several stories emerged from the results. Awo's Action Group, more disciplined and based on a principle of individual membership, defeated Zik's looser and less organised NCNC in the west, which became the opposition there. The NCNC won in the east. The Northern People's Congress, only founded in 1948, dominated in the north. And, although the representatives from the different regions hardly knew each other before they met in the central house of representatives in Lagos, there was genuine talent in the new council of ministers. But behind the scenes there was a shadow of potential corruption, an awareness that politics could be a way of making money.

The most striking result was that Zik, who had been courted by Governor Macpherson and put on a Nigerianisation commission, was no longer the charismatic strongman of southern nationalism. Observers remarked that his star had been 'completely eclipsed' by Awolowo[12] and, although Zik argued that in a more democratic system the NCNC would have won in the west as well as the east, he chose to 'retire' for some months and anathematised the Action Group as the 'Reaction Group'.

The NCNC and its allies had won elections for Lagos Town Council in 1950 by 18 to 6, but greater discipline and attention to detail by the AG enabled it to win a majority in the first western region elections the following year. It had published its list of candidates in advance and brought them all to Lagos for a rally; the NCNC thought that some successful candidates had betrayed it, but in reality they had never been as firmly committed.[13] Zik was not even a member of the central house of representatives.

There was an element of personal as well as national tragedy here. Azikiwe in himself encompassed the country's three main cultural groups, speaking Igbo, Hausa and Yoruba – an Igbo by origin, he had grown up as a Hausa boy and, living in Lagos, had given his children Yoruba names. Commenting on the Richards constitution in 1946, he foretold accurately that it 'divides the country into three zones that are bound to departmentalise the political thinking of this country'.[14] But by the late 1940s he was being seen by others as Igbo. In 1948 he agreed to become president of the Ibo State Union and, in an ill-conceived speech the following year, he said that the God of Africa had specifically created this nation to lead the children of Africa from bondage.

The AG, which had skilfully drawn together both monarchical and democratic elements in Yoruba society, was also feeling threatened by Igbo educational advance. Education became a watchword for the western regional government (see below). The north also suffered from a dangerous fusion of pride and paranoia. In the Ibadan conference of 1950, the final stage in negotiation of the Macpherson constitution – in which each regional delegation was pushing a different agenda – the northern representatives had seriously threatened going back to the separation of 1914. This was a genuine challenge to 'one Nigeria', but Macpherson's team persuaded them to back down with the guarantee that they would have half the seats in the central legislature. The Sardauna made it clear that he would not tolerate any attempt to divide the north into more than one state.

For the north, with its different culture and traditions, was marching to a different beat. Even its understanding and practice of Islam was rather different from the more westernised south, where Muslims had been a majority of the population of Lagos in 1931 and were still 41% of the population in 1950.[15] The politicised north, a thin veneer of feudals and the western-educated class that ruled both peasantry and nomads, was in no hurry for self-government. Over

90% of the people were illiterate, and critics argued that students who did get into the education system were disadvantaged because time was guaranteed for Koranic instruction.

In 1948 the Northern People's Congress had been founded in a Zaria reading room while Abubakar Tafawa Balewa was in the UK for an African conference and for a meeting of the Empire Parliamentary Association opened by Clement Attlee. Tafawa Balewa and the Sardauna of Sokoto did not join immediately, and while the first stood for a more critical approach to the emirates the second – who had had his frictions with the Sultan of Sokoto – nonetheless represented a more conservative, aristocratic wing. Even in 1952 an observer could dismiss the NPC, by then ruling the north and with key ministers at the centre, as 'far from being a political party…it is at its best a reunion platform for old boys of Katsina College'.[16]

One of the surprises of the late 1940s was the growth of politics of a kind in the north, with the 'cultural' NPC becoming a type of party, and Tafawa Balewa, the educator from Bauchi, becoming a nominated member of the Legislative Council and 'the silver voice of the north'. He was from the Jere tribe, not closely linked to the more powerful Fulani or Hausa clans. In August 1950, in the northern house of assembly, he proposed a resolution 'to appoint an independent commission to investigate the system of native administration in the northern provinces, and to make recommendations for its modernisation and reform'. This was a dagger aimed at the colonial indirect rule system and the feudals. Yet there were still more radical voices heckling the NPC, for in the same month Aminu Kano and others set up the Northern Elements Progressive Union. This was encouraged by the Hausa page of Zik's Kano newspaper, *The Comet*, and it attacked imperialism as well as the conservatism of the north and its native authorities. In the middle belt around Jos, which was technically part of the northern region but Christian and animist in belief, there were political stirrings with an anti-Muslim flavour.

Chapter 9
Regional governments and the coming of independence

The issue of Nigerian unity took on a different flavour in the 1950s, as the administrative regions of the colonial government became political regions with significant powers, responding to electorates whose priorities were largely ethnic. 'The Nigeria of the 1950s had been made unviable by centrifugal regional tendencies, and barely held together by British colonial administrative politics,' wrote one commentator.[1] There were a series of clashes between the regions that followed the row at negotiations on a new constitution in Ibadan in 1950, when the north demanded half the seats in the central house of representatives and the west and east feared they could never control the centre. There were quarrels in 1953 over the Action Group's demand for self-government in 1956, and in 1954 over the status of Lagos.

There were different forces at work. The British, who were also promoting federations in the West Indies, Central Africa and Malaysia, thought that federation was the only formula that could hold such diverse geography and ethnicities together. John Macpherson, Governor of Nigeria 1948–54, was determined that, when independence came, there should neither be dictatorship nor chaos. The north was anxious that a rush to self-government meant handing over its people and culture to rule by southerners. This was not an unreal fear. Most civil service and many business jobs in the north were dominated by southerners, and there were only a handful of northern university graduates. The southerners were still living in their own *sabon gari* enclaves adjoining northern towns.

Macpherson tried to get Zik to understand the reasons for northern caution in the complicated run-up to London talks on self-government in 1953, which both Zik and Awo had wanted to boycott. He told him, 'Every postmaster, every stationmaster was from the South. By the time their young men were qualified all the jobs would be filled from the South. White pegs were easier to remove than black pegs.'[2] Hence the northern leaders were keen to gain time to catch up and, in looking at a federal solution, they favoured a weak centre and strong regional governments.

Were the northerners actually willing to secede? In 1950 an article about Tafawa Balewa in *West Africa* stated that he was ready to contemplate the political separation of the north. In his autobiography, Ahmadu Bello, Sardauna of Sokoto, wrote of the debates in 1953: 'Lord Lugard and his Amalgamation were far from popular amongst us at that time. There were agitations for secession; we should set up on our own; we should cease to have anything more to do with the Southern people; we should take our own way. I must say it looked very tempting…'[3] On 31 March he described Lugard's amalgamation as 'the mistake of 1914'.[4]

Passions were running high in 1953, with northern leaders insulted in Lagos and serious riots in Kano's *Sabon Gari* in which 46 'nationalists' died.[5] The north was seen in the south as an obstacle to the campaign for self-government in 1956 – a resolution moved by Chief Anthony Enaharo, which led to withdrawal of the AG ministers from the central government. There were threats that northern exports and imports might be stopped from using southern ports. Nonetheless the British were desperately keen to keep Nigeria together, and it is not clear that the northern leaders really contemplated secession. Their Eight Point Plan did, however, demand complete regional autonomy, with no central legislature but a 'central agency' to manage defence and foreign affairs, all revenues to be regional and each region to have its own public service.

In the south the perspectives were different. The AG and National Council of Nigerian Citizens came together in a marriage of convenience to obtain independence – 'the Axis' as Macpherson described it to London, in an unhappy echo of the Second World War. They organised demonstrations in protest at the coronation of Queen Elizabeth in London and declared the day of the coronation a 'day of mourning' for the 'victims of imperialism' in Kano. The NCNC, which still had significant support in the west and had made an alliance with Aminu Kano's Northern Elements Progressive Union in the north, was the most 'national' in its thinking and keenest to see a strong central government. The AG was still Yoruba and regional in its approach; though it was leading the charge for self-government in 1956 it also sought a right of secession in the next constitution. Hence it was not so enthusiastic about a strong central authority and concerned that 'backward' northerners might be able to dictate to what it saw as the most sophisticated and urban electorate in the country. The personal antipathy between Awo and Zik was comparable to their shared hostility to the Sardauna and Tafawa Balewa.

By late June 1953 Macpherson had managed to get Awo and Zik to lift their threat to boycott the London talks on the basis that they would examine the defects in the Richards commission, agree what changes were necessary and decide how to implement them. Oliver Lyttleton, Secretary of State for the Colonies 1951–1954, chaired the meetings in two phases in London and then, in January 1954, in Lagos. Opening it in London, he claimed that the only cement holding the rickety structure of Nigeria together was the British, and the British were getting little if any material gain from the country. Awo, in a note on federalism he circulated to delegates, argued that the British, having tried to create a nation, were now trying to break it up again. Student leaders at the new University College, Ibadan, petitioned against federalism; Emeka Anyaoku, later to become Commonwealth

Secretary-General, was one of these who wrote to Awo, Zik and the Sardauna in favour of a strong unitary state with up to 22 provinces and none bigger than the rest.[6]

In fact Lyttleton did not have a preconceived plan and the 'Lyttleton Constitution' launched in October 1954 was inevitably a compromise. But it was a compromise that tilted towards the regions, which were allowed to choose when to achieve self-government. In fact the east and west were self-governing in 1957; the north, significantly, was not self-governing until 1959, only a year before the whole country became independent. Lagos, as the federal capital, had a separate status. Awo had wanted it to be part of the western region; the northerners, who wanted to guarantee access to the sea, and Zik, who was conscious that there was a significant Igbo population in Lagos, wanted it kept apart. The mandated Cameroons strip, whose representatives had been crucial to NCNC gaining power in the east, had a distinct federal status. Fissiparous tendencies among the smaller ethnicities, which were keen to get their own recognition, received a boost. Opportunities for corruption increased as regional marketing boards, commercial developments and revenues available to the regional governments were now responsible to politicians.

Able leaders, such as the Sardauna and Awo, chose to govern their regions rather than seek power in a weak centre. Only in 1957 did Nigeria acquire a Prime Minister, Abubakar Tafawa Balewa, of the Northern People's Congress. A thoughtful, unassuming man, he was an educated northerner who did not belong to the powerful Fulani or Hausa clans. His negotiating skills meant that, prior to independence, he brought the opposition AG into a government that, following post-Lyttleton elections, had been an alliance of the NPC and NCNC. Southerners thought he was not his own man and was taking orders in Lagos from the Sardauna. Another constitutional conference, in London in 1957, agreed that independence should take place in 1960.

At a Nigeria-wide level, and in a last throw by the British to deal with the ethnic complexities prior to independence, a commission was set up to examine the problems of minorities and respect for human rights. This was led by Sir Henry Willink. It worked from November 1957 to April 1958 and, disregarding much pressure, it held firm to the regional formula that had evolved over the previous decade. Although Alan Lennox-Boyd, Secretary of State for the Colonies in 1954–59, had indicated that it could recommend new states – and both the NCNC and AG had proposed them – it ruled them out, stating that 'a separate state would not provide a remedy for the fears expressed'.[7]

Willink acknowledged that in each of the regions he found either a minority or a group of minorities who described 'fears and grievances which they felt would become more intense when the present restraints were removed'.[8] He observed that with the approach of independence there had been 'a sharp recrudescence of tribal feeling'.[9] But his principal argument against creating new states was that it would be hard to draw clean lines between ethnicities. The principal political case against – accepted by the parties and the British – was that any such attempt would delay independence. However, Willink did propose a special development status for the Ijaws of the Niger Delta and two 'minority areas' for the Edos in Benin province and in the Calabar area. His report stated that the fears of minorities in the north could be reduced if non-Muslims could choose non-Muslim courts and there were a judicial services commission to appoint and administer Alkalis, the Islamic judges.

The report called for a single police force for the whole country, guarantees of fundamental rights in the constitution and an election commission to oversee both federal and regional elections. But in retrospect, so close to independence, it is clear that these measures were likely to be too frail to hold together a structure where the concept of 'Nigeria' still lacked ownership. Willink recognised problems that originated in indirect rule and the compromises necessary to bind different peoples together under British administration, yet it was too late for the British to do much about them.

As constitutional talks dragged on through the 1950s, the British officials who had most to do with Nigeria and its leaders were often cynical and pessimistic. In January 1956 Ralph Grey, Civil Secretary and later deputy Governor-General, wrote in private, 'Never before, so far as I know, has a unitary country been dismembered in order that it might be reconstituted as a Federation. And I should doubt if there is anywhere in the world a true, democratic Federation which has parts differing so widely one from another as here.' Clem Pleass, governor in the eastern region, wrote to a colleague in October, 'The fact is that once self-government is achieved, the political party in power in this Region at that time...will devote their attention to ensuring that they remain in power for as long as possible and that no other political party has a chance of getting elected to office. And they will do this by every conceivable kind of gerrymandering and intimidation they can think of.'[10]

It was not until 1959, on the eve of the whole country's independence, that the north attained self-government. Significantly it was treated by the British with the respect and bombast appropriate to full independence for most of its colonies. There was a huge durbar at Kaduna racecourse in May, described as probably the biggest party the north had ever seen. Alongside the durbar was an educational pageant. But the educational disparity between the north and the other states was still terrifying; 1958 statistics showed only 3,000 teachers being trained in the region, compared with 11,000 in the east and 10,700 in the west; with a population thought to be more than half that of Nigeria as a whole, the north had only some 10% of the country's children in school.

What were the regional governments of the 1950s actually like? Two key aspects worth emphasising were the desire of all three to press hard for educational advance and the discouraging signs that political status was being used as a shortcut to acquire economic resources. Throughout Africa, as colonies looked to become independent, the educational deficit became a major concern. This was true at all levels: there was a need for trained civil servants, doctors and health workers, teachers and professionals of all kinds. There was also a demand for improved literacy. Estimates for 1959–60, from a Nigerian development plan supposed to last from 1960 to 1965, saw 43.9% of the federal budget allocated to education.[11] In the west the Action Group government led by Awo campaigned for free primary education, and the unpopularity of its 15-shilling health and education taxes led to defeat by the NCNC in federal elections in 1954. Awo had argued that primary school attendance was only 35% in the west, as compared with the 65% in the east, and whereas there were 105 secondary schools in the east there were only 25 in the west. By 1955, when the free primary schooling took off in the west, the AG was rewarded by victory in regional elections. In the east the NCNC government also sought to introduce free universal primary education, but hit financial problems to pay for it. Although the north did spend more on education the gap in achievement between north and south widened, and led to a campaign for 'northernisation' – the promotion of northern civil servants and statutory business, and the restriction of southerners to short-term contracts.

The nexus between political and economic power, and the opportunities for corruption, increased enormously as the regional governments became more powerful. Between 1951 and 1957 the Western Regional Tenders Board awarded building contracts worth £5M or more to twelve Nigerian firms, all owned by members or supporters of the Action Group. In the north the Northern Amalgamated Merchants' Union and Northern Contractors Union were closely associated with the NPC, and in the east the Eastern Nigeria Civil Engineers and the Building Contractors of Enugu had close links with the NCNC.[12] The AG was taking loans from the National Bank, which was also banker to the western regional government. The NCNC was taking loans from the African Continental Bank, largely owned by Zik, which was also official banker to the eastern regional government and subsequently nationalised by it; this had led to a scandal and an inquiry in 1957. Regional MPs were put on boards that enhanced their income.

These cosy relationships marked a significant extension of the assistance that the colonial authorities had given to British trading and shipping companies. Accusations of corruption became a useful stick with which to beat opposing groups of politicians. An instance of this came in 1953, when a Mr Storey, the Town Clerk of Norwich, was invited to investigate corruption in Lagos council, run by the Democratic Party, allies of the NCNC. He noted that the council had voted £2,500 a year for its part-time mayor, which was a large sum at the time; it had also appointed the unqualified Prince Adedoyin as Town Clerk, in a ruse designed to make room for Zik to move into the federal house of representatives. Awo, then western premier, used these events, and the Storey report, as an excuse for dissolving the Lagos town council.[13]

But the 1950s were an exciting time in Nigeria, with a growth in middle-class jobs and a sense of possibilities opening out as independence became inevitable. Following a wartime inquiry into higher education in west Africa, Nigeria had its first university, with the launch in 1948 of the University College of Ibadan, linked to London University. Zik insisted that the east should have its own university too; it opened two years later in Nsukka, on the model of the US land-grant colleges, paid for by £4.5M from the Eastern Marketing Board. High-life music became popular in the south. Queen Elizabeth paid the country a visit in 1956, some 30 years after her uncle, the Prince of Wales, who had come during the early colonial period. The Korean War, 1950–53, led to a global demand for commodities that was helpful for the economy, although the Commonwealth division that fought with the UN coalition on the Korean peninsula did not include Nigerian or other colonial troops.

Few major Nigerian-owned businesses were yet to emerge, but the grip of British and European firms on the import-export trade diminished. Louis Odumegwu Ojukwu, father of the future Biafran leader, made a fortune in transport, his lorries driven all over west Africa; the NCNC put him in as chairman when it nationalised the African Continental Bank (London telegraphic address: ZIKBANK). Interregional trade increased and the north, the country's poorest region, was the main beneficiary; it ran a substantial surplus with the other regions, exporting cotton, groundnuts and other produce through southern ports. The east, with its palm produce, was actually a food deficit region and relied on out-migration for remittances and to reduce land pressures. This was to lead to tragedy in the 1960s, for the Igbo traders in Kano's *Sabon Gari* market surpassed the city's traditional market in numbers and profit, leading to fatal resentments.

But the west was the richest of the three regions and the big economic winner in the 1950s. Although Awo started talking about 'democratic socialism', the more striking aspect was the success of the cocoa business in private hands and of small, entrepreneurial firms. The region benefited from a system of revenue allocation based on agricultural produce and certain imported items. Although Awo lost the battle to get Lagos as part of the west, the region gained from having the country's biggest city and commercial port as its neighbour. In 1959–60 the west was able to spend £29.6M in recurrent and capital expenditure, as compared with £18.7M in the east, £23M in the north and only £75.8M in the federation.

Ever since 1914, when an ordinance had made sub-soil minerals the property of the Crown, the colonial state had controlled the exploitation of tin and coal. By 1938 it granted a monopoly in oil exploration to the Shell Oil Company. In 1956 Shell-Mex and BP Ltd found commercial quantities 80 km west of Port Harcourt, which rapidly became a boom town. Prior to independence in 1960 the government was operating a 50–50 revenue share with the company. Following the debacle of the Anglo-French withdrawal from the Suez Canal in 1956, this Nigerian oil was of strategic importance to the UK. The growing significance of oil royalties would cast a baleful shadow over the first decade of a sovereign state.

Chapter 10
The joy of independence

Nigeria became independent on 1 October 1960, and the royal representative for the ceremony was Princess Alexandra, the attractive and personable cousin of the Queen. She arrived in Lagos from London on 26 September, in pouring rain. This was not just Nigerian history in the making. With some 40M Nigerians ruling themselves and independence in 16 neighbouring countries in the same year, the majority of Africans were in command of their destinies for the first time in over a century.[1]

The whole country celebrated with fireworks, dancing and flood-lights on public buildings. The federal government allocated £1.75M for events and £100,000 to each of the three regions, and it took the opportunity to improve street lighting in the capital. The *jeunesse dorée* of Lagos enjoyed themselves at the Kakadu nightclub and cabaret.[2] Prime Minister Abubakar Tafawa Balewa, now a British knight and still a pious Muslim, made it clear that he did not wish to invite the princess to join him for the traditional first dance at the independence ball. He initially suggested that Maitama Sule, his 29-year-old Minister of Mines and Power, should have the honour. Sule sent to London for evening wear and started learning the steps. But he was upstaged by Festus Okotie-Eboh, the flamboyant Minister of Finance, who said that an older man like himself should dance with the princess.

Beneath the excitement there were big issues at stake. With Nigeria's independence the majority of African states were freed from colonial rulers, leaving only the Portuguese, Rhodesians and white South Africans as minorities ruling black majorities. This continuing domination would be a major foreign policy concern for Nigerian governments until South Africa's multiracial election of 1994 brought Nelson Mandela to power. Further, this was a nation's birth at the height of the Cold War. In September, a week before Nigerian independence, Patrice Lumumba, first president of an independent Congo, was overthrown in a coup led by General Mobutu Sese Seko. The former Belgian colony seemed to be falling into chaos, and western spy agencies were heavily implicated in the coup. The United States, United Kingdom and Belgium were among those worried that Lumumba would take Congo into the Soviet sphere, along with rich minerals, including uranium. The Cuban revolution had taken place in 1958; Nikita Khrushchev was boasting that the Soviets would 'bury' the west; and soon Yuri Gagarin would be the first man in space.

The colonial regime had been anxious about any signs of sympathy for the Soviet bloc, and in 1957–58 Chief Minister Abubakar Tafawa Balewa, already in charge of passports, refused to renew one for Mrs Ransome-Kuti. She had travelled widely in communist countries on behalf of Nigerian women's organisations, and he remarked, 'In the past when it was thought that Mrs Kuti might be the innocent victim of Communist schemes, she was informed officially…but now it can be assumed that it is her intention to influence the various Nigerian women's organisations, with which she is connected, with Communist ideas and policies.'[3]

There were elements of continuity, as well as change, in the foreign policy stance of the newly independent country, and the continuities were criticised by more fervent nationalists, who were inspired by the growing radicalism of Kwame Nkrumah, Prime Minister of Ghana 1957–60. Even before Nigeria became independent, Nkrumah had declared a republic, moved towards a one-party democracy with a single-chamber parliament, passed the Preventative Detention Act and deported critical journalists. Although the manifesto of the National

Council of Nigerian Citizens was more neutralist than either the Action Group or the Northern People's Congress, which were more pro-west, the government of Balewa was cautious. It was against racism and colonialism on the African continent and unwilling to be put in a Cold War box. Prior to independence the prime minister had led a delegation to London to protest at French nuclear tests in the Sahara. Departing from the independence festivities to go to the UN, he mischievously said, 'It is a pity in my view that nations who are members of the UN have constituted themselves into blocs or groups. I do not like the word neutrality and I agree with Mr Nehru's statement that when a neutral country joins a neutral bloc it ceases to be neutral. We want to pursue an independent view, which is not the same as neutralism.'[4]

How was it that Balewa became the first elected prime minister of a sovereign Nigeria, in what in retrospect was called the First Republic? Had the British, possibly for Cold War reasons, fixed the 1959 elections so that this cautious and Anglophile northerner, with several wives as a good Muslim and 22 children, became the leader at independence? For the results in December showed that, in the federal House of Representatives, the NPC had won 142 seats, the NCNC had 87 and the AG had 73. With many illiterate voters and only men voting in the north, the party symbols were important: a hoe for the NPC, a cockerel for the NCNC and a palm tree for the AG.

Technically the NCNC and the AG could together have had a majority. But this possibility broke down for two reasons. The British feared that it would raise the prospect of southern domination, which could have led the north to secede, so undoing Lugard's sticking-plaster merger after 45 years of laborious administration. Officials pressed Nnamdi Azikiwe, who was serving as President of the Senate of Nigeria – in this office only from January to October 1960 – to continue with the NPC–NCNC alliance that had been running the federation prior to independence, but which had gone through a temporary divorce for the elections. The second reason was that Obafemi Awolowo, Premier of Western Nigeria in 1954–60, overplayed his hand. He offered to serve in a government under Zik on condition that Zik agreed to the creation of three new regions; Zik turned this down when he found that Awo was making a similar proposal to the NPC.

Two of the three most prominent leaders now opted to work at the federal level: Zik was initially President of the Senate, and Awo led the federal opposition. Dr Michael Okpara took over from Zik as NCNC Premier of Eastern Nigeria, and Chief Samuel Akintola replaced Awo as AG Premier of Western Nigeria. Only the Sardauna preferred to keep to his fiefdom in the north, leaving the unassuming but clear-minded and skilful Balewa as Prime Minister. It was symbolic of the continuing difference of the north that the first person to vote in Sokoto was the Sultan, Ahmadu Bello, who walked about 800 yards to do so – 'the first time he has ever walked in public'.[5]

Controversy continues as to whether the British actually rigged the 1959 elections to favour the NPC, as was alleged by a former colonial official, Harold Smith.[6] The three regional governments were using their public resources to win seats, the British had vetoed any break-up of the disproportionately large north, as had the Sardauna, and the outgoing Governor-General was leaning on Zik to continue the NPC–NCNC agreement with a ceremonial recognition of Zik's long service to the nationalist cause. It is conceivable that the British had some information they could have used against Zik, but this was probably not necessary. For Zik was content initially to be President of the Nigerian Senate. He became Governor-General at independence and remained so until the country became a republic in 1963, when he became President.

More substantially, of course, the construction of the federal state and the in-built advantage of the north in the federal constitution reflected a long-running paternalist bias in British policy. The Sardauna had made it clear that, as a direct descendant of Dan Fodio with spiritual and temporal powers, he would not be a party to the break-up of the northern region. The British had gone along with the delaying tactics of the NPC and in March 1957 launched the BBC Hausa service in an effort to make up the information deficit in the wider population. It was striking that, when the north did get self-government in May 1959, the British treated it as if it were the independence of another colony. As described earlier, there was a huge durbar at Kaduna racecourse with 8,000 men and 3,000 horses. The Duke and Duchess of Gloucester and Alan Lennox-Boyd, Colonial Secretary, were in attendance.

The British establishment was nervous about what was happening in Africa, with Nkrumahism in Ghana, chaos and white flight in the former Belgian Congo and the massacre in Sharpeville shining a harsh light on racism in South Africa. It was important to keep an independent Nigeria as a friend, but the country was too big and volatile to be controlled in the way that France was seeking to control its ex-colonies. In 1958 the UK Army Council withdrew its command over Nigerian forces, and, when in December 1960 the UK signed a defence agreement with Nigeria, it seemed lacking in content; the UK would provide training, but it would not have a base, and the mutual assistance clauses seemed nebulous. Behind the scenes the favourable balance of payments that the UK had enjoyed had fallen from around £27M to around £15M in the three years up to 1959.

However, when Harold Macmillan, British Prime Minister (in office 1957–63), visited Nigeria in early 1960 as part of his swing through west and southern Africa – made famous by his 'wind of change' speech to the South African parliament on 3 February – he would have been satisfied that Nigeria would remain a friend to the UK and the west. In a sign of the importance he attached to the country he made a political appointment of Anthony Head, his former Minister of War, as the first British High Commissioner to Nigeria.

Independence inspired genuine feelings of comradeship and optimism in the political leaders. An editorial in *West Africa* on 19 November stated, 'Even if Nigeria sounds sometimes too good to be true, the Nigerian story is one of the most remarkable and creditable in the modern world.' At the age of 57, Nnamdi Azikiwe, independent Nigeria's first and last Governor-General, took an oath of allegiance to the Crown and promised to 'well and truly serve' in his new office. In his inaugural address, entitled 'Respect for Human Dignity', Zik appealed to the Sardauna, Awo and other prominent politicians to join in national reconstruction and 'this great adventure of restoring the dignity of man in the world'. He argued: 'Representative democracy has been tried in Nigeria and we have proved more than equal to the task...When Britain transferred power to us on 1 October 1960 we were no longer an expression of geography but a reality of history. During all our years of political vassalage we became socially and economically integrated. We have also developed an identity of interest and we have crystallised a common nationality.' Referring to the Sharpeville shootings in South Africa, he stated firmly 'under no circumstances shall we accept that the black race is inferior to any other race'.

His peroration quoted Frank Buchman, the apostle of Moral Rearmament, who looked forward to a hate-free, fear-free, greed-free world. Zik said, 'Let us bind the nation's wounds and let us heal the breaches of the past so that, in forging our nation, there shall emerge on this continent a hate-free, fear-free and greed-free people, who shall be in the vanguard of a world task force, whose assignment is not only to revive the stature of man in Africa, but to restore the dignity of man in the world.'[7] Shortly after independence Awolowo dismissed the idea that his party, or the NPC, were interested in secession; the fact that he had wanted an option for secession written into the federal constitution did not mean that he wanted to secede.[8]

Yet within seven years of Zik's fine words Nigeria had suffered two military coups and was in the grip of civil war. This was not the future that the crowds celebrating in the streets in October 1960 had foreseen. It was not what the young and educated Lagosians of different ethnicities, enjoying life in the Kakadu nightclub, with all the white men's jobs now within their reach, could have imagined. Yet there were early hints of continuing problems, only partially concealed in euphoria.

A fortnight after independence there were major disturbances among the Tiv, who had voted overwhelmingly for the United Middle Belt Congress; they wanted a middle belt state cut out of the north, with which the Tiv felt they had little in common. Fulani nomads left the area with their cattle. There were 4,800 arrests, 2,830 convictions – with whipping the commonest punishment – and 18 died.

Not everyone was happy with the Nigerian state as it was then constructed, and this was shown again in early 1961 when those in the Southern Cameroons, administered with Nigeria as a mandate by the UK, voted by four to one to join Cameroun; those in the Northern Cameroons voted by 145,265 to 97,654 to become Nigerian. There were ethnic factors involved, but most Cameroonians had rebuffed an attractive offer from Balewa. He had promised them their own state and twelve seats in the Nigerian Senate; for years Cameroonians had played a part in Nigerian politics, both federally and in the east, and both Nigerians and British were surprised at the result of the referendum.

In addition, the fundamental inequality between north and south had not been bridged. Those in the north, where the average annual income was estimated at £30 and only men could vote, were massively disadvantaged in education. Although the city of Kano was embarking on a crash expansion of primary schools, the overall differences were enormous. In 1958 there were over a million pupils in school in each of the eastern and western regions, but only 238,000 in the more populous north; around 11,000 had enrolled to train as teachers in each of the southern regions, but only 3,000 in the north.

The trouble for Balewa and those trying to make a success of an independent Nigeria was that public expectations were excessive, the economy would have difficulty paying for them, and politics seemed the easiest way to make money. 'Nigeria' was becoming a deadly combination of zero-sum game and roulette. The honeymoon joy of independence was the prologue to a deepening crisis.

Chapter 11
Overture to disaster

The early 1960s, an era of youthful experiment and optimism in western Europe and North America, was reflected in Nigeria also. Artists and writers dug into indigenous history and achievement to find new inspiration for a new nation. In 1963 Fela Kuti, who had been studying music at Trinity College of Music, London, moved back to Nigeria with his first band, Koola Lobitos. Son of the Rev. Israel Oludotun Ransome-Kuti and the activist Funmilayo, Fela was starting on a career that would fuse music and politics in a new style, enthralling young Nigerians and getting up the noses of successive rulers, especially in the military. Writers such as Chinua Achebe, whose *Things Fall Apart* (1958) was quickly recognised as a classic novel, and the young Wole Soyinka, who won a prize from London's *Encounter* magazine after writing his play *A Dance of the Forests* in 1960 to celebrate independence, were showing the world what Nigerians could do.

The federal government in 1960 had declared English to be the national language, which gave Nigeria full participation in the dominant language of the second half of the twentieth century. When an attempt was made later to create Wazobia, a kind of Nigerian Esperanto made from Hausa, Igbo and Yoruba, it fell foul of other language groups, which was why English had been adopted as a bridge language in the first place.[1]

The most immediate assertion of the new statehood was in foreign affairs. This happened even before its new green-and-white flag had been raised at independence and before Nigerians had learnt to sing the words of the national anthem, which was written by Miss

Lillian Jean Williams of the Federal Ministry of Labour and adopted in October 1960:

Nigeria, we hail thee,
Our own dear native land,
Though tribe and tongue may differ,
In brotherhood we stand.
Nigerians all are proud to serve
Our sovereign Motherland.[2]

In June 1960 Balewa sent Maitama Sule to Addis Ababa to a conference of independent African states. At the time Sule was being groomed to be the first Foreign Minister in the independence government and African states were divided. There was a smaller group, the Casablanca group, which included Ghana and Senegal, which was keen to move rapidly to pan-African unity; this would have included, for example, a unified military force. The rather larger Monrovia group, to which the about-to-be-independent Nigeria belonged, was more concerned about improved functional connections, including in road and air transport, which were still dominated by export corridors and European colonial links. For the cautious Balewa, whose north had only just become self-governing, it seemed premature for Nigeria to surrender significant sovereignty so early in its new status.

As luck would have it, Sule was invited to make the first speech at the Addis conference, and he made a strong pitch for the two African groups to unite. In this he had been encouraged by the then US Ambassador to Nigeria, who was presumably concerned with preventing Soviet communism from spreading on the continent.[3] Two years later in Ghana, the Organisation of African Unity was born.

This was just the first of many examples of Nigeria taking a leadership role with a generally pro-western bias. In addition to promoting African unity the government made serious contributions in two crises affecting the continent: in the Congo, where it supplied the United Nations with peacekeeping troops, and in the debate over South African apartheid and the Commonwealth. The Congo crisis, in which Katanga had tried to secede, around 100,000 people died and UN Secretary-General Dag Hammarskjold lost his life in a plane crash, had mesmerised the world. It led to much negativity in the western media about the capacity of African states to rule themselves. Nigeria sent both police and troops to shore up the government and protect lives. There were two battalions of Nigerian troops in the Congo between 1960 and 1964; this was a significant undertaking from an army that only consisted of five battalions and 7,000 men, and each of the five battalions saw service there in turn. It was the start of a series of UN peacekeeping deployments that were to continue under both civilian and military regimes into the 21st century.

The Congo experience was important in giving confidence to Nigerian officers, who subsequently hijacked governments and fought a civil war. It was not entirely without blemish, for there was a mutiny in the fifth battalion, commanded by Lt Col. J. Aguyi-Ironsi, when they were ordered to rescue an Austrian ambulance under fire. Seven soldiers were dismissed and ten NCOs were demoted. Aguiyi-Ironsi, who later was given command of the whole UN force, was withdrawn for a while. But the widespread respect for the professionalism of this small army was illustrated in 1964 when Nigerian troops were airlifted to Tanzania to retrain soldiers after a mutiny. Julius Nyerere, at the start of his long-running presidency of Tanzania from 1964 to 1985, was strongly critical of UK appeasement on Rhodesia and apartheid South Africa; but he had been forced to appeal to the British for help.

UN service in the difficult conditions in the Congo involved serious action for a youthful cadre of officers, who were beginning to develop their own ideas for Nigeria's future. It was not until February

1965 that Sir Christopher Welby-Everard, the last British commander of Nigerian forces, handed over to Aguiyi-Ironsi, who was the senior Nigerian but not necessarily an automatic replacement. Reporting to the government on his Congo deployment, Aguiyi-Ironsi had written a document headed 'For Nigerian eyes only' that included two paragraphs of criticism of the forces from NATO countries in Congo. Emeka Anyaoku, then a junior official in Lagos who had been asked to arrange the typing of this report, persuaded a reluctant Aguiyi-Ironsi to remove the paragraphs, as they might jeopardise his chances of succeeding Welby-Everard.[4]

Public opinion in Nigeria, and also Zik and Awo, persuaded the Balewa government to toughen up its stand on South Africa. Travelling to London in 1961, prior to the Commonwealth conference that led the apartheid regime to depart, the Prime Minister had said that he did not wish to force the South Africans out of the association. Nigeria was a dominion – its army was called the Royal Nigerian Army – and it had invited South African representatives to its independence celebrations. But from this uncertain start it became such a champion of freedom for Africans under colonial or racist domination that, by the late 1970s, it was recognised as an honorary member of the frontline states and Nigerian passports included a condemnation of apartheid. In his first speech to the UN General Assembly, on Nigeria's admission, Balewa had committed the country not only to the total liberation of Africa and African unity, but also to the 'promotion of the rights of all black and oppressed peoples throughout the world'.

There were hints of anti-west defiance in the conservative, gradualist position of the government. Even before independence it had joined protests at French nuclear tests in the Sahara, in southern Algeria, with Nigerians anxious about nuclear fallout; in 1963 the government broke diplomatic relations with France over the same issue, which may have influenced French support for Biafra later. It also abrogated the defence treaty with the British that, although of limited significance, became an object of strong criticism for radical nationalists. The same sectors led pressure for Nigeria to become a republic in 1963, precisely three years after independence, with its governor-general becoming a ceremonial president instead. There had been something distinctly odd about Dr Azikiwe, as governor-general, having to swear allegiance to the British monarch.

For after the good fellowship of leaders and publics, which had been put on display at independence, the structural and ideological divisions in the Nigeria construct became more threatening in the early 1960s. These showed up in political crisis, in economic disappointment exacerbated by corruption, and in dangerously anti-democratic ideas among the younger officers who were influenced by a rash of military takeovers elsewhere in Africa. Whereas in the 21st century there was a nostalgia for the simplicity of parliamentary rule in the First Republic, there was a lack of historical awareness of what it had seemed like at the time.

The dysfunctional federation, with its disproportionately large northern region, created constant frictions between the powerful regional governments and also within the NPC–NCNC coalition at the centre. The NPC used its federal position to strengthen the appointment of northerners in the military and the bureaucracy and to economic posts. To southerners this seemed like an overture to northern domination. The NCNC, which had hoped the coalition would give it access to plum positions and economic resources, was forced back into exploiting its eastern heartland. Zik himself had difficulty in accepting that his roles, first as governor-general and then as president, did not give him real authority.

The crisis burst in the western region, where the AG split at its party conference in Jos in 1962, affecting its ability to govern the west. There were divisions over attitudes to the federal government, where

Chief Samuel Akintola, Premier of Western Nigeria, wanted a more cooperative relationship, and over the policy of Awo's opposition in the federal parliament, which had been advocating nationalisation of basic resources, which was anathema to the NPC. Awo had been trying to build support around the country, allying with minority tribes to make the federal opposition more effective; Akintola wanted the AG to focus on its Yoruba heartland. A constitutional formula by which a party could be simultaneously a government and an opposition was hard to manage in Nigerian circumstances.

On 25 May the political dispute became a fight with broken chairs on the floor of the Western House of Assembly, and police had to clear it with tear gas. Showing unexpected ruthlessness Balewa declared a state of emergency in the west, suspended the AG regional government and installed Moses Majekodunmi, Federal Minister of Health, as administrator in the west. A commission of inquiry went after Chief Awolowo and his principal lieutenants for the misuse of funds for party purposes from the National Investment and Properties Corporation and the National Bank, both of which were owned by the regional government and seen by it as piggybanks, and four other parastatals.

This was followed up by something more serious: Awolowo and his principal aides were put on trial for treason. The suggestion was that the accused 'between December 1960 and September 1962, in Lagos and various other places in Nigeria, formed an intention to levy war against our Sovereign Lady the Queen within Nigeria'. It was alleged that they had recruited volunteers, arranged for their training outside Nigeria in the use of explosives and firearms, imported arms and reconnoitred the power station, airport and naval base for takeover.

Balewa was in London for the 1962 Commonwealth Prime Ministers' conference when he was told of these charges. 'I couldn't believe it,' he said afterwards. 'I thought it would make us a laughing stock and told them to release him. But they assured me it was true. I just couldn't believe Awolowo would be so foolish.'[5] The prosecution claimed that the AG had set up a 'tactical committee' after Awo was defeated in the 1959 election, and that it planned to take power in a coup on 23 September 1962. The trial dragged on and final judgement was passed in July 1964, when Awo was sentenced to seven years in jail after an appeal. Public opinion in the south held that the case was not proven, and the murky financial dealings of the western regional government seemed no worse than those in the east and north.

Nonetheless, shortly after the AG split and the fight in the House of Assembly, Chief Akintola became western premier again, heading a new party, the United Peoples' Party, which ruled in coalition with the western regional NCNC.[6] The United Peoples' Party then morphed into the Nigerian National Democratic Party, not becoming notably more democratic along the way. Not surprisingly these events caused turmoil in Yorubaland. The sense that the NPC, abetted by the NCNC, was intent on knocking out the west as a regional power and diminishing Yoruba influence in the federation was underscored in 1963 when a mid-west state was carved out and then controlled by the NCNC. Awo had long called for more states, but that was to break up the vast northern territory and give more scope to minority tribes, condemned to permanent opposition. A creeping authoritarianism at the federal level led to a preventive detention act in 1963 and a press bill to restrain the famously exuberant and unreliable Nigerian media in 1964.

An issue that had both political and economic consequences, and which helped to raise the already steamy political temperature, was the census. Censuses under the British had shown that most Nigerians lived in the north, and this had been used as justification for the allocation both of parliamentary constituencies and of development resources in the run-up to independence. But in 1962, under the eye of a retired British official, 45,000 enumerators sought to count the Nigerian population properly for the first time; a decade earlier there had been a 'group count' in which only the names of the heads of each family or compound were counted, with an estimate for the number in each group. The 1962 results were never published, but highly similar stories published in Zik's *West African Pilot* and *Tribune*, an AG paper, suggested that more people now lived in the south than the north.[7]

This was dynamite. Mr J.J. Warren, the British official who had overseen the count, said that the eastern figures in particular were inflated. Balewa did not extend Warren's contract and took control of the census himself. In spite of 180,000 enumerators, rules against 'census migrations' and that individuals should be counted by sight – even women in purdah in the north – the revised 1963 population figures showed an implausible rise from 1952 to 1953. Whereas the total population a decade earlier was thought to be 30.4M, it had nearly doubled within a decade to 55.7M. But crucially the north stayed ahead of the rest combined, with a claimed total of 29.8M. Extraordinarily, Nigeria has never been able to mount an impartial, accepted census ever since, and more recent numbers have been reached by estimated adjustments to the revised 1963 totals.

The crisis then pitted President Azikiwe, who had wanted the election postponed, against Prime Minister Balewa, who met the service chiefs and announced arrangements for an election 'that will be held tomorrow' (30 December 1964).[8] The election was due by the end of 1964. A joint action committee of trade unions called for a general strike to postpone the election, but only railmen and port workers stopped work. The electoral commission was deadlocked, and when the Sardauna refused to attend a meeting of governors and premiers called by the president prior to the poll, he said it had been convened 'to organise secession from the Federation'.[9]

There had been thuggery and corruption in the 1959 elections, but worse was to come in the 1964 federal elections, the first after independence. Southern hostility to northern domination had increased, and the NCNC and AG joined with minority parties in the north in an effort to end the rule of the NPC and its unpopular Akintola ally in the west. They called their grouping the United Progressive Grand Alliance. On the establishment side the Sardauna, Balewa and Akintola put together a Nigerian National Alliance. Every kind of obstruction was used to stop the UPGA and, in a caricature of democracy, they were prevented from nominating candidates.

The result was that 88 out of 174 seats in the northern region went unopposed to NNA candidates, and nearly a third in the west went unopposed to the Akintola faction. Late in December the NCNC had called for a UPGA boycott of the election, but this was only a success in its eastern heartland. In the end the NNA had an overwhelming majority: 198 out of 312 seats in the federal assembly.

After this unsatisfactory election was over, boycotted in the Igbo east, President Azikiwe initially refused to call on Balewa to form a government. But conciliation led by Sir Adetokunbo Ademola, Chief Justice of the Supreme Court of Nigeria, produced a 'Zik–Balewa' pact: Tafawa Balewa promised to create a broad-based government and the eastern region elections could be run again. In reality the northern-based establishment had won.

Nigeria had come close to the brink. Michael Okpara, NCNC Premier of Eastern Nigeria from 1959, had threatened secession; there had been talk of a coup to remove President Azikiwe on grounds of ill health; the scale of electoral malfeasance was huge, so that, for example, no opposition candidate had been allowed to run in the Prime Minister's Bauchi constituency and he had been returned unopposed. Nigerians could have little faith in a democracy that seemed so unfair and kleptocratic.

The ugliness of Nigerian democracy was not balanced by any widely appreciated economic dividend from independence. The educational drives by western and eastern regional governments meant that more people were emerging from schools with aspirations for employment that were not being met. In December 1961, for instance, some 200,000 leavers came onto the labour market in the west.

Managing expectations was not easy. Shortly after independence Finance Minister Chief Festus Okotie-Eboh had raised import taxes sharply, and the country ran an adverse trade balance of £50M in that year. At the same time an educational expansion plan, proposed by a commission led by the British educator Sir Eric Ashby, was expected to cost £75M over ten years to combat illiteracy of 85–90%. An ambitious six-year development plan for 1962–68 – in reality a collection of regional plans – was budgeted at £160M in the first year, rising to £220M in the sixth. How would Nigeria, which broke parity with UK sterling in 1962, raise the funds that were needed? Tax revenues were insufficient, and the country was relying on international loans.

Okotie-Eboh became notorious, like Kingsley Ozuomba Mbadiwe, Minister of Transport, as one of the 'ten per centers', the ministers who were collecting commissions on projects they approved. Walter Schwarz, a British journalist in Nigeria, commented of Okotie-Eboh that 'He never allowed his ministerial duties to interfere with his continually expanding business interests. He triumphantly survived a storm in the House of Representatives after he had started a shoe factory and then increased the duty on imported shoes.'[10]

But not all the ministers were corrupt. In retrospect Maitama Sule, who was responsible for minerals including oil, which was beginning to take off as an industry, has been rated as the least corrupt oil minister the country has ever had. He did not take or award oil blocks on an improper basis, and he negotiated with ENI, the Italian firm that owned AGIP, to break the stranglehold of Shell-BP and the 'Seven Sisters' cartel. When in January 1966 the government of which he was part was overthrown by young majors, he was so short of money that it was his permanent secretary who loaned him the money to return home to Kano.

Sule told the author that Balewa never asked him for favours, either, and that after the prime minister's murder there was no suggestion that he had personally profited from his position: 'He did not have a kobo.'[11] But what the public and the media realised was that some politicians, and their friends, were profiting enormously from their opportunities. This tarnished the image of the First Republic, making it vulnerable to a puritan reaction, yet it also embedded the idea that politics provided a shortcut to wealth. Balewa completely failed to call any of his ministers to account or punish them for their misdemeanours.

Seeing the impact of independence and Nigerianisation, a number of foreign companies invested in new factories and enterprises in the early 1960s. Guinness breweries started making stout in Ikeja, Lagos, in 1962; this became one of most globally profitable centres for the firm, and its advertising of 'Guinness for power', hinting at sexual potency for Nigerians, became as familiar as the Guinness pelicans in advertising in Britain. Although the British share in Nigerian trade was in decline, the UK still held just over half the stock of foreign investment in 1967, and foreign capital still dominated large-scale manufacture. In 1963 it was estimated that the structure of equity in large-scale manufacture was: 10% private Nigerian, 68% private foreign, 3% federal government, and 19% regional governments.[12] Regional competition and corruption led to duplication and waste; the federal government could not exert control and rationality; and contractor finance and supplier credits were popular with the regional politicians because they obtained kickbacks or 'commissions'.

The failure of the economy to deliver real benefits to an increasingly educated labour force led to a successful general strike, which started at midnight on 31 May 1964. The labour movement had been divided along Cold War lines but Michael Imoudou, a flamboyant leader of the railwaymen who wore a red tracksuit as his battledress, managed to unite them to get implementation of wage rises proposed by a Morgan Commission. This had been set up the previous year and attacked absurd wage differentials and insecurity of tenure. Whereas the minimum wage for government employees in Lagos was £7.10 shillings a month, the commission, whose published proposals were delayed by the government, reckoned that a man, one wife and two children would need £16.16 shillings a month. It recommended a minimum wage of £12 with consequential rises elsewhere in the country.

But the government and employers were dilatory and high-handed. Balewa said he would not negotiate while the workers were on strike and threatened them with dismissal. By the end of the first week 800,000 workers were on strike, ignoring such threats. The strike officially ended on 13 June, by which time the government had accepted most of the Morgan recommendations. But the weakness of labour had also been demonstrated. When the Union Trading Company, owner of a department store in Lagos, dismissed strikers, the police had to be called to control the crowds of applicants for their places. Market women raised food prices even before the settlement was announced.[13]

The dissatisfaction with the Nigerian body politic was wide-spread, and it was displayed in the press, in the labour movement, in the dubious federal election at the end of 1964 and in its aftermath. At independence, only four years before, it would have been inconceivable that, so few years later, Chief Awolowo would have been incarcerated for treason in the 19th-century prison in Lagos. What few realised was that anger with the slow pace of decolonisation and the corruption of politicians was beginning to take hold in the military.

At its most senior level the officer corps held fast to the apolitical tradition of the British Army. Major-General Sir Christopher Welby-Everard, in the crisis at the end of 1964, had to inform President

Azikiwe that he took orders from the prime minister, not from a president who in theory was his commander-in-chief. After creation of the mid-west region the ethnic balance of the military was supposed to mimic the supposed balance between the regions: 50% from the north, 25% from the east, 21% from the west and 4% from the mid-west. But the situation was more complicated than it appeared. Going back to British stereotypes about warlike tribes the north was over-represented, yet a significant number of 'northerners' were actually from minority groups, not Hausa. Because of their educational advantages the Igbos were well represented in the technical arms and services, and among officers just below the top. Whatever the intentions of the senior officers, it was impossible to isolate their juniors from anguished discussion about the volatile political scene in Nigeria. The very smallness of the Nigerian armed services meant that it was easier than in other countries to mount a successful coup, and the biggest stumbling-block was the geographical extent of the country.

Section 3

1964–89: The shadow of the generals

Chapter 12
Military coups, Biafra and civil war

Nigeria's third quarter-century was disastrous. This bridged a tumultuous era from the leadership of the civilian Prime Minister Tafawa Balewa to that of the military President Ibrahim Babangida, who ruled from 1985 to 1993. It included two breakdowns of civilian democracy; a war between Nigerians with anything up to three million casualties; institutionalised corruption at the level of the state, which was linked to extraordinary national dependence on oil revenue, alongside continuing poverty; and the arrival of the military in politics that, purporting to be an instrument of national unity, came to be seen in the south as an armed agent of northern hegemony.

In 1962 Tafawa Balewa had decreed a state of emergency in the west after scuffles in the House of Assembly, but he failed to intervene in the far more serious riots that broke out in 1965, after western regional elections in November. These saw an angry Action Group, now part of a United Progressive Grand Alliance with its leader Awolowo in prison, trying to defeat Samuel Akintola's Nigerian National Democratic Party which was overtly backed by the federal government. The NNDP argued that it was championing the Yoruba cause against threats of Igbo domination, and that for the first time the west was getting a share of federal benefits, from scholarships to appointments. However, many Yorubas saw Akintola as a quisling, a northern representative ruling them with an iron rod. Rigging was on a huge scale, from the manipulation of nominations to the biased returns of electoral officers.

The eastern radio, responsible to the United Progressive Grand Alliance/AG alliance ruling in the east, announced one set of results;

the western radio, under the control of Chief Akintola, stated that the NNDP had won 71 seats, the AG 15 and the NCNC two. The governor of the western region called on Akintola to form another government. In the words of Eghosa Osaghae, a leading Nigerian analyst, 'The 1965 Western regional elections turned out to be the final Waterloo for the young Republic.'[1]

In late 1965 and the first weeks of 1966, the western region, the richest part of the country with the federal capital on its coastline, became ungovernable as a wave of riots, arson and political murders gradually engulfed the area. Tax was not collected, Balewa seemed incapable of acting to quell the riots and Major-General Johnson Aguiyi-Johnson, Chief of Staff of the army in 1966, withdrew troops that had been deployed in the region because many of them sympathised with the rioters. There were many deaths and injuries.

Summing this up, the British journalist Walter Schwarz wrote:

Popular disillusionment about democracy, already far advanced after the federal elections, was now almost total. At first, details of the violence were published in the newspapers; but the threat implied in the 1964 Newspaper Amendment Act [of a fine of £200 or a year's imprisonment for publishing 'false' reports or rumours] progressively damped the story down. Within four weeks of the election the official death toll had reached 46, but most people considered this a fraction of the true figure. In the town of Isho police opened fire on a group of demonstrators, killing eleven on the spot, while a further 19, including four policemen, were seriously injured. In Ijebu province, Awolowo's home area, a customary court judge was driven from his house by armed men and beheaded. Many Hausa from the North were killed.

Altogether, the *Nigerian Tribune*, the AG paper in Ibadan that had managed to keep going in spite of censorship, estimated in January 1966 that 567 had been killed and 1,000 injured. A later estimate suggested that as many as 2,000 had been killed in the western region between August 1965 and January 1966.[2]

In the middle of this mayhem, and on the eve of his murder in the first Nigerian coup, Balewa was hosting a meeting of Commonwealth presidents and prime ministers in Lagos on 11 and 12 January. This aimed to coordinate a Commonwealth response to the recent Unilateral Declaration of Independence by the white minority regime of Ian Smith, Prime Minister of Rhodesia from 1964 to 1979. It showed how Nigeria's international reputation seemed unaffected by the state's own internal fragility, which had barely registered with western media.

This was the first gathering of Commonwealth leaders to take place outside the United Kingdom and the first to be organised by its international secretariat, set up the previous year with the Canadian Arnold Smith as Secretary-General. Several African presidents, including Kenneth Kaunda of Zambia and Julius Nyerere of Tanzania, were highly critical of Harold Wilson, the British prime minister, for his lame response to UDI. For Wilson, Lagos would have seemed the most pro-British venue he could have hoped for in Africa in which to defend his feeble policy.[3]

On the morning of 15 January 1966 a group of young army officers launched a coup and succeeded in assassinating Balewa, members of his cabinet, the Sardauna of Sokoto Ahmadu Bello, Chief Akintola and senior military figures. But the coup, though bloody, was only partly successful. Major Chukwuma Nzeogwu, one of the five Igbo majors responsible and its leader in the north, explained at his first press conference that the plot had not gone according to plan in Lagos and Enugu. 'We carried out our assignment: the others did not,' he said.[4] In Enugu, the presence of Archbishop Makarios III of Cyprus, on the last leg of a tour of the federation following the Commonwealth conference, meant that the life of Michael Okpara, NCNC Premier of Eastern Nigeria, was spared. In Lagos, Aguiyi-Ironsi, who had been tipped off about the plot, pulled rank at a rebel checkpoint and drove to the Ikeja barracks. He spoke first to the regimental sergeant major before briefing the officers that he intended to take control of key points in Lagos. Yakubu Gowon, a lieutenant colonel who had just returned from a joint services staff course in England, escaped assassination by going straight to Ikeja rather than to the Ikoyi Hotel. He advised Aguiyi-Ironsi, who was talking of taking three hours to move troops, to get them moving in half an hour.[5]

Aguiyi-Ironsi was the General Officer Commanding. With so many leaders dead and President Azikiwe out of the country, Aguiyi-Ironsi was asked by Alhaji Dipcharima, Federal Minister of Transport, who was chairing the remnants of the cabinet, to take power. On 17 January he broadcast to the nation. He told it:

> The Government of the Federation of Nigeria having ceased to function, the Nigerian Armed Forces have been invited to form an interim military government for the purpose of maintaining law and order, and of maintaining essential services. This invitation has been accepted and I...have been formally invested with authority as the head of the Federal Military Government and Supreme Commander of the Nigerian Armed Forces.[6]

He suspended the federal and regional constitutions and parliaments and appointed a military governor in each region.

This coup, which brought the military to power for the first time, was initially greeted with much enthusiasm by a public fed up with election rigging, corruption and a sense of drift. Even in the north the results were not immediately unpopular. An official who had worked closely with the Sardauna told a British friend that a great burden had been lifted from his shoulders; the Sardauna, who had been so dominant for 15 years and had become more religious as he aged, was no longer so popular in a changing north. Yet, with the terrible advantage of hindsight, the coup can be seen as a foretaste of the bloodshed to come.

There are still mysteries about this takeover. It is not entirely clear what the young majors who launched the coup really wanted and whether there was any element of complicity or prior awareness from Aguiyi-Ironsi or President Azikiwe, who was conveniently out of the country on sick leave.[7] The majors were bright young men – Patrick Nzeogwu, Chief Instructor at the Nigerian Defence Academy and a fluent Hausa speaker who had been born in the north, and whose body was thought to have magical properties after he died fighting for Biafra; Major David Okafor, head of the Federal Guard; and Emmanuel Ifeajuna, perhaps the key conspirator, who seems to have been responsible for the deaths of Balewa and Chief Festus Okotie-Eboh, had been a national hero after winning a gold medal for the high jump in the 1954 British Empire (now Commonwealth) Games in Vancouver.

Because this first coup was so quickly overlaid by Aguiyi-Ironsi, its content is obscure. It has left an impression of scatter-gun idealism, with attacks on 'political profiteers, the swindlers, the men in high places that seek bribes and demand 10%, those that seek to keep the country divided permanently so that they remain in office as ministers and VIPs, the tribalists, those that make the country big for nothing before the international circle, those that have corrupted our society and put the Nigerian calendar backward'.[8] Major Nzeogwu followed up this broadcast in Kaduna by prescribing the death penalty for looting, arson, homosexuality, rape, embezzlement, bribery or corruption, obstructing of the revolution, sabotage, subversion, false alarm and assistance to foreign invaders. But Nzeogwu, who at one point was leading a column of troops advancing south on Lagos, gave up when it was clear the Aguiyi-Ironsi had control over most of the country. He and others were given safe conduct and detained.

This was certainly not a bloodless coup. Balewa had been warned by Sir Francis Cumming-Bruce, British High Commissioner, that an assault was planned and was offered refuge. But the Prime Minister, who had survived other death threats and was somewhat fatalistic, ignored this offer. He was killed after praying, and his family did not recover his body until some days later, lying in bushes by the Lagos–Abeokuta road. Nearby was the body of the rich and unpopular Okotie-Eboh. When Ifeajuna had come for him, Okotie-Eboh offered him US$3M if his life was spared. 'That's what's wrong with you,' said Ifeajuna, and then shot him dead.[9] At an English prep school the young Mukhtar Balewa learnt of his father's death from a transistor radio; a compassionate headmaster kept him on for a year gratis until Yakubu Gowon, by then the head of state, authorised the payment of fees.

That the coup had been launched by junior officers was not fortuitous, for their seniors were trained in an apolitical, Sandhurst tradition. However west Africa was enjoying a rash of military takeovers; by mid-January soldiers had seized power in Togo, Dahomey (now Benin), the Central African Republic and Upper Volta (now Burkina Faso), and before the end of February, Major-General Joseph Ankrah had overthrown Kwame Nkrumah, the iconic pan-Africanist, in Ghana. The justifications varied, but there were common threads in attacks on corruption, the disappointments of independence and a desire to break away from the colonial heritage. But above all, making a coup was relatively easy to do, those holding the guns were hard to challenge and, although this was never in a manifesto, corrupt politicians had shown that power could lead to rich pickings.

In a hint that coups can spawn coups, and that other parts of the country were fissiparous, Isaac Adako Boro launched a twelve-day revolution on 23 February in the Niger Delta. His Niger Delta Republic was soon crushed by the military, and he and his two lieutenants were tried for treason and sentenced to death. But it was a sign that a federal Nigeria could not take for granted the increasing oil wealth being pumped from the Delta.[10]

Very soon Aguiyi-Ironsi was demonstrating that the army prepared officers neither for politics nor for civil administration. The military governors depended heavily on civil servants. A hundred days after Aguiyi-Ironsi took over, the influential journalist Peter Enahoro – who wrote under the pseudonym Peter Pan in the *Daily Times* and was a brother of Chief Anthony Enahoro – offered a damning assessment: this was not a good government, and Enahoro implied that Aguiyi-Ironsi was overwhelmed and hitting the bottle. But what did for the short-lived Aguiyi-Ironsi regime was a perception that this was an Igbo takeover, and that it threatened the north.

Aguiyi-Ironsi, himself an Igbo, relied on a small caucus of Igbo advisers. He failed to put on trial the Igbo majors in the January plot, and he promoted 18 Igbo officers to the rank of colonel against the advice of his Supreme Military Council. His public moves were centralist and anti-democratic. Decree 33 abolished 81 political parties and cultural organisations. On 24 May he issued Decree 34, which, at a stroke, abolished Nigeria's federal system. In a situation where northerners were alarmed at an Igbo takeover – some Igbos in the north were triumphalist – educated northerners, civil servants and staff and students at Ahmadu Bello University spearheaded violent anti-Igbo riots. Lives were lost in massacres, property was destroyed and Igbos began to retreat to safety in the east.

Meanwhile a group of northern officers and NCOs, including Major Murtala Muhammed and Captain Theophilus Yakubu Danjuma, planned a revenge coup. This took place early on 29 July. Aguiyi-Ironsi was staying at Ibadan with Colonel Adekunle Fajuyi, Military Governor of Western Nigeria, when a detachment of northern soldiers arrived at Government Lodge. Both were killed. At the same time, hundreds of primary schoolchildren were lining the roadside in Ibadan, waiting for hours in the sun to wave flags as Aguiyi-Ironsi was due to drive by; they were taken back to their schools without explanation, where their parents dashed to collect them on learning he was dead.[11]

Brigadier Babafemi Ogundipe, Chief of Staff in Lagos, ordered troops to quell the mutiny, but they were ambushed with heavy losses. Ogundipe felt he had to negotiate with the rebels. Colonel Emeka Ojukwu, military governor in the east, phoned Ogundipe to offer his support if he wished to declare himself supreme commander. But Ogundipe was losing control of the army and declined. The rebels said there was strong pressure in the north for secession – the code name for the coup was Operation Araba ('secession') – and there were ideas circulating for a simultaneous breakaway by both the north and the west.[12]

For two or three days 'Nigeria' was adrift until Lieutenant Colonel Yakubu Gowon, then Chief of Army Staff, who had at first been taken prisoner by the rebels, agreed at their request to take over as Supreme Commander. He was only 31, a Christian and from a small tribe, the Ngas (Angas), in the Bauchi/Plateau area; this categorised him as a northern minority figure, but from that middle part of Nigeria that was always likely to get squeezed in struggles between north and south and with an interest in keeping the polity together. When Gowon prepared his first broadcast to the nation, he was due to announce the secession of the north. But Adetokunbo Ademola, Chief Justice of Nigeria, and British and US diplomats persuaded him otherwise.[13]

In his first broadcast Gowon said, 'As a result of the recent events and of the other previous similar ones, I have come to strongly believe that we cannot honestly and sincerely continue in this wise, as the basis of trust and confidence in our unitary system of government has been unable to stand the test of time…the base for unity is not there.'[14] For easterners, beginning to think that the only way to protect themselves lay in secession, this was taken as a broad hint.

For the next ten months, until Emeka Ojukwu declared Biafran independence for the east on 30 May 1967, Nigeria oscillated on the edge of break-up or a radical reconstruction. More Igbos were murdered in a pogrom in the north, in September–October 1966, which precipitated the departure of a million refugees; Igbo soldiers returned from the north and northern troops returned from the east; and in April 1967 Chief Awolowo threatened that the west would also secede if the east did so. When in January Ojukwu met Gowon in Aburi, Ghana, under the auspices of the Ghanaian military leader, General Ankrah, they were at cross purposes. All four military governors took part.

Ojukwu arrived with detailed proposals. Gowon wanted a more open agenda and to start talks that could continue in Nigeria. Ojukwu argued for a 'drawing apart' of the four regions, to put an end to the killings; the central government would be weak, requiring the concurrence of the four regional commanders, who in effect would have their own armies. On a generous view the Aburi formula could have resulted in something like the Swiss confederation, Europe's most successful plurinational state. Gowon was intellectually outgunned by Ojukwu. Ojukwu, with the confidence of an Oxford degree and the heir to one of the biggest fortunes in Nigeria, was also Gowon's senior in the army and had little respect for him. When Gowon returned to Lagos his civil servants told him that he had given away too much. In Decree 8, which said that all senior appointments had to be approved by all regions, he had given ground, but even so the decree had the effect of annoying Ojukwu by stating that a state of emergency could be declared in any region with the agreement of only three out of the four military governors.

Attempts at mediation and efforts by 'leaders of thought' in each region to find a constitutional solution came to nought. On 31 March 1967 Ojukwu expropriated federal revenues in the east. Awo's threat of western secession, which would have blocked northern access to Lagos and the sea, forced the northern emirs into a revolutionary change of stance. The northern 'leaders of thought' proposed that more states should be created, including in the north, as a way of saving the federation and the north. This was an abrupt change, which the late Sardauna would never have countenanced. Yet it opened the door to an alliance between the north and west, strong enough to preserve a federal Nigeria in the war that was now inevitable. Gowon reorganised his government, mixing civilians with the military and bringing in Awolowo, so recently a jailbird, as Deputy Chairman of the Supreme Council and a surprisingly efficient Commissioner of Finance.

On 26 May, Ojukwu's consultative assembly in the east author-ised him to go for independence and, on the same day, Gowon announced that Nigeria was being divided into twelve states. While the north was divided into six, the east was turned into three. Significantly, only one of the three was predominantly Igbo and the increasingly valuable oil belt went into a Rivers state, comprising tribes that had had minority status in the east. However, if the Rivers tribes thought they were going to be the bankers to the federation in future they were sadly mistaken. In 1969 Gowon promulgated a Petroleum Act that stated that ownership and control of all petroleum in Nigeria should be vested in the federal government.[15]

Gowon initially saw the war as a 'police action' that he and others thought might be over quickly. It lasted much longer, causing much suffering. All civil wars have complex causes, but many have profound issues at their heart. In seventeenth-century England there was a quarrel between parliament and an autocratic monarchy; in nineteenth-century America there was a struggle to end slavery; in twentieth-century Spain republicans and communists fought fascists. In Nigeria, where the slogan was 'One Nigeria', it was simply about preserving the country as a single entity.

Biafra lasted longer than expected because of the resourcefulness of the Igbos, and the power of a propaganda campaign that stressed that they had been and would be the victims of genocide. Igbo deaths in the north prior to the secession may have numbered 5,000, but the Biafran leadership and Markpress, its energetic public relations firm in Geneva, promoted the idea that 50,000 had died.[16] Gowon, whose political position was not entirely secure, failed to pursue what he described as a war 'between brothers' as ruthlessly as he might until Biafran forces advanced through the mid-west, and reached Ore, only a hundred miles from Lagos. He gave his three divisions great freedom, and their competing commanders were slow to coordinate their attacks. However, by the end of 1967 the federals had taken Enugu, the old eastern capital, and by May 1968 they had captured Port Harcourt and most oilfields. By then Biafra was cut off from the sea. All arms and relief supplies were being flown into a road, converted into an airstrip, at Uli.

The world was slow to wake up to what was going on in west Africa. The Nigerian civil war coincided with another Middle Eastern conflict, the Six-Day War, and the continuing struggle in Vietnam. However, western media, including television and photographers, increasingly focused on hunger among Biafrans, particularly among children. It was alleged that starvation was being used as a weapon of war – Chief Awolowo had implied that all weapons were permissible – and denials by Gowon were not readily accepted.

Catholic relief agencies, sympathetic to Biafra because many Igbos were Roman Catholic, publicised and tried to offset a humanitarian crisis and many able British journalists, including Frederick Forsyth, who resigned from the Reuters news agency, Michael Leapman and Auberon Waugh attacked what became a strong pro-federal position from the UK government. Leslie Kirkley, director of Oxfam, who visited Biafra in June 1968, reported that unless food arrived in six weeks up to 400,000 children would die of *kwashiorkor*, the hunger-related disease. Commenting on this, Michael Gould, historian of the war, added, 'Unfortunately, these reports were a major contributory factor in helping maintain the war for a further eighteen months, and arguably why it proved impossible for either side to find a peaceful solution to the conflict.'[17]

Economics and international alliances became entwined as the war dragged on. Ojukwu's calculation was that the longer Biafra could hold out, the better its chance of securing international recognition and survival. However this meant the Organisation of African Unity would abandon its 1963 commitment to the sanctity of colonial boundaries. In the circumstances Ojukwu did well, with Biafra getting formal recognition from Tanzania, Zambia, Gambia and the Ivory Coast and sympathy from pariah states like Rhodesia, established states like Portugal and even largely Muslim states such as the Sudan and Niger – although so much of the propaganda was of a 'Muslim threat' to 'Christian Biafra'.[18]

Biafra's key ally was France, which provided arms and subsidies but not formal recognition; in July 1967 Biafra entered into an agreement with the de Rothschild Frères, Paris, to sell oil and mineral rights for ten years for £6M. In reality Biafra was unable to export oil, though it had enough for its own purposes, for the federals first blockaded and then captured Bonny and its terminals early in the war. Official hesitation by France was illustrated by a meeting in Paris in September 1968 with a Biafran delegation that included Azikiwe and Michael Okpara, the former eastern premier. The French said they could not offer recognition unless more African states recognised Biafra. The delegation then advised Ojukwu to start negotiating with Gowon, but he refused. At this point Azikiwe, significantly, began to call for the reunification of Nigeria; in effect he changed sides.

In fact, the federal government had the better of the economic war. Between the third quarter of 1967 and the fourth quarter of 1968 the index of industrial output rose from 121.2 to 229.8. The federals changed the Nigerian currency in January 1968, causing Biafra to introduce its own – there was continuous trading across permeable battle lines – and did not devalue when the UK devalued sterling in November 1967. While prices rose and there were problems from inflation, Awo's strategy of deficit financing kept the federal treasury afloat as war costs increased and the federal armed forces rose to as many as 250,000.[19]

The Wilson government in the UK had supplied the federals with ammunition from the start, and it went on to provide armoured cars also. But when Biafran planes bombed Lagos, Gowon asked for aircraft. The British prime minister, under attack from humanitarian quarters, refused.[20] At this point, in an important move for Nigerian foreign policy, the federal government turned to the Soviet Union, which provided Ilyushin and MiG aircraft. This tilt, from what had been seen as a reliable pro-western ally, strengthened Wilson's resolve to maintain support for the federals.

The war itself was largely a matter of skirmishes rather than pitched battles, with poorly trained federal soldiers loosing off ammunition and Biafran troops melting into the countryside even as the federals advanced through the towns and main roads of the Igbo heartland. Gowon issued a code of conduct to the Nigerian Army, but its soldiers were responsible for at least one serious war crime at Asaba, on the east bank of the Niger in October 1967, when an estimated 700 men and boys were massacred. Gowon claimed not to have known about this at the time, but many years later he made a public apology in the town.[21] But the endless drumbeat of accusation that the federals intended to carry out genocide of Igbos led the government to appoint an international observer mission to investigate. Although it listed occasions when the code of conduct had not been followed, it cleared the federals of any policy of genocide. Nonetheless, the last two years of the war were punctuated with continuing debates about how best to get relief to hungry Igbos in their shrinking territory. There was discussion of an overland route for relief, but it was never agreed. Ojukwu preferred the airlifts to Uli, in which food alternated with ammunition.

Understandably, with increased attention to the suffering of civilians, there were several attempts at mediation between the two sides, all unsuccessful. Two key players in this were the OAU, chaired by Emperor Haile Selassie of Ethiopia, and the Commonwealth, whose Canadian Secretary-General, Arnold Smith, chaired peace talks in Kampala in May 1968. However, the Organization of African Unity – which sent delegations to Nigeria, invited Ojukwu to speak in Addis Ababa and was still pressing for negotiations as late as December 1969 – was seriously encumbered by its charter commitment to the sanctity of colonial boundaries.

The Commonwealth involvement was interesting – the Kampala talks lasted for six days – as its new international Secretariat had had no impact on the Indo-Pakistani War of 1965 and had witnessed the frustration of African states with Britain after Ian Smith's UDI in Rhodesia in the same year. Arnold Smith's activism in attempting to make peace in Nigeria was assisted by Emeka Anyaoku in his international affairs division; Anyaoku's London home hosted visits by both Biafrans and federals, but he himself had refused to take the oath of allegiance to Nigeria, which was required by Gowon of all civil servants, on the grounds that Gowon had failed to protect his fellow Igbos.

Anyaoku, still technically on secondment from the Nigerian diplomatic service, flew into Uli on a mercy flight to try and persuade Ojukwu to accept Smith's terms, but Ojukwu refused to agree to anything less than his version of Aburi. In fact both Gowon and Ojukwu were intransigent, in spite of the international pressure for compromise. Gowon thought he was bound to win militarily and was no longer prepared to tolerate a weak central government; Ojukwu thought that nothing less than recognition of Biafra would safeguard the Igbos.

When it came, Biafra's collapse was sudden. On 11 January 1970 Ojukwu flew into exile in Ivory Coast; his army commander, Lieutenant Colonel Philip Effiong, surrendered on behalf of Biafra the next day. The world held its breath, fearing the genocide that Biafran propaganda had forecast, and the federal government refused permission to charities that had sent supplies to Biafra to continue doing so. Hundreds of thousands of Igbos were by then in refugee camps, and there was a hiatus before the federal relief lorries got through. Bridget Bloom, one of the best international journalists covering a war that was hard to report accurately, visited the former Biafran enclave within days of the collapse. She found many hungry people, but few walking skeletons; there were, however, women raped or who 'had been conscripted', and problems arising from the shortage of transport and the sudden worthlessness of the Biafran currency.[22]

However, Gowon's promise that there would be 'no victor, no vanquished' – a recognition that all Nigerians had lost in the bloodshed – was by and large justified. Devastation in the eastern regions had been huge, with the destruction of roads, bridges and infrastructure as well as of former industrial capacity. Awo estimated that the war had cost the federal government N£230.8M in local currency and N£70.8M in foreign exchange. Oil revenues were sharply reduced.

The human cost was huge, but unquantified and unquantifiable. Several authors suggest a wide range of deaths, between one and three million, with another three million displaced.[23] Most of these fatalities were not the result of shooting or bombing, but direct or indirect consequences of hunger and starvation. Those who were injured but could not get proper medical help, or who suffered from conditions that would have been cured in peacetime suffered for the rest of their lives. Most of the deaths were among Igbos in the east, but this numerical vagueness reflects both poor statistics that went back to the census controversies and a remarkable desire among many Nigerians to leave the past behind. Chinua Achebe, the celebrated author who had represented Biafra abroad, was an exception. He maintained a sense of bitterness up to his death in 2013, publishing *There Was a Country: A Personal History of Biafra* (Allen Lane, Harmondsworth) the year before he died. By contrast Ojukwu, who on departing said, 'So long as I live, Biafra lives' and died in the same year Achebe's memoir was published, had made peace with Nigeria and was given effectively a state funeral.

The federal victory in the civil war did not put an end to the existential question about the Nigerian state – whether so many different peoples can live together amicably in one polity. But it recast it. It demonstrated that there are military, political and economic forces strong enough to counteract and defeat the centrifugal and fissiparous tendencies. It showed that there was not some southern unity, of Igbos, Yorubas and the ethnicities in the Delta, that could overthrow a perceived hegemony of the north. It showed that the north itself was not a single uniform bulldozer, but a mosaic of groups with different interests and different appreciations of Islam. And above all it showed that the minority tribes all over the country were committed to the survival of a reorganised federation, in which their voices could be heard and that the Nigerian Army would not allow the Nigerian experiment to fail. Key civil servants, working with Gowon, were also from the minorities.

The confused Biafran advance into the mid-west early in the war, when it seemed as if Biafra was not just about Igbo protection but an attempt to end northern rule over the south, failed to galvanise Yoruba support. When Lieutenant Colonel Olusegun Obasanjo, a senior Yoruba officer but a convinced 'Nigerian' in the army, refused the siren calls of the east,[24] and Chief Awolowo threw his political weight behind the Federal Military Government to his lasting cost in eastern electoral support, that particular option was closed off. An alliance of the north and west, along with eastern minorities, was bound to defeat Biafra.

But the federation that emerged at the end of the civil war was not the one that had won independence from Britain. The decree that created twelve states opened the door to a greater sense of ownership of Nigeria beyond the hitherto dominant Hausa-Fulani, Yoruba and Igbo; it also opened the door to continuing pressure for more states, recognising even smaller ethnicities, which was still not entirely assuaged when the Abacha regime moved to a total of 36 in the 1990s. But whereas the three regions at independence could act like countries in their own right – and they had overseas representatives, for example – the twelve and subsequently more numerous states were much less powerful, particularly in an era of military regimes and central government control of finance.

Finally, the war gave an enhanced significance to the Nigerian military. This was particularly true for the army, although the Navy blockaded Biafra and the first military governor of the new Rivers state was Lieutenant Commander Alfred Diete-Spiff, a naval person. The two coups in 1966 had disrupted hierarchies, creating jealousies and suspicions. Deaths and withdrawals among the Igbo officers made gaps that could not be filled quickly by competent successors. Whereas the first division, commanded by General Murtala Muhammed, a Gowon rival, had inherited possibly the best and most cohesive elements of the pre-Biafran federal army, the second and third divisions created hastily as the war began had more raw recruits. Lieutenant Colonel Benjamin Adekunle, who commanded the third division that liberated Port Harcourt, was nicknamed 'the Black Scorpion' for his speed and cunning, and obtained much publicity.

Shortly before the war ended, Gowon changed the commanders of his three divisions that were closing in on Biafra. This meant that Obasanjo, rather than Adekunle – whom Gowon may have suspected was politically in league with Awolowo – took the surrender of the bulk of the remaining Biafran troops. This almost chance event was the first of a series of flukes in the career of a young officer, then in his early thirties, who went on to be both a military head of state and an elected president of the country.

In fact the civil war, and the experience of the senior officers who won it, were to change politics in Nigeria for the next 40 years. Whereas the outcome of the American civil war did not fundamentally alter a commitment to civilian democracy rooted in public support and well-understood principles, the Nigerian polity had been and was still fractured. Military rule, justified either on 'one Nigeria' grounds or for anti-corruption and modernisation, became dominant. The fact that these arguments were spurious – 'one Nigeria' was felt in the south as northern domination, and corruption under Presidents Babangida and Abacha was world-class – did little to shake the faith of the military rulers concerned.

Yet the friendships and jealousies of senior comrades on the federal side had lasting effects. All were young, with long lives ahead, catapulted from regional barracks in a tiny army to commanding large numbers in a shooting war under the eyes of international television. Gowon was only 31 when he became head of the military government, a year younger than Ojukwu. Murtala Muhammed's removal on the eve of victory stoked his rivalry with Gowon. Obasanjo comforted the future dictator Sani Abacha and persuaded him to stay in the army after he had a breakdown during the war.[25] And there were gender aspects, too: a number of Federal officers took Igbo brides in the heat of conflict, which led to intelligence networks among wives which were still important in the civilian political era after 1999.[26]

Chapter 13
Reconstruction, another coup and the craving for democracy

The immediate post-war era, up to the establishment of the Second Republic in 1979, saw Nigeria blessed and cursed by an oil boom; adopting an aggressively pan-African foreign policy, focused especially on ending the white minority regimes in southern Africa; and involved in an endlessly protracted transition to civilian democracy, which became a pattern of procrastination by military regimes after 1983.

In spite of international scepticism the regime of Yakubu Gowon, who was Head of State of Nigeria from 1966 to 1975 sought to follow through the 'no victor, no vanquished' policy with a programme of 'Reconstruction, Rehabilitation and Reconciliation' in the shattered east. There were several features. Adults in the east were given a nominal £20 each to restart a cash economy; civil servants and the military were reintegrated into federal service on the basis that they lost promotion for their 2.5 'Biafran' years; and Igbos were encouraged to return to northern cities like Kaduna and Maiduguri to reclaim their property, where chiefs were told to make them welcome. Gowon himself promoted magnanimity in the aftermath of the surrender by ordering his troops to 'become soldiers of peace', to share their food and medicines with the impoverished Igbos, and to help transport them to their homes. One exception was a crackdown on expatriate missions perceived as supportive of Biafra; the state confiscated schools and hospitals built by these religious orders.

Physical and psychological scars took long to heal. Friendships and commercial relationships were disrupted, and the cosmopolitan pre-war artistic community of Lagos had dispersed. But most observers felt that Nigeria – with its religious and ethnic divisions and widespread poverty – acquitted itself well. Gowon's claim that this was 'a peace never before achieved in the history of the world' was perhaps an exaggeration, and reconstruction was aided by a rapid increase in oil income after the war.[1] Igbo commercial drive, stimulated by limited land availability in the heartland that had led to migrations both westward and northwards, took a few years to recover, as did infrastructure in the east. Igbo influence in the political sphere was also weakened, while Igbo recruitment into the upper levels of the army was delayed for years, which meant that Igbo voices were muffled during the military regimes of the 1980s and 1990s.

The successful end to the war put Gowon in a much stronger political position, and soon after it was over he announced a nine-point plan that promised Nigerians a return to civilian rule – initially no later than 1974. He wanted to reorganise the civil service, recognising the impact of the new twelve states; to put the military onto a peacetime footing, reducing the numbers while learning the lessons of the war; to end official corruption; to invest in the country's development, using the anticipated increase in oil revenues; to draw up a new constitution and make even more new states; to carry out another, more accurate census; and to establish nationwide political parties as a prelude to elections and a civilian government.

But he failed to deliver, and grumbling increased both amongst the military and from civilian politicians who wanted to renew electoral games that had been brutally halted in 1966. Initially the military governors chosen by Gowon, who lost their commands on appointment, often seemed overwhelmed by their responsibilities. What became obvious subsequently was that most of them were corruptly enriching themselves – inquiries after his overthrow in 1975 showed that only two out of the twelve, the governors of Lagos and

Ibadan, had not done so – and that there was colossal mismanagement of state resources, symbolised in that year by enormous congestion in the port of Lagos as ships poured in with cement, over-ordered for a grandiose army barracks, and claimed demurrage for each day's delay.

The Gowon regime seemed incapable of dealing with corruption, and its leaders became hubristic. In 1974 there was a scandal in one of the new states – Benue-Plateau, Gowon's home region – where Joseph Gomwalk, Military Governor of Benue-Plateau State in 1966–75, and Joseph Tarka, Federal Commissioner of Communications in 1966–74, were implicated. Tarka resigned, but Gowon failed to discipline Gomwalk, who was a friend. A sense of hubris had been shown even during the war. Gowon had had a lavish wedding when marrying his wife Victoria in Lagos in April 1969 with horse-drawn carriages. The following year, just as the war ended, Alfred Diete-Spiff, Military Governor of Rivers state, commandeered an aircraft allocated to journalists who were desperate to get into the former Biafra to check on the condition of survivors. While the journalists fumed for nine hours, the plane was used to transport guests to his wedding.

The media and politicians became impatient with delays in return to civilian rule. Whatever the defects of the pre-war system, many Nigerians had become enamoured with democracy. But whereas Gowon had first promised that the military would hand over two years after the end of the war the target then became 1974, then 1976, then some time after that; he was in no hurry to get a new constitution written. Obafemi Awolowo, the most powerful of the pre-war politicians in the Federal Military Government, resigned in 1971. While resuming his legal career he was impatient to get back to elected governments, and there was a gradual opening up to political organisation and discussion. But at the same time a number of powerful voices were urging a permanent governing status for the military. These included Allison Ayida, one of the powerful civil servants on whom the

Gowon regime depended, and Nnamdi Azikiwe, whose 'Grand Old Man' status had survived his political wobbles before, during and after the war.[2] Ayida argued that the new, more intelligent, army would not be content to stay in the barracks and a constitutional settlement must recognise that it could be interventionist. Zik proposed a diarchy, a formal sharing of power between the military and civilians.

In 1973 the military regime sought to administer an accurate census, but it ran into the same troubles of inflated figures and public disbelief that had undermined the exercise a decade earlier. Not only did it purport to show that the northern states now had a growing preponderance in the federation, 64% of the total, but it claimed that the numbers in Kano and the northeast had virtually doubled in only ten years. Even the military governor of Lagos cried foul, and Gowon decided that the country was not ready for rule by squabbling civilian politicians. In an attempt to overcome the continuing inter-ethnic tensions he launched a National Youth Service Corps, by which student-age Nigerians had to spend a year in a different part of the country. The concept of 'federal character', or a balance between ethnicities in appointments, was promoted.

But military plotters had decided that Gowon's time was up. Brigadier Murtala Muhammed had always been jealous of Gowon, and the fact that the military governors of states had been in place since the war blocked opportunities for others. When Gowon told the Supreme Military Council that by November 1976 he would rotate the governors and senior officers, Muhammed, in a whispered aside heard by Diete-Spiff, said, 'What about your own job?'[3] At the end of July 1975, when Gowon was at an OAU meeting in Kampala, Muhammed and a group of lieutenant colonels and colonels who had helped bring Gowon to power and win the war overthrew him in a bloodless coup. Muhammed was a northerner with battlefield prestige who promised a corrective government that would restore the dignity of the military. Nigerian commentators, critical of the corruption and ineptitude of Gowon's government and relieved that there were no more killings, generally praised the coup.

This reaction was reinforced as it soon became clear that Muhammed was determined to do the things that Gowon had promised: to introduce a new constitution prior to elections, clean up corruption and the ballooning public service and create new states. Within weeks of taking over as Head of State on 30 July, the new leader had dismissed or retired some 11,000 civil servants and purged the police, the judges and four Vice-Chancellors. In retrospect some analysts believe that this drastic action, though applauded by the media and public, was counter-productive: in a kleptocratic society where lucky and wealthy individuals are expected to finance extended families, it meant that civil servants in future might grab what they could while they could, knowing that their tenure was uncertain. Some of the sacked 'deadwoods' had also been more competent than their successors. Gowon's twelve states became nineteen, work on a new constitution was expedited, and a four-year timetable, leading to a transfer of power to elected civilians on 1 October 1979, was announced.

There was a nationalistic and statist streak to the Muhammed regime. This showed in economic affairs, with a serious effort to effect the 1972 indigenisation decree designed to increase Nigerian influence in the economy, and in foreign affairs, with a leadership role against the racist minority governments in southern Africa. At home he announced a panel to transfer the federal capital from Lagos to the interior, a strategy similar to that adopted 20 years before in a similarly large country, Brazil. By February 1976 the decision was taken to move the capital to Abuja, a central site dominated by a huge rock that looked like a sleeping elephant, in a small Hausa emirate ruled by Sulamainu Barau. This emir had studied at the famous Katsina Training College and made the progressive decision that his followers need no longer go down on their knees and pour dust on their heads in obeisance.[4]

Muhammed took control over universities and primary schools, tightened controls on journalists and broadcasters and reorganised the trade unions. His regime cut back FESTAC, the second World Black and African Festival of Arts and Culture, which was to be a global demonstration of African artistic achievements floated on Nigerian oil wealth. Anthony Enahoro, Gowon's commissioner for culture, had ordered an off-the-peg Bulgarian design for a National Theatre for FESTAC – also to be a Palais de Sports – and insisted that it be 50% larger. Costs of the building project, with over-invoicing and other dodges, had ballooned. Muhammed reorganised the upper tiers of government and insisted that its members should not flaunt their wealth, although a 1976 Public Officers (Protection Against False Accusation) Decree would also protect them against both false and true allegations.

On 13 February 1976 General Muhammed was murdered in a failed coup. He had been travelling with minimal security, part of his commitment to austerity, when his car was riddled with bullets. It seemed like a throwback to the excesses of 1966, which had put Nigeria on the path to war. But there was little risk of the country's break-up this time. The plot, led by Lieutenant Colonel Bukar Dimka, resulted from factionalism in the army and the resentments of those who had done well with Gowon and were now sidelined by Muhammed. There were few ideological or ethnic factors. Nonetheless a significant number of officers were implicated and Major General Iliya Bisalla, the Commissioner of Defence, one colonel and three lieutenant colonels were among 32 people sentenced to death and executed on the evening of 11 March outside Kirikiri Prison, Lagos, and on Bar Beach, a popular swimming resort. There was a continuing question as to whether Gowon, who denied it, was in any way responsible. But

Nigeria demanded the withdrawal of the British High Commissioner, to whom Dimka had turned with a request to make contact with Gowon after the assassination of Muhammed. Gowon, a student at Warwick University on an army pension, was then asked to return to Nigeria for questioning, but refused.[5]

The mourning for Muhammed was national and authentic, and Lagos airport would be named after him. Cynics later wondered whether his enduring popularity rested on the fact that such a short period of power had protected his reputation. But his successor as Head of State was Olusegun Obasanjo (in office 1976–79), a Yoruba, who drove the transition to civilian rule with equal vigour. He oversaw a considerable reduction in the size of the army. He seems to have understood that its continuing involvement in government was damaging and ultimately fatal to the military. He took steps to reassure Hausa-Fulani officers and leaders that he would not pursue a 'southern' agenda or threaten their interests, and this was only one reason why he never had the full confidence of his fellow Yorubas.

For the more radical and artistic Yorubas, Obasanjo was never forgiven for the assault on Fela Kuti's 'Kalakuta ("Rascal") Republic', a compound in Lagos from which Fela launched a series of musical broadsides at the government, the rich and neocolonialists. After several raids it was surrounded by a thousand armed soldiers in February 1977, set on fire, and the 77-year-old Funmilayo Ransome-Kuti was thrown from a first-floor window; she died later from her injuries, and two of her sons, Fela and his younger brother Beko, were both seriously hurt, which fuelled a lasting anger. In a characteristic gesture of defiance, Fela presented his mother's coffin at the Dodan barracks and wrote a popular song in pidgin English, 'Coffin for Head of State'. In it he accused Obasanjo and Brigadier Musa Yar'Adua, another coup plotter against Gowon who had taken Obasanjo's place as number two in the army, of corruption. With civilian politicians building dubious war chests in the run-up to elections, the perceived probity of the military under Muhammed was under threat.

There was a high degree of continuity between the Muhammed and Obasanjo governments, but Obasanjo was responsible for a reorganisation of local government, for dealing with a student rebellion over the cost of food at universities and for a constitutional settlement regarding federal appeals from state-level sharia courts. He was also responsible for the Land Use Act, 1978, which decreed a kind of nationalisation that was subsequently embedded in civilian constitutions. It vested all lands within the states in the military governors to be held in trust 'for the use and common benefit of all Nigerians.'

The 1979 constitution stuck, like most in Africa, to the concept of an elected executive president; there was little desire to return to the Westminster parliamentary system of 1960. Much later, as a democratically elected president in the 21st century, Obasanjo would again be haunted by the sharia issue that the constitution tried to side-step. A Federal Election Commission was set up and a new revenue sharing formula was adopted, under which the federal government would get 57%, state governments 30% and local governments 10%, with special grants accounting for 3%. After the near independence in finance of the pre-war regional governments, there had been a drastic move to federal control under Gowon and Awolowo. This, in the era of the oil economy, was now somewhat eased.

For the most remarkable fact about Nigeria in the 1970s, which assisted post-war reconstruction and led to ostentatious wealth among a few, was the arrival of oil money. Oil money was internationally denominated in US dollars, and this largesse coincided with increased US involvement in the economy; it was a belated gesture of nationalism, on 1 January 1973, which saw the British pound sterling abandoned in favour of the Nigerian Naira (N), at a rate of £1 = 2N. Between 1970 and 1979, when the elected President Shehu Shagari took office, oil output doubled from 396M barrels a year to 840M barrels. More pertinently, oil exports as a percentage of total exports rose from 58% to 93% in the same period, government oil revenue jumped from N166M to N8,881M and oil revenue as a portion of total revenue went up from 26% to 81%.[6]

What were the consequences of this bonanza? They included inflation, a leap in public service salaries, the neglect of agriculture, an expansion of parastatals, the wasteful allocation of resources and rent-seeking and prebendalism among those who could access the honeypots. The money greatly increased the power of the federal government. Gowon was quoted as saying that the only problem for Nigeria was how to spend the money, but by the time Obasanjo was Head of State, when oil prices had come off the boil, he was trying to manage down the expectations of a predominantly poor population: 'I wish to stress that, although this country has great potential, she is not yet a rich nation.'[7] There was a craze for luxury imports, and the Udoji Commission, which was supposed to reform the public service in 1974, actually led to wage rises of between 130% at the lower end and 90% at the top in order to bring the public sector into line with the private sector; awards in 1975 were backdated by nine months and in the first four months of 1975 the money supply rose by 47%.[8] Government spending was outrunning income; the external reserves dropped from N4.1bn at the end of 1974/5 to N3.1bn at the end of 1975/6; there was a deficit in the trade balance, and Nigeria had to raise loans on the international market.[9]

In theory the large sums available to the Nigerian government were being ploughed in a methodical way into successive national development plans, but implementation was poor and even under the military it was exposed to sectional and regional interests. As Forrest noted in 1995, 'There has never been a planning mechanism in Nigeria.'[10] A group of northern intellectuals close to the military, nicknamed the 'Kaduna mafia', were adept at obtaining regional benefits from the wealth being sucked out of the ground in the southeast. Oil wealth was erratic, and after the spurt arising from the Yom Kippur war in 1973 there was a fall in prices in the late 1970s. An admirable attempt to introduce universal primary education, in part an attempt to make up for the deficiencies in the north, was hitting financial limitations by the late 1970s, and the federal government tried to shift the cost to the states.

The 1970s saw a steady expansion in the number of state-financed parastatal corporations, of which the Nigerian National Oil Corporation was the most strategically important and the Nigerian Steel Development Authority, founded in 1971, the most wasteful and ineffectual. Part of a fashion for state-led development in the postcolonial world, they were overwhelmingly dependent on federal funding. However, their ambitions outran their capacity, and they were targets for theft and misappropriation. Many, including the NNOC, failed to publish regular accounts. The state also acquired a monopoly in fertiliser, salt, pulp and paper, with a presence in other sectors. While the US overtook the UK as an investor in Nigeria in this decade, an analysis under the Muhammed government showed that many international firms had bypassed the indigenisation decree, maintaining a significant grip on the economy.

As a member of the Organisation of Petroleum Exporting Countries cartel, Nigeria had benefited from the boom and followed the example of other members in increasing royalties and getting more involved in the industry. The government, through the NNOC, took a 100% interest in new concessions, and first a 35% and then a 60% participation in existing oil-producing contracts. It demonstrated its power over the companies in 1978, when it nationalised the local operations of the British Petroleum Company. BP, holding 20% of a joint operation with Shell, had helped pioneer oil production in Nigeria. But it was still controlled by the UK government, and Obasanjo took action partly because he wanted to put pressure on the UK to solve the Rhodesia conflict and partly because he was horrified to learn that Nigerian oil had ended up in South Africa as a result of a BP oil swap. Barclays Bank operations in Nigeria were nationalised at the same time.

By the late 1970s, with non-OPEC oil coming on stream from Alaska, the North Sea and elsewhere, prices fell. The heavy dependence on one source of revenue and domestic extravagance led to relative austerity for Nigeria. Obasanjo launched Operation Feed the Nation, for the country had lost its self-sufficiency in food. On 31 May 1976 he took his staff to an area behind the Dodan barracks in Lagos where they dug the land, cleared weeds, applied fertiliser, planted seeds and collected eggs from chickens already there.[11] While the campaign was only moderately successful, it had a lasting impact for Obasanjo. By the 21st century his Ota farms were major suppliers of eggs and chicken to the Nigerian market, and promoting agricultural self-sufficiency in Africa was to be a first priority for his charitable foundation.

The most striking aspect of Nigeria, seen as an oil-rich power in the 1970s, was its increasingly aggressive foreign policy. It played a key role in its region, with the establishment of the Economic Community of West African States in 1975. It pursued a more neutralist line in international affairs, following the improved federal relations with the eastern bloc during the civil war, and tackled the United States head-on by supporting the Movimento Popular de Libertação de Angola in the Angolan civil war. This was an era when the US was backing the 'pro-west' Angolan leader Jonas Savimbi, and indulging in 'constructive engagement' with the apartheid regime in South Africa, while Cuban troops were fighting alongside the MPLA in solidarity. After the MPLA appeared to have won, Nigeria gave Angola N13.5M in 1976.

Nigeria also backed the armed struggle in South Africa and used its largesse for both political and humanitarian purposes. It became an aid donor, lending N225M to the IMF oil facility, US$80M to the African Development Bank and US$52M to the OPEC special fund.[12] It helped coordinate the Africa, Caribbean, and Pacific Group of States, which assisted newly independent states in trade negotiations with the European Community and joined actively in contemporary struggles by developing countries for a new world international economic order. It continued to supply the UN with peacekeeping troops.

But the heart of this independent Africanist policy lay in the ceaseless effort to end European colonialism and white minority rule in the south of the continent. While some of the aid efforts were criticised at home – Nigeria funded a new presidential palace in Togo, for example – this was a genuinely popular cause, and every Nigerian passport included a statement about ending colonialism in Africa. While the military governments in the 1970s were in sync with public opinion, it was left to a civilian, President Shagari, to see Rhodesia turn into Zimbabwe.

Chapter 14
A second republic, its short, inglorious life and its overthrow

Few would have anticipated that independent Nigeria's second try at a civilian, democratic government would last an even shorter time than its first. The military government of General Olusegun Obasanjo, Head of State for three years, was meticulous in keeping to its handover schedule, running up to 1 October 1979, and a turbulent public and media had a genuine appetite for the free choice of rulers. Yet by the time the military overthrew President Shehu Shagari on 31 December 1983, his government had lost credibility and another coup was widely welcomed.

What had gone wrong? There were several factors. The civilian politicians and the structure of a federation, which now contained 19 states with continuing campaigns for state creation, were partly to blame. The extraordinary levels of corruption and mismanagement of the economy angered all who were not immediate beneficiaries. A resurrection of always dangerous north–south and Muslim–Christian frictions provided a threatening background. And issues in the military, which was annoyed by cutbacks and Shagari's spending on militarised police forces, turned parochial concerns into a rapidly successful challenge to the civilian-run state.

The civilian politicians had a year to campaign, for the official ban on politics was lifted in September 1978 and a Federal Electoral Commission subsequently cleared five parties to compete. The military had tried to reduce the ethnic character of pre-war elections by insisting that all parties should have their headquarters in the national capital with branches in at least two-thirds of the states. But these precautions were inadequate. The Unity Party of Nigeria, led by Chief Obafemi Awolowo, remained Yoruba-based although it sought backing from minorities elsewhere; Nnamdi Azikiwe's Nigerian People's Party could not rebuild the 'national' character of the NCNC of the 1940s and lost support in the north when a Borno leader broke away to form the Great Nigeria People's Party. Aminu Kano led a more radical but also pro-sharia People's Redemption Party in the north.

The most federally inclusive was the National Party of Nigeria led by Shehu Shagari, who came from Sokoto and had had, under the patronage of the Sardauna, a big career in the NPC in the first republic. But its base was in the north. Starting as parliamentary secretary to Tafawa Balewa, Shagari had gone on to hold three ministries before the war. He was brought back by Gowon in 1970 to be successively Minister of Economic Affairs and then Minister of Finance. Giving a nod to the party's federal character, although its political heart lay in northern conservatism, Shagari was the presidential candidate, Alex Ekwueme, an Igbo and an architect by profession, was his vice-presidential running-mate, and the party's secretary was a Yoruba, Adisa Akinloye.

There were few genuine policy differences between these parties that were based on personalities, calculations as to who was most likely to deliver spoils, and ill-disguised ethnicity. Awolowo maintained the welfarist and somewhat social democratic stance of the former Action Group. Eghosa Osaghae, a modern historian, writes of the NPN that it was 'a conservative party committed to maintaining law and order, human rights, a free market and respect for traditional institutions.'[1]

In all there were five elections, between 7 July and 11 August 1979 – for the Senate, the House of Representatives and Houses of Assembly in the states, for governorships, and finally for the presidency. The electoral commission ruled out a large number of candidates but the various elections went off peacefully, with the UPN winning in the Yoruba states, the NPP in the Igbo east, and the NPC controlling seven states and collecting seats everywhere except in Lagos and Ogun, two Yoruba states. But a great row enveloped the presidential result, where Shagari obtained 5,688,857 votes compared with 4,916,651 for Chief Awolowo, his nearest rival. Awo, who unsuccessfully went to court to try and overturn the FEDECO's prompt ruling in favour of Shagari, took issue over its interpretation of the constitution.

As part of the commitment to 'federal character' the constitution prescribed that the winning presidential candidate must win at least a quarter of the votes in at least two-thirds of the 19 states. In fact Shagari achieved this in twelve states, but fell short in the northern state of Kano where the leftist but sharia-supporting party of Aminu Kano kept Shagari's vote down to around 19.4%. While mathematicians argued as to what two-thirds of 19 should be, and Awo and his lawyers argued that he was entitled to a run-off, both the electoral tribunal and Supreme Court ruled against him.

But the vocal opposition of the southwest, and its media, weakened the new republic from the start. Shagari and the NPC made an agreement with Zik's NPP, which saw the NPP gain eight ministries including foreign affairs, and a working majority in the house of assembly. This agreement did not last. There were continuing frictions between federal and state governments, and within parties with weak discipline. The democratic experiment was also vitiated because the majority of states were effectively one-party, and state governments squashed efforts at independence in local government. The federal government sought to intervene directly in the states by appointing 'presidential liaison officers'.

Shagari's government had no coherent domestic policy, apart from its willingness to spend money on education both at the primary level and on establishing new universities in the states. It invested heavily in the Abuja project for a new capital, and in new steelworks at Ajaokuta in Kwara state, built with Soviet help, and Aladja near Warri, erected with German and Austrian assistance. Three steel rolling mills were built in other locations, scattered across the country. But the steel projects were expensive, uneconomic, dependent on foreign ore and technology, and never delivered industrial benefits. Much money was wasted in contracts for Abuja. Recollecting this era, an Indian High Commissioner at the time thought that the Shagari government was more incompetent than corrupt.[2] But such investments reflected political pay-offs, and corruption had grown with the need to repay loans amounting to N$7M (US$11.9M) advanced by rich businessmen for the NPN campaign in 1979.[3]

A sense of cluelessness was exacerbated by conflict in the north where there was an uprising in 1980 by followers of an Islamic leader known as Muhammadu Marwa; the Maitatsine riots were put down by the military but resulted in 5,000 dead, including Marwa. Debates about sharia prior to the 1979 constitution had led to increased Christian/Islamic frictions in religiously mixed cities in the north, where southerners in *sabon gari* quarters were a visible target. In 1982 there were clashes in Kano, which spread to Kaduna and Zaria, with deaths, churches burnt and damage to southern-owned businesses. Shagari annoyed the military by increasing police numbers tenfold, to 100,000, and giving the police arms. The increasing authoritarianism of his government – involving use of state media and security services – sharpened hostility in opposition media and in a civil society that would grow in importance in the 1980s.

A key factor in the undoing of the second republic lay in economic mismanagement, and the government's failure to respond to the oil glut of the early 1980s. It had been misled into extravagance by a doubling of the oil price from US$19 a barrel in 1979 to US$38 a barrel two years later. It thought it was sailing into office on a tide of oil revenue. But this was followed by a sharp fall in demand, and although Nigeria and other OPEC and non-OPEC producers reduced prices and output the country saw its annual revenue from oil drop from N12.9M in 1980 to N7.8M in 1983. GDP fell by 8.5% in real terms between 1981 and 1983, while consumer prices rose by over 20%.[4] Foreign currency reserves were run down, and talks for a loan from the IMF, embarked on as a last resort, broke down; Nigeria and its western creditors were far apart in a dispute over the amounts owed in debt and as usual the IMF was pressing for a drastic structural adjustment programme. Meanwhile the public sector and poorly managed parastatals continued to expand, and new agencies were set up to promote presidential initiatives that merely duplicated existing bodies.

This was an era of capital flight, extensive cross-border smuggling, and manipulation of the prices of key commodities such as sugar and rice – where a Rice Task Force under Umaru Dikko was to become notorious. Dikko's corruption had already been exposed when a 1975 tribunal looked into his misuse of FESTAC monies, and it was typical of Shagari and his party's carelessness about probity that he was ever employed in such a post. As a consequence of changing diets, and a weakening of domestic agriculture, many Nigerians had come to depend on imported rice.[5] The government tried to reinvigorate domestic agriculture, with a Green Revolution Programme that took over from Operation Feed the Nation, and sought to combine self-reliance with multinational and World Bank investments. Analysts dispute how far local food production was damaged by the oil boom, but imports declined as austerity hit after 1982.[6]

When in April 1982 the government introduced a belated austerity programme, involving import controls and monetary restrictions, it opened the door to corrupt misuse of licences of many kinds. Its approach was more statist, and more reluctant to remove subsidies and privatise parastatals, than the prescriptions for austerity plus privatisation that were becoming the donor formula of the 'Washington consensus'. In particular it responded to ordinary Nigerians' view that, as a major oil producer, they should enjoy cheap petrol – a subsidy issue that led to demonstrations again in the second decade of the 21st century.

For the man and woman in the street the reality was one of inflation, and recession, while those who had their tongues in the political gravy-train were getting richer. The son of a senator under Shagari – the senator was murdered and his funds in Switzerland were never located – told the author he remembered toting bags of half a million dollars along London's Oxford Street.[7] After a considerable struggle by the Nigerian Labour Congress the minimum wage was raised from N70 in 1979 to N125 in 1981, but this was inadequate. Forrest commented, 'The rule of the politicians was disastrous for the material advancement of Nigeria and for the living standards of its citizens. The real income of urban households declined by 34%, between 1980 and 1984.'[8]

The Shagari government launched diversionary tactics in the face of the economic crisis – expelling two million 'illegal aliens' in 1983, and purporting to promote a hardly credible ethical crusade. Half of these foreigners were English-speaking Ghanaians, some highly qualified but many working on construction sites or as petty traders; another significant group were from Niger. These expulsions were not unprecedented, for Nigerians had been expelled from Ghana by Dr Busia in 1969, but they damaged the country's status as a regional good neighbour and founder and pillar of ECOWAS, with its commitment to the free movement of labour. Shagari's ethical crusade carried little conviction because it was obvious that his party people were feathering their own nests, and there was no systematic crackdown on misbehaviour.

The economic decline in the second half of Shagari's first term also hit one of the country's most prized resources, the education of its children. Some teachers were unpaid for months and, unable to survive if far away from their families, were forced to return to their villages.[9] State and local budgets, suffering cuts and misuse, failed to maintain school and other essential services.

Nigeria also lost some of its international standing as a campaigner against racism in southern Africa and for current causes in the developing and postcolonial world. During the final phase of military government, under the Muhammed/Obasanjo regime, it had nationalised major British companies and stood up to the United States; these stands had public appeal, with all Nigerian passports including a commitment to freedom throughout the African continent. But the incoherence in domestic policy of the civilian government was reflected in a more cautious approach to foreign policy.

This was not immediately apparent. Maitama Sule, a survivor of Tafawa Balewa's government, was appointed by Shagari to represent Nigeria in the wings of the 1979 Lancaster House conference. This was negotiating the transition of Rhodesia into Zimbabwe, the terms of democratic elections, and an end to the bitter civil war. On arriving in London he called on Margaret Thatcher, the new Conservative Prime Minister, whose sympathies lay with the whites in Rhodesia and who had not been best pleased by Nigeria's nationalisation of BP and Barclays.

Recalling this meeting, Sule said that Thatcher started by telling him that he had arrived too late. It was her intention to close the conference – presumably to revert to the 'internal settlement' that had been Conservative policy prior to the crucial Commonwealth conference in Lusaka that led to Lancaster House. Sule responded with a mixture of flattery and threat. He told her that it would give his president a heart attack if she was to close the conference as soon as the special representative of Nigeria arrived; this was a veiled threat that there could be further damage to British interests. But he also flattered her. He said that here she was – a young, intelligent and pretty woman, the first female prime minister – who had achieved something that had defeated three male prime ministers before her: she was in sight of a solution to the intractable Rhodesian problem.

'So what do you want me to do?' Sule recalls Thatcher asking. He told her she should keep the conference going. He personally would stay as long as necessary – in fact he stayed in London for 42 days – and 'would scold my African brothers' if they seemed unwilling to make an agreement.[10] Shridath Ramphal and Emeka Anyaoku from the Commonwealth Secretariat, along with leaders of frontline states were also working behind the scenes to keep the talks on track, even when it looked as if they might break up over the issue of white farmers' control of agricultural land.

Sule advised Robert Mugabe and Joshua Nkomo to hang on to the white farmers, but to encourage them to bring in black partners. In fact the farmers were given a ten year guarantee, and the issue only became explosive two decades later with the 'fast track' occupations of white-owned land. But the role of Nigeria in Lancaster House was not unimportant, and followed the trajectory marked most clearly by Muhammed and Obasanjo. For the country had leverage not only on the British, because of continuing if reducing investments and trade, but on the Zimbabwean and southern African nationalists, which it was supporting politically and financially. After Zimbabwe's independence, and Mugabe's election victory, the Nigerian government funded Ziana, a state news agency; it also gave Mugabe US$10M to buy out the *Rhodesia Herald* (now *The Herald*) – the settler organ founded in the days of Cecil Rhodes – which became central to Mugabe's increasing control of the media.

The civilian government continued its aid for the liberation movements in southern Africa, where the balance had sharply altered against white domination as a result of independence for the Portuguese colonies and Zimbabwe. It opposed the US policy under Reagan for 'constructive engagement' with the Pretoria regime, and it was a sign of Nigeria's importance, not least as a supplier of oil to the US, that Vice-President George Bush visited the country in 1982. With less emphasis on indigenisation, US multinationals had become active investors. In 1980 Fela Kuti released his famous musical attack on the International Telegraph and Telephone Corporation (ITT) – 'International Thief Thief'. Shagari's government remained active in ECOWAS, though it could no longer afford to fund its west African neighbours so generously, and promoted a grandiose 'Lagos Plan of Action' for the OAU that looked forward to an African economic community, a visionary concept that was beyond the immediate capacity of member states.

Two small border disputes, with Chad, where a Nigerian peace-keeping force had to be withdrawn, and with Cameroun, where there was a simmering quarrel over the Bakassi peninsula, led to the deaths of Nigerian soldiers and embarrassment for the military. In late 1983 one officer, disobeying Shagari, led an unauthorised attack on Chadian troops who had crossed the border and were holding Nigerian soldiers hostage; he was Muhammadu Buhari, soon to become a military ruler and, in 2015, an elected president. Some 30 years later a permanent secretary of the Foreign Ministry told the author with pride that Nigeria had never gone to war with any neighbour, although it had assisted several with peacekeepers.[11] But what seemed like a feeble response to the deaths of Nigerian soldiers became another item on a charge sheet that military plotters were drawing up to justify another intervention.

In late 1983, after an election that precipitated the death of the second republic, there was a 'what-might-have-been' for Nigerian foreign policy. The coup took place after Emeka Anyaoku had been nominated as Foreign Minister, but before completion of senate hearings that were a condition of approval under the constitution.

He had resigned from the Commonwealth Secretariat, where he was Deputy Secretary-General to Shridath Ramphal, responsible for political and international affairs, to take up the post in Nigeria. Married to a distinguished Yoruba woman from the Abeokuta heartland, he had resigned from the diplomatic service during the Biafran war, and combined an unrivalled empathy with Nigeria with exceptional international experience. Had he taken up his post and the Shagari government survived, it is likely that his country would have played a more vigorous role in the final unwinding of South African apartheid. Instead, after the coup, he returned to London to resume his position at the Commonwealth Secretariat.

On 31 December 1983 Brigadier Sani Abacha went on the radio to announce that 'I and my colleagues in the armed forces have – in the discharge of our national role as promoters and protectors of our national interests – decided to effect a change in the leadership of the Government of the Federal Republic of Nigeria and to form a Federal Military Government.' In a New Year broadcast the new head of state, Muhammadu Buhari, who had been a Petroleum Commissioner and chaired the Nigerian National Petroleum Corporation under the previous military regime of which he said this was an offshoot, justified the coup on grounds of corruption, economic mismanagement, and election rigging. In a conscious echo of Murtala Muhammed's takeover broadcast he concluded on a note of national unity: 'This generation of Nigerians and indeed future generations have no other country but Nigeria. We shall remain here and salvage it together.'[12] Buhari, who had been a brigade major for the federals in the civil war, was one of the small group of officers who had been involved in all the coups since Murtala Muhammed had organised the overthrow of Aguiyi-Ironsi in 1966.

What on earth had happened? Only a few months earlier, in August 1983, Shagari and his party had won a comfortable election victory. In an article that appeared on 2 January – written before the coup but unluckily appearing just after it – a contributor to *West Africa* had opined that 'Damaged, but still surviving, is the judgment that many would now pass on Nigeria's constitutional democracy.' Yet there was no internal opposition to the military takeover, although an officer who had gone to tell Shagari in Abuja that he was history was shot dead, and public reaction was one of relief. African comment was less enthusiastic, particularly among civilian presidents, although Master-Sergeant Doe, the military leader of Liberia, offered his congratulations.[13] The coup could be seen as part of a pattern. In ECOWAS alone ten out of the 16 states could be said to be ruled by the military, to a greater or lesser extent, compared with only five at the end of 1979.

But the elections were fraudulent; the cost of living crisis for Nigerians had worsened; corruption was visible; and plotting in the military was untroubled by the security services. There were several problems with the elections. As the press had pointed out earlier in the year, FEDECO had given the government an advantage by changing the order in which they were held, so that the presidential vote came first, cascading benefits down to NPN candidates standing for governor, in state houses of assembly, and in local government. Voters' rolls were inflated in all states, but the majority were held by the NPN, so the governing party was more advantaged by rigging. 'There was no doubt that the voters' register had been fraudulently inflated...The attitudes of the parties clearly showed that they relied more on rigging and other malpractices than on the support of the electorate to secure victory,' commented Osaghae.[14]

Finally, the opposition was once more divided along its 40-year-old rifts between Awo's largely Yoruba UPN and Zik's largely Igbo NPP. An attempt to bring them together in a 'Progressive Parties Alliance' was a failure. As a result Shagari, who had refused to stand down to permit a non-northerner to lead the NPN, was declared to have won nearly half the vote in the presidential election, with Awo a distant second on less than a third. The winner had got the mandatory quarter of all votes in 17 of the 19 states, and the NPN elected governors in twelve. Throughout the elections there was much violence and intimidation, and opposition parties complained of NPN misuse of the police and security services, and its monopoly of state broadcasting.

The NPN, where members boasted that there were only two parties in the country, itself and the military, was badly tainted and critics worried that it was aiming to build a one-party state. Nicknamed by one commentator 'the Party of National Patronage' it seemed to be held together principally by manipulation of the spoils and rent-seeking systems.[15] Its popularity was wearing very thin after the August 1983 elections. Yet earlier Shagari had tried to bind up the wounds of the civil war by simultaneously offering pardons to Ojukwu and to Gowon. Ojukwu returned from exile in 1982, greeted by cheers from Igbo supporters and awarded the chiefly title of *Ikemba* ('strength of the nation'). Gowon, who had had his military pension removed by Obasanjo, spurned this offer on the grounds that he had committed no crime. He had settled in England for a while to study, where he received a doctorate from Warwick University in 1982.

Two representative but rival figures in the final days of the Shagari government were Umaru Dikko, who ran the president's re-election campaign, and Chief M.K.O. Abiola, the wealthy owner of the *Concord* newspaper group, who was alleged to have tried to buy votes to replace Shagari as the NPN's presidential candidate. Dikko, from Kaduna in the north, had backed Shagari to be NPN presidential candidate in 1978–79 and, when Shagari won, was made Minister of Transport and chairman of the presidential task force on rice. He was 'alleged to have stashed away billions in foreign exchange due to his privileged position as the task force's chairman'.[16] His fundraising for the re-election campaign was murky and, when the military

government sought his extradition from the UK in 1985 after failing
to bring him back from Heathrow in a trunk, there were two charges.
The more serious was that, as chairman of the rice task force, he had
corruptly received N4,525,000 (US$7.7M) in return for a favour to
Eurotrade Nigeria, a firm that had secured a contract for customs
clearance and distribution of rice imported from the US.

Just before Shagari's overthrow Dikko had fallen out with
the president. Moshood Kashimawo Abiola, one of the NPN's vice-
presidents and the party's chairman in the Yoruba state of Ogun, fell
out both with Dikko, who suspected that he had made off with the
Concord newspaper, which Dikko thought should be an NPN party
organ, and with Shagari, who he felt should have made way for a
southerner in the 1983 election, in the interests of displaying the
party's 'federal character'.

By the 1980s Abiola was a multimillionaire. He had trained
in Scotland as an accountant, getting a first-class degree, and had
made much of his money in the US. His big break had come when
he was appointed chairman of the Nigerian subsidiary of ITT, and
subsequently vice-president for Africa and the Middle East. ITT at
the time was one of the world's biggest multinationals and Fela Kuti's
attack on it was related to a row over a record label that was part of
the ITT stable.

Paul Slawson, then with ITT, recalls selecting 'Kashi', as he
knew him, to run the Nigerian operation in place of an old-style
British businessman. Abiola was physically big and intellectually astute
and had the star quality shown later by Bill Clinton in that he could
light up a room. Slawson remembered him turning up in his robes and
wowing an ITT meeting in the US.[17] Abiola, like many Yorubas, was a
Muslim. He was also prepared to be patient in nursing his ambitions.
When the military government impounded paper destined for *Concord*
he remarked placidly that it was 'the will of Allah.'

By the end of 1983 the Nigerian establishment was looking sleazy and its politicians arrogant, while at the same time the public was hurting more. Some consumer goods had become scarce, with prices rising by up to 200%. A six litre container of vegetable oil tripled in price from N4 to N12. Some of the scandals, in rice and sugar, were only exposed after the fall of the government. But suspicious cases of arson to cover up frauds, listed by Buhari in his first broadcast, were known and visible. These included fires that gutted the Post and Telecoms building in Lagos, the broadcasting building in Anambra, the Ministry of Education building and the Federal Capital Development Authority's accounts office in Abuja. A major scandal involved British Aerospace, which supplied 18 Jaguar air force jets for £300M, where NPN figures were said to have skimmed off £22M.[18] Capital flight between 1979 and 1983 was officially estimated at N18bn (over US$14bn).[19]

The senior officers' coup, which swept away the president as their commander-in-chief as well as the chief of the defence staff, had been prepared at least four months earlier and may have been designed to pre-empt action by more junior officers. Analysis showed that at least two-thirds of the new Supreme Military Council had belonged to a similar body under Muhammed and Obasanjo, or had worked as military administrators for the previous military government. The idea that all the senior military had gone into retirement after 1979, suggested then by Obasanjo at his handover to Shagari, was rubbish.

But the disruptive impact of military interventions on discipline and hierarchy was illustrated by the fact that the key organiser of the 1983 coup was Major-General Ibrahim Babangida, who became chief of the army staff, and who was on Dimka's 'extermination list' in 1976. He was lucky still to have been alive to go on plotting. Buhari was the fifth military head of state, but each time a new military leader took over there were consequential changes in promotions and sackings, and there was always a fear that younger officers might take matters into their own hands, as they had in 1966. For officers who were on the wrong side of a coup, or unpopular with the new leader, there could be expulsion and hardship if not worse.[20]

The leaders of the 1983 coup were from the north, and some had trained at the Pakistan and Indian military academies rather than in the UK. There had been complex political debates during the civilian period involving the 'Kaduna mafia' – the group of northern businessmen and intellectuals close to the military who lost ground in the NPN and even made contact with Awolowo. Babangida, Buhari and Abacha pursued a northern agenda under the guise of national unity. The military had always offered an attractive career to northerners and middle-belters who lacked the qualifications of their contemporaries in the south. After the war there were no Igbos in the upper echelons and there were not many Yorubas. With the enormous significance of oil in the national economy, the 1983 coup offered an opportunity to the military not only to control this wealth, but to do so on behalf of the still poorer northern part of the country. With Buhari's appeals for belt-tightening and against corruption these factors were not immediately apparent. What Nigerians could not have guessed, as they listened to Buhari speaking on the radio on New Year's Day, 1984, was that they were starting on a 15-year course of military dictatorship, including the harshest and most corrupt the country has ever faced.

Chapter 15

Buhari, IBB and a new military era

The backdrop to the new military government was an economic crisis. The 1980s were a bad time for Africa. At the end of the decade the UN Economic Commission for Africa found that there had been a negative gross national product per head, largely due to population increase and the high cost of debt, while living standards on the continent had fallen by 20%.[1] In Nigeria successive military regimes continued with the austerity started by the Shagari government, and there was an inevitable reaction on the part of labour, students, civil society, human rights groups and, when they felt free enough to protest, the media. Decree 4, the Public Officers' Protection against False Accusation decree of 1984, which was issued by the Buhari regime, was designed to silence the press. Decree 2 allowed for the detention of critics without trial. The apparatus of repression, dusted down from the previous military regimes, was brought back with minimal changes.

Muhammadu Buhari, Head of State from 1983 to 1985, and his strong chief of staff, General Tunde Idiagbon, increasingly ruled without consultation with the senior military. They wished to run a 'corrective' government, cleaning up corruption, declaring a 'war on indiscipline' and putting the economy to rights before considering any return to civilian politics. Initially even the Nigerian Labour Congress welcomed the return of the soldiers. But, before long, Nigerians could see that this hairshirt administration might have elements of hypocrisy. For example, Festus Marinho was reinstated as managing director of the Nigerian National Petroleum Corporation. He had had the same post under Obasanjo but was removed in 1980 after a judicial inquiry into N2.8bn that had gone missing; although he was cleared on this, the inquiry concluded that 'there had been serious lapses in NNPC'. General Idiagbon took his son on a pilgrimage to Mecca, even though there was supposed to be a clampdown on external travel.

The 1984 War Against Indiscipline is still remembered by Nigerians, as local troops sought to persuade them of the virtues of queueing and taking turns in post offices and of a stronger work ethic. NCOs were deployed in secondary schools to help keep discipline. The attitude of Buhari in this 'war' was dangerously close to Bertolt Brecht's joke in 1953 about the 'people's democracy' of East Germany: that it was necessary to change the people. In Nigeria the people were seen as the problem, being factious, lazy, anarchic and in need of repression to achieve anything. This could not provide a long-term solution to the nation's problems.

But in the meantime there was a spate of political trials against corrupt politicians and others and a major quarrel with the UK over the attempt to smuggle presidential adviser Umaru Dikko through Heathrow in a trunk labelled 'diplomatic baggage' in 1984.[2] Trials of hundreds of politicians were handled by military tribunals that assumed guilt unless innocence could be proved, with lengthy jail terms handed down. Publicity about corrupt payments and the misuse by governors of 'security votes' for which they had never had to account helped persuade the public of the rottenness of the Shagari republic. However southern observers noted that northerners generally got off more lightly in the sentences handed down.

Dikko was a serious irritant to the generals. Discovering that service chiefs had been rounded up in the Buhari coup he drove to Seme, on the border with the republic of Benin, walked across, took a taxi to Lomé, the capital of Togo, and flew to London on KLM via Amsterdam. In London he went onto BBC television, made a vituperative attack on the coup plotters and vowed to wage a jihad against them. He was particularly angry when he discovered that all members of his family and servants, still in Nigeria, had been detained, including his 90-year-old father. On 5 July he was captured outside his house in London's Bayswater by an Israeli group hired by the Nigerian government and drugged. By sheer good fortune he was still alive when British anti-terrorist police opened the crate at Stansted airport and impounded the Nigerian Airways plane that would have taken it to Lagos.[3]

Inevitably there were diplomatic repercussions, with withdrawal of High Commissioners and negative publicity in the British press. In January 1985 the UK rejected a request for the extradition of Dikko, who went on to qualify as a barrister. Fundamentally, however, Nigeria–UK relations remained friendly, even though Nigeria subsequently failed in a formal legal attempt to get other exiles extradited, which could have opened the way to bringing back Dikko.[4] Shortly after the military coup Nigeria had paid US$60M in trade debts, comforting British and other western creditors that it would not renege. The author, then deputy director of the Commonwealth Institute in Kensington, which was planning a major educational and cultural focus on African countries in 1984, agreed to go ahead with a significant Nigerian participation in a private conversation with Dr Garba Ashiwaju, Federal Director of Culture, in spite of the breakdown in diplomatic relations.[5]

In August 1985 General Buhari was overthrown in a bloodless coup – he was in his hometown of Daura in Kaduna state, celebrating Eid-el-Kabir, and Idiagbon was on pilgrimage in Saudi Arabia. The new head of state, the only military dictator in Nigerian history who preferred to describe himself as 'President', was Ibrahim Babangida, known as IBB from his initials. A senior officer who was in the army for 35 years, observing several coups, recalled this as a very self-serving takeover.[6] Babangida did not really represent any policy or national interest but was motivated by power and greed. But the new ruler, a hail-fellow-well-met figure in the mess, was initially popular. He had qualified in the Indian Military Academy and masterminded the overthrow of Shagari but supported Buhari to succeed him, and he was one of the clique of young officers who had come to the fore in the war and been close to power ever since. He was only 44 when he assumed office.

In addition to his private desire to rule, Babangida criticised the Buhari regime publicly for its conservatism and arrogance, for trampling on journalists and human rights and for failing to get an agreement with the IMF. He repealed the hated Decree number 4 and ordered the release of all journalists who had been detained. Although this did not diminish the 'northern' aspect of the coup, he returned the passports of Chief Obafemi Awolowo and his son, who was publishing *Nigerian Tribune*, within a fortnight. Interestingly, he complained in his first broadcast that the growing unpopularity of the Buhari regime was separating the troops from the people and the Nigerian Armed Forces 'could not, as part of this government, be fairly permitted to take responsibility for failures'. Like his predecessor he concluded on a note of national unity – Nigerians had to stay together and salvage the country.[7]

Although Babangida embarked on a long-drawn-out process of democratic transition, considered below, the immediate crisis he faced was in the economy. While he pointed out in his opening broadcast that to spend 44% of national income on servicing debts was unsustainable, he was at once reminded by a freer press and civil society that to go cap-in-hand to the International Monetary Fund offended national pride. His approach showed a much greater subtlety and sensitivity to public relations than Buhari's. He launched a public debate as to whether the country should take a US$2.5bn IMF loan in a typical IMF structural adjustment programme with severe cuts in public spending and other conditions, or whether it should reject the loan but make its own choice of cuts in an atmosphere of national sacrifice. Predictably, public opinion supported an anti-imperialist Nigerian variant of the structural adjustment remedy, but this went sour when citizens realised the extent of their sacrifices.[8]

In reality Nigeria ended up doing much as the IMF prescribed, although it did not take the loan. Its own agreement included tougher management of demand; an aim to expand domestic output through import substitution and a lower exchange rate for the Naira; reduction of controls, deregulation of the financial sector and liberalisation of trade and payments; privatisation of 96 public corporations and parastatals; and rescheduling external debt so that most would be paid from and after 1991. Crucially Babangida made an agreement with foreign creditors under which debt service was limited to 30% of export income. In all, this was reckoned to be the most comprehensive structural adjustment programme negotiated in Africa in the 1980s.

But the economic impact was mixed, and the programme became increasingly unpopular and harder to enforce. Although it was supported by western donors, there was no influx of foreign investment and foreign debt rose from about US$18bn in 1983 to about US$33bn in 1990.[9] Exporters and importers were up to their old tricks in exploiting a two-tier foreign exchange system with under-invoicing and non-repatriation of foreign exchange receipts from non-oil exports. There was a growing disparity between good-looking statistics and a worsening cost of living for the middle class and urban poor.

On the statistical side, agricultural output rose by 5% a year between 1985 and 1989, helped by two good harvests, manufacturing output rose 14% between 1986 and 1990 and GDP went up by 5.3% a year during the same period. Although the economy was still dominated by oil income, the non-oil exports doubled in value in two years from 6% to 12% of total exports in 1988. The real exchange rate saw a huge fall in the value of the Naira between 1984 and 1987.[10] Importers and Nigerians used to foreign travel hated this, and many bakeries closed after the government banned the import of flour.

The structural adjustment programme was introduced in two phases in 1985 and 1986, and in theory would only last until 1988. It included an 80% cut in subsidies on petroleum products, which did not put an end to public exasperation with fuel shortages, a 30% surcharge on imports and a number of extra taxes at both federal and state levels. The benefits of what had been 'free' primary education were undercut when parents were required to pay school fees. The costs of electricity, rent and many basics rose sharply and inflation rose, too, with the government printing money and making extra-budgetary allocations. The manipulation of foreign exchange, and smuggling to and from neighbouring countries over porous borders, eroded the structural adjustment programme.

The pauperisation of Nigeria was such that the 1991 World Bank report ranked the country as the 13th poorest in the world, annual per capita income having fallen vertiginously from an estimated US$778 in 1985 to US$175 in 1988 and US$105 in 1989.[11] The result was violent opposition from the Nigerian Labour Congress, students, the media and particularly affected groups. Babangida, who had named himself as Minister of Defence and had dictatorial powers – even though he had complained that Buhari and Idiagbon were not consultative – became ever more repressive. The evolution of events in the 1980s undercut the more liberal human image he had presented when he took power and made for suspicion over the 'democratic transition' that he claimed to want, initially to take place by October 1990.

When he first took over, Babangida sought to co-opt critics of the military regime. A prominent example was Olikoye Ransome-Kuti, who became Minister of Health and a national and international protagonist of efficient basic health services. But he was also the brother of the musician Fela Kuti, the unstoppable firebrand who had married 27 of his dancers on stage and was constantly being arrested for offences ranging from attacks on authority to drug use and financial misdemeanours. A third and younger brother, Beko, also a medical doctor, was imprisoned by Buhari as a 'threat to national security' after his government dissolved the Nigerian Medical Association, which he led, and which had been campaigning for more hospital drugs. By 1989, Beko was a major human rights activist, setting up the Committee for the Defence of Human Rights and organising demonstrations to 'Free Femi Arborisade', a socialist militant who had fallen foul of the Babangida regime.[12] Babangida did not give up on the co-option strategy. In 1988 Wole Soyinka, who had won the Nobel Prize for Literature in 1986, was made first chairman of the Federal Road Safety Corps.[13]

But the transition programme, promoted with the aid of a Political Bureau that organised a national consultation in 1986, seemed to go on forever, and a restless public concluded that the generals did not really wish to relinquish control. Babangida's justification for delays and amendments was that Obasanjo's transition had been too hurried and that much more needed to be put right if Nigerians were to handle democracy. Although Babangida had released gaoled civilian politicians, he was keen for 'new breeds' to appear, and the transition process was tortuous: it involved another constitutional assembly that produced amendments that were mostly ruled out by the military and a ban on debates on sharia, and the handover was postponed to 1992. Party organisation was permitted from May 1989, but within six months the 13 parties that appeared were all dissolved, and Babangida decreed that there would be only 2 parties, one a little to the left, the Social Democratic Party, and the other a little to the right of centre, the National Republican Convention. He did not want to go back to the ethnicity and multiparty system of the Tafawa Balewa era, was not attracted to the one-party states that were going out of fashion with the collapse of east European communism, and was influenced by the two-party structure of US presidentialism.

Babangida had made himself Chief of Army Staff, and, as said earlier, was the only military ruler to style himself as President, not just Head of State. But even though he manipulated appointments to protect himself, the dire history of coups meant that there were always military risks to military rulers. The first overt threat emerged in December 1985, when the regime said it had uncovered a plot by General Mamman Vatsa, who had been an ally of Babangida's and, unusually, was also a published poet. Along with some air force officers, who were supposed to be planning to bomb the Dodan barracks in Lagos, the plotters were picked up and executed. The rationale of this plot, which was said to be a protest against the possible IMF loan and the regime's initial friendliness towards human rights, remains unclear: its suppression showed Nigerians that behind Babangida's smile lay an iron fist.[14]

A rather different critique came from a retired general and former head of state, Olusegun Obasanjo, who still knew many serving officers. In 1980 he had published a memoir of the war, *My Command*, which opened the door to a flood of books by others and which had focused on his command of the Third Marine Commando when he took over from Brigadier Benjamin Adekunle in the closing stages.[15] Predictably it irritated Adekunle because he claimed the division was a rabble when he took over, and Wole Soyinka, who said that Obasanjo's betrayal of the talks with Biafran Army Colonel Victor Banjo had led to his brutal imprisonment for three years.

In August 1985, in a speech at Ibadan, just prior to the Babangida coup, Obasanjo argued that after two democratic failures, which were the fault of the operators rather than the system, the great needs in Nigeria were for socioeconomic progress and a wider spread of prosperity. But he warned, 'I believe it is very dangerous to parcel the country up into political ruling group, economic-controlling group, and military-dominating group.'[16]

Obasanjo, who courted controversy, followed this up with a nuanced memoir about his unlikely friendship with Major Nzeogwu, the 1966 conspirator who had died fighting for Biafra and who had been Obasanjo's comrade in the Congo. It was published in early 1987 as *Nzeogwu: An Intimate Portrait of Major Chukwuma Kaduna Nzeogwu*.[17] He admired Nzeogwu for his patriotism and ambition for Nigeria but disliked his naivety, recklessness and resort to violence. In a passage that reflected some of Obasanjo's own thoughts at this point, he wrote:

> Chukwuma had a dream of a great Nigeria that is a force to reckon with in the world…He had a dream of an ordered and orderly nation, through a disciplined society. He also dreamt of a country where national interest overrides self, sectional or tribal interest. He wanted a country where a person's ability, output, merit and productivity would determine his social and economic progress, rather than political and ethnic considerations.[18]

While some Igbos felt Obasanjo had been less than flattering about a hero, the reaction in the north and from Babangida was much sharper. The book was launched provocatively on 15 January 1987, the exact anniversary of the majors' coup and the Sardauna's murder, and copies were burnt at a demonstration at the Ahmadu Bello University. At a time when other southern officers were complaining that they had been passed over in promotions and it looked as though Obasanjo was rebuilding a southern alliance in the democratic transition, he seemed to be calling for the military to withdraw from governance. The high command ordered retired officers to 'refrain from making indiscreet and unguarded statements'.[19]

Babangida tried to buy off military discontent by giving powerful and remunerative jobs to senior officers. By 1992 he had used at least 80 senior and middle-level officers as governors or administrators in the states. Senior officers were also put in to run federal and parastatal organisations. Such men, criticised as 'tourists in government', were often less competent than their civilian predecessors, and the president changed them round when he felt like it. The strategy had the advantage of divide and rule, creating rival patronage cliques and ambitions.[20]

The later 1980s saw Nigerians endure an increasing tyranny as the desire for democracy came up against the effects of the military-backed structural adjustment programme. Suspicions were rife that the military and its friends were helping themselves to spoils. The promotion of Maryam Babangida as a 'First Lady', building army support for her husband as president of the Nigerian Officers' Wives Association and then in rural areas through her Better Life Programme for Rural Women, was symptomatic of an 'Eva Peron' aspect to dictatorship that was new to Nigeria. While a role model for some, her inflated status was also an annoyance to educated urban women. Students, organised labour, professional bodies and a growing civil society fought the authorities with demonstrations, strikes and appeals for solidarity from the outside world. Although northern millionaires financed their own papers to offset the southern press, southern journalists pursued the regime where they could.

This animus came to a head with the parcel-bomb murder in October 1986 of Dele Giwa, editor of *Newswatch*, the Lagos-based investigative weekly.[21] Like the rest of the media it always walked a tightrope, but it had been pursuing several stories that embarrassed the government. There are differing accounts as to the cause of the murder. One is that Giwa had a tape of Mamman Vatsa's statement to the tribunal prior to his execution. Another is that he was interested in a scandal close to the president and his wife, involving Gloria Okon, a person accused of drug trafficking, who was spirited to the United States although she was said to have died in Nigeria. However, the parcel that killed him was marked as coming from the presidential cabinet, and it was clear that senior figures in the regime were implicated.[22] *Newswatch* was internationally renowned, and the death of its editor became a rallying point for all those concerned for freedom of the press and human rights. It spurred the growth of what was called 'guerrilla journalism', which became even more significant during the Abacha dictatorship in the 1990s. By the end of 1987 several papers had had periods of closure, or seen their journalists detained for leaks or allegedly libellous comments.[23]

With Babangida dangling the prospect of a democratic transition, however often postponed, the agitation for new states to accommodate more ethnic groups continued to bubble. Babangida was not enthusiastic. Nonetheless in 1987 he agreed to two new states: Katsina in the north, cut out of Kaduna, which included the home town of Muhammadu Buhari, and Akwa Ibom in the Niger Delta between Port Harcourt and Calabar, cut out of Cross River. The federal government gave each of them N23M to get started and then an additional N10M to implement urgent projects, but there was rancour over the sharing of assets between the new and old states and at least six other claimants to statehood around the country were frustrated that they had not been recognised.

For ordinary citizens suffering from the woes of the economy and structural adjustment, there were additional anxieties in the 1980s from the growth of a sense of insecurity. Street robberies in the big cities, the growth of banditry in the Delta and even aircraft hijacking made crime front-page news that hit home. Underpaid and often corrupt police, who would stop cars for a bribe, provided little sense of protection. It was pointless for victims to appeal to the law. The thuggish 'area boys' of Lagos said they were victims of the structural adjustment programme;

the increasingly restive minorities in the Delta claimed to be obtaining some recompense for the federal government's rip-off of their resources by 'bunkering' (the illicit draining of oil from the pipelines). Where he thought it appropriate Babangida bought off individuals and groups by overt or covert bribery, known as 'settlement.'

In 1988, for instance, there was a general strike, ten universities were closed and the National Association of Nigerian Students was banned. Several died in violent clashes between police and protestors, with reduction of petrol subsidies as a result of the government's austerity programme as a trigger for unrest. Those in a position to do so appealed for international solidarity. Dr Festus Iyayi, President of the Academic Staff Union of Universities, was awarded the Commonwealth Writers' Prize for his book called *Heroes*. He urged the international community to appeal to Babangida to restore human rights, release all labour leaders and members of pressure groups in detention and hand back union buildings, documents and other property to their owners.

But while life for Nigerians could be grim, their government was walking tall on the world stage. Babangida took Nigeria into the Organisation of Islamic Conference (OIC, rebranded as the Organisation of Islamic Cooperation from 2011) as a full member in 1986, a body in which it had already been an observer; he strengthened relations with the West, in the dying days of the Cold War, and particularly with the United Kingdom; and he invested heavily in the Economic Community of West African States and the sub-region at a time when the ECOWAS structures were looking weak. There was confidence, if not swagger, in Nigerian foreign policy. Babangida took on the Italian government when an Italian businessman dumped toxic waste in the port of Koko, Bendel state, and he insisted that Italy should pay to ship the material back to Italy.

The decision to become a full member of the OIC, which may have had financial aspects when Middle Eastern oil states were known to be looking for investment destinations, was Babangida's. It set off reactions and riots in religiously mixed parts of the country, and especially in the north; Christian activists, during a decade when pentecostals were making converts to a 'prosperity religion', saw this as a preliminary to a government policy of Islamicisation. Religious divides and suspicion had been worsening since the sharia constitutional debates in the late 1970s. Full membership of OIC, though not significant in itself because it was difficult to get Muslim solidarity at a time of all-out war between the Sunni dictatorship in Iraq and the Shia ayatollahs of Iran, seemed to be symbolic. As a gesture in a different direction, Babangida also established diplomatic ties with Israel, which helped him with his personal security.

Nigeria, while doubtful of the sincerity of Britain in diplomatic attempts to end South African apartheid, rebuilt links with the former colonial power. Margaret Thatcher, the tough right-wing British prime minister, visited the country twice, in 1988 and 1989, and Babangida met Queen Elizabeth in London on a state visit in May 1989; loyal Nigerians complained that the only broadcast publicity he got was a public warning against likely traffic jams in Victoria. Thatcher had never had compunction in dealing with dictators; Augusto Pinochet of Chile had been a key ally in the reconquest of the Falkland islands in 1982. She was supportive of structural adjustment. Nigeria had now overtaken South Africa as the UK's most important market in Africa, and the UK government supported a debt rescheduling agreement with commercial banks worth US$5.5bn, signed in London in April 1989.

Babangida and Obasanjo had their differences, but the Nigerian president acceded to a request from Emeka Anyaoku, Deputy Secretary-General of the Commonwealth, that the former head of state should be joint leader of a negotiating team to go to South Africa.[24] Grandiosely called an Eminent Persons Group, it was the product of a compromise at a Commonwealth meeting in the Bahamas in 1985 at which the

UK was urged to impose sanctions on a South Africa veering towards civil war. Its visit in 1986, when it saw Nelson Mandela in jail and the white leaders of the government, coincided with a peak in the brutally suppressed revolt of black townships. The EPG's effort was destroyed when the white South Africans launched aerial offensives against three neighbouring Commonwealth capitals and the team departed. It is thought now, however, that its 'negotiating concept' was a contribution to the peacemaking of the 1990s and that it helped white businessmen in particular to recognise that it was time for a change.

Babangida's willingness to work with Nigerians with whom he might disagree was illustrated again in 1989 when his diplomatic machine was put at the service of Chief Emeka Anyaoku, soon to become Commonwealth Secretary-General (in office 1990–2000), in a successful campaign to elect the first African to that role. At a summit in Kuala Lumpur later that year, the Chief comfortably beat Malcolm Fraser, former Prime Minister of Australia, when the heads of government had to select a successor to Shridath Ramphal.

Nigeria remained the key funder of ECOWAS, paying a third of its budget and hosting its offices in the new capital of Abuja. In 1981 the organisation had agreed a defence protocol, which became the justification for military involvement when the Liberian and Sierra Leonean civil wars took hold in the 1990s. But in the 1980s the organisation seemed weak, threatened by lack of interest on the part of its Francophone members still tied to France and the regional ambitions of the Libyan leader, Muammar Gaddafi. Babangida was a personal friend of Samuel Doe, President of Liberia, who ran into increasing difficulties at home as a result of his favouritism to members of his own tribe.[25] Nigeria brought together Presidents Doe and Joseph Saidu Momoh of Sierra Leone to sign a peace accord. Nigeria subsequently led the ECOWAS Military Observation Group intervention in the Liberian civil war in 1990.

Nigeria also helped its neighbour Benin, where traders were caught by surprise by a Nigerian anti-smuggling decree. There were strikes, and the country's treasury ran out of money. Benin was given US$2.5M in hard currency, N5M to buy Nigerian services and 12,000 tonnes of finished petroleum products.[26] But what Nigeria saw as a good neighbour policy could also be seen as overbearing by the smaller, poorer states with which it shared west Africa. The enormous disparity in size and its access to petrodollars made it difficult for others to stand up to Nigeria when they saw their interests challenged in the region.

Section 4

1989–2014: A decade of pain, then disappointment in democracy

Chapter 16
The annulment of an election puts Nigeria on edge

Nigeria's most recent quarter-century has seen both the worst of times and the best of times. It has left many citizens uncertain as to where their country is heading and still feeling poor in a country where leaders and external economists proclaim its wealth. Religious faith, often inspirational, may also be a badge of division. Corruption at all levels has not gone away. Globalisation has amplified crime and opened long borders to jihadis, introduced new ideas along with false rumours, speeded change and linked diasporas more closely with home communities. Some have been spooked by a US intelligence prediction, picked up by Wikileaks, that Nigeria will break up in 2015, and Boko Haram has spread insecurity beyond the three northeastern states where a state of emergency was declared in 2013. And, at the forefront of the new century, Nigeria witnessed a withdrawal of the military from government. For an unequalled period, from 1999 on, it has been ruled by elected politicians.

Yet this decisive change had, as a prologue, an immensely damaging false start, which was followed by a cruel and kleptocratic dictatorship. For IBB's claims to be reforging the country as a more viable democracy were undermined when the outcome of a long-sought presidential election on 12 June 1993 was suspended.

The famous transition to democracy with all its tergiversations – the latest experiment was called 'Option A4' – had run into the buffers, and with it Babangida's own credit had run out. For the transition programme had been lengthy, arguably starting with the formation of a Political Bureau in 1986 to recommend a new system, at a time when Babangida was talking of a return to civil rule in 1990. It had involved attempts to exclude old politicians and those guilty of corruption, to inculcate a two-party system that would avoid the regionalism and ethnic identities of the two earlier attempts at democracy, and to renew local government. Babangida claimed to want a more secure, educated democracy based on a stronger economy and a new social order. He created the Mass Mobilisation for Self-Reliance, Social Justice and Economic Recovery (MAMSER) to involve the public in this endeavour and, at a more elite level, a Centre for Democratic Studies designed to train new, improved politicians.

But while the government was calling for a democracy to be built from the grassroots up, it was actually imposing a top-down system with a number of booby traps, as Olusegun Obasanjo memorably described it in 1992.[1] Many of the purposes to which the government aspired were admirable, including a reduction of the role of money and violence in politics and a stronger institutional basis. However the route taken tended to negate them. When politicians were freed to establish their associations in 1989 and 13 appeared, they were then dissolved. Primary elections to produce presidential candidates for the two manufactured parties were twice postponed in 1992. Above all, the Social Democratic Party and National Republican Convention, which were orchestrated and funded by the National Elections Commission, were 'GONGOs', government-organised non-governmental organisations, which lacked authenticity and were given identical constitutions.

Below the level of presidential elections, the regime greatly increased the number of local government areas from 301 in 1989 to 589 in 1991 and reversed its position on the creation of states, approving nine more in 1991 to make a total of 30. A constituent assembly had argued for more states, and the Igbos felt unfairly treated with only two. However, the new dispositions did not exactly meet the demands of the agitators for state creation, and they reflected political factors compelling for the president. Hence, as an example, the new Delta state had its capital illogically in Asaba, hometown of Babangida's wife Maryam and scene of brutality in the civil war. Nor did these changes put an end to the agitation or the continuing quarrel over the proportion of federal income that should go to state governments. The current allocation formula gave 48% of revenue to the federal government and 24% to the states.

For instance Ken Saro-Wiwa (1941–95), a popular writer who was also well connected, had launched a national and international campaign for substantial self-determination for his Ogoni people, who were suffering from oil extraction in the Delta. Saro-Wiwa had backed the federal cause in the war, had been the civilian administrator in Bonny after it was recaptured by the federals, and served in the Rivers cabinet until he fell out with Alfred Diete-Spiff, military governor of Rivers state during and after the war. In the 1980s he was responsible for a popular TV comedy show featuring a Mr Basi.

But by the 1990s he was speaking up for the Ogoni and calling for more money to go back to the oil-producing areas that were suffering from serious environmental damage from oil spills, pipeline leaks and gas flaring. He denounced the Hausa-Fulani and Yoruba for ripping off his people. In July 1992 he spoke at the UN Working Group on Indigenous Populations in Geneva and published *Genocide in Nigeria: The Ogoni Tragedy*. On 30 November, in the Lagos-based *Guardian*, he wrote, 'What we must have is a confederation of Nigerian states, or a commonwealth of independent states of Nigeria. Each ethnic group, large or small, would be free to administer itself in its own way.'[2] Saro-Wiwa helped set up the Movement for the Survival of the Ogoni People. This was only one of several ethnically based campaigns in the Niger Delta whose resistance activities, including sabotage and theft from pipelines, began to have a major impact in reducing output. This hit federal revenues as well as the companies, and it was not helped by the inefficiency of the state-owned Nigerian National Petroleum Corporation. In 1992 Babangida set up a commission to carry out development works in six oil-producing states, but this did not mollify local communities.

The perennial problem of military governments, which are themselves illegitimate, is that they are always exposed to attempts to dislodge them from power. Ambitious or idealistic junior officers do not see why their seniors should hang on to a monopoly. In the case of Babangida, whose zig-zagging and dribbling route to democracy earned him the nickname 'Maradona', an attempted coup took place after many Nigerians were already fed up with his delays. On 22 April 1990, Major Gideon Orkar led an unsuccessful coup, ruthlessly put down by Lieutenant General Sani Abacha, who then became Defence Minister in August, bidding to be Babangida's natural successor. In Orkar's broadcast, he claimed that it was not just another coup but 'well conceived, planned and executed for the marginalised, oppressed and enslaved people of the middle belt and the south, with a view to freeing ourselves and our children yet unborn from eternal slavery and colonisation by a clique of this country'.

The coup-makers echoed the feelings of the civil-society opposition in the south against perceived Hausa-Fulani domination, and they had links with minorities in the Delta state who were angry at the north purloining their oil wealth. Their most radical proposal was to expel five northern states (Sokoto, Borno, Katsina, Bauchi and Kano) from the federation. In this the coup was standing on its head the previous history of all those unhappy with Lugard's and post-independence Nigeria; in the past such regions had wanted to leave voluntarily by themselves, not to extrude others. This proposal assumed there was a greater commonality in the rest of Nigeria, but it would also have put at risk the southerners and Christians who lived in the *sabon garis* of the northern cities.

But while the government claimed that the coup was the bloodiest, its vengeance was equally fierce. A hundred officers and civilians were tried by a military tribunal, and around 67 officers were executed; family members, not directly involved, were also hounded. Babangida made gestures to the oil-producing areas, including a doubling to 3% of federal revenue to cope with ecological damage, and also strengthened his personal security by moving from the Dodan barracks in Lagos to the fortress of Aso Rock in Abuja. Abuja, which was declared as the Federal Capital Territory by Murtala Muhammed while he was Head of State in 1976 and whose construction was a feature of Shehu Shagari's presidential election campaign in 1979, formally became the capital of Nigeria in December 1991. Gigantism in its central area architecture bears testimony, as with Islamabad, Pakistan's capital, to its dictatorial provenance. It took a while for embassies and other significant institutions to move there from Lagos.

Despite the growing internal opposition to military government, Nigeria was still playing a highly visible role on the international scene. Regionally, it was throwing its weight around. In Liberia, where Babangida was friendly with President Samuel Doe, he endowed the Babangida Graduate School of International Relations. The United Kingdom provided assistance in 1992 when he set up a National War College.

But it was not always possible to disentangle the domestic from the international. The fall of the Berlin Wall in 1989 and Nelson Mandela's release from a South African prison in 1990 had an impact throughout Africa. The collapse of east European communism undercut one-party regimes and, more ambiguously, seemed a victory for capitalism plus liberal democracy. Mandela's freedom, the start of a lengthy negotiation that resulted in full democracy in 1994, seemed like a triumph for Nigerian foreign policy in alliance with the front-line states. Yet it was a body blow to the standing of all military regimes in Africa: continuing military rule in Nigeria became harder to defend.

These cross-currents were illustrated in late 1991, first when Commonwealth leaders issued a declaration in favour of democracy and human rights at Harare in October, and secondly when Olusegun Obasanjo was a serious runner to be UN Secretary-General in November. Chief Emeka Anyaoku, who had been Nigerian Secretary-General of the Commonwealth since 1990, was passionate in his belief in democracy. He seized the moment created by change in eastern Europe and the release of Nelson Mandela in South Africa to give a new direction to this post-imperial club.

However, the Commonwealth declaration at once raised questions about Nigeria. Democracy was becoming the norm and a military regime an embarrassing oddity. As it happened the activist Beko Ransome-Kuti had been nominated by the Commonwealth Medical Association to serve on a non-governmental group called the Commonwealth Human Rights Initiative. Chaired by Flora MacDonald, former Foreign Minister of Canada, it published 'Put Our World to Rights', a campaigning manifesto that was influential at Harare; Beko himself, often harassed or imprisoned like other rights activists in Nigeria, had had to slip clandestinely across the border on foot or motor-cycle to get to meetings in Auckland and Delhi. Democracy struck in Zambia, at the conclusion of the Commonwealth conference in Harare, when the long-serving and former one-party president Kenneth Kaunda was defeated in a multi-party election in his 27th year of office.

It is possible that the want of Nigerian democracy in what was seen as a new era was one factor in the failure of Obasanjo to get elected as UN Secretary-General in November 1991, when a vote was taken to decide Javier Pérez de Cuéllar's successor. Obasanjo had not been the only Nigerian candidate to begin with. He faced criticism at home, not least from his bitter first wife Oluremi. But he toured the world, learnt French and was supported by the Babangida government with which he was not on the best of terms. Although the Organisation of African Unity could not agree on a candidate, it was thought to be Africa's turn this time. In the end the United States backed an Egyptian, Boutros Boutros-Ghali, a choice it later regretted. Obasanjo came in a respectable third in the Security Council election, with six votes, to seven for Bernard Chidzero, the Finance Minister of Zimbabwe who had worked in the UN system, and eleven for Boutros-Ghali. The nationalist positions taken by Obasanjo when he was Head of State in the 1970s – support for the Movimento Popular de Libertação in Angola and nationalisation of UK multinationals – may also have counted against him in Washington.

It was impossible to separate the public anger at Babangida's dilatory approach to democracy, particularly in the south, from continued economic setbacks and the suffering blamed on structural adjustment. In the north there were Muslim–Christian clashes, and around a thousand people died in fighting in 1992 in Zangon, where disagreement between Hausa and Kataf over the siting of a traditional market turned violent. A military government, backed by a sinister State Security Service, was no guarantee of security for citizens. A collection of rights groups, including the Constitutional Rights Project, the Campaign for Democracy, the Committee for the Defence of Human Rights and the Civil Liberties Organisation as well as professional and labour bodies saw clearly that a military dictatorship was a hostile oppressor, not a custodian of the national interest.

The government's privatisation programme had gone slowly and not attracted the expected injection of foreign capital.[3] In August 1992, officials said that inflation was running at 33%, but independent experts thought it was 90%; for three years the capacity utilisation of industry was running at only 30–40% and agriculture was not growing fast. The fiscal deficit of the federal government, which had been 8.5% in 1988, had risen to 12.4% in 1991. The value of the Naira was continuing to slide. In March 1993 the employees of the state won a 45% pay rise following a strike. It put more pressure on states' budgets where Ondo, for instance, was having to spend 35% of its revenue on debt servicing; the federal government was having difficulty in persuading Paris Club creditor nations to treat it as a highly indebted poor country eligible for relief. Early in the year Ernest Shonekan, who was now heading a Transition Council that was part of Babangida's elaborate machinery, failed to win debt relief in a trip to Europe. Shonekan, who had been Chief Executive of the United Africa Company Nigeria, which had been spun out of the Unilever multinational, got a cautious response of sympathy only from John Major, UK Prime Minister, who as a young man had worked for the Standard Chartered Bank in northern Nigeria.

In 1993 it looked as though Nigerians would at last get to elect their president, albeit from the two state-created parties, the SDP and NRC, and that Babangida had accepted that he should stand down. The wheels started turning in February with primaries at ward and local levels, followed by state choices in March and then large national conventions for the SDP and the NRC involving some 9,000 participants. Keen candidates splashed their money around. The upshot for the NRC was that Bashir Tofa, a Kanuri businessman in his forties who was backed by the Kano state governor, won comfortably. Although Tofa chose a Christian as his running mate, he lost Christian support when questioned in a TV debate about a call he had made for jihad in 1990.

The result within the SDP was more interesting. Moshood Abiola, often called M.K.O. Abiola, narrowly beat Babagana Kingibe by 2,683 votes to 2,256. He then chose Kingibe as his vice-presidential running mate, creating a Muslim–Muslim ticket that was thought to be risky in a country where religion could spill into conflict. Abiola had joined the SDP only a month before nominations, and he was a wealthy businessman with substantial baggage. This included the multinational ITT Corporation, for whom he had once won a large telecoms contract from the Murtala Muhammed government; the *Concord* press group; a reputation for philanthropy that included large donations to all the Nigerian universities; and a campaign that he coordinated with some in the Congressional Black Caucus in the US for reparations to Africans and African-Americans for the transatlantic slave trade.[4]

At a time of economic hardship, it was thought that a poor boy from Abeokuta who had become wealthy could be the right person to lead Nigeria out of the doldrums.[5] He was a symbolic figure. He was the only one of his father's 23 children to live beyond four months, which is why his father named him Kashimawo, 'let's watch and see if this one lives'. He had known Olusegun Obasanjo at the Baptist Boys' High School in Abeokuta and had blocked a doorway for Murtala Muhammed when Muhammed was responsible for communications in the Gowon government to persuade him to repay debts owing to ITT.

It was difficult for anyone in the military era to make a fortune without connections. Abiola, who had thrived, was generally supposed to have backing in the corridors of power. This was illustrated by an endorsement he received for his reparations campaign from no less than Babangida himself. In an interview on the Nigerian Television Authority in February 1993, the president said, 'Well, I think basically that Chief Abiola is the baby of Nigeria, so his championing anything to do with Nigeria is perfectly in order...I think what we are trying to do is to see if the crusade could bring to the attention of the world the injustices done to the black man.'[6]

Nonetheless, as the real prospect of a civilian government grew closer – the presidential election was to be on 12 June, with the new president taking office on 27 August – the drumbeat from acolytes and praise-singers of the military regime grew louder. The Association for a Better Nigeria put up advertisements in Abuja calling for an extension of term for Babangida and his 'peace, unity and stability'. Chief Arthur Nzeribe, the ABN's key organiser, was a colourful Igbo businessman who had created the Fanz Organisation in the UK, which dealt in construction and arms sales in the Middle East, and Sentinel Assurance Group in Nigeria. Along the way he had been a director of Charlton Athletic Football Club. Illustrating a family nexus that could connect businessmen with generals across ethnic divides, his second wife was the sister of the wife of General Shehu Musa Yar'Adua, who was Vice-President of Nigeria under Olusegun Obasanjo in 1976–79. At one point Nzeribe had been an SDP presidential candidate, and Yar'Adua led an SDP faction.

In earlier state elections the NRC had won more governorships than the SDP, so it was slightly surprising that the Abiola-Kingibe ticket triumphed on 12 June. Although the announcement of the results and Tofa's concession letter were halted by the government, enough had come out from the Independent National Electoral Commission and the press to make it clear that the SDP had won over 8.1M votes to the NRC's over 5.8M. The SDP took 19 states to the NRC's 11, comfortably exceeding the constitutional requirement. Abiola, a Yoruba, scored huge majorities with over 80% in five southwestern states, including Lagos; he even won in Tofa's own ward. His worst performance was in the northern Muslim state of Sokoto, where he only won 20.79% of the votes.[7] He ought to have been declared the winner.

The election, so long awaited, went off relatively smoothly although the turnout at 35% was low. This was probably due to the confusion sowed by ABN as to whether the election would actually take place and a certain apathy. But Abiola's win set off a struggle within the military hierarchy between those who were willing to accept him as president, those who wanted Babangida or one of his confidants to continue, and those around Abacha, whose Ministry of Defence was still in Lagos when other ministries had moved to Abuja, who saw this as a chance for Abacha to succeed. After a hectic couple of months of military politicking, Babangida handed over power to an 'Interim National Government' of civilians with Abacha as the sole military member and Ernest Shonekan as its chairman.

Meanwhile, the suspension of the results and annulment of the election led to major demonstrations in Lagos, with the National Labour Congress calling for a general strike and motorists decking their cars with leaves in a traditional gesture of protest. Some fearful Igbos and northerners left the city. Rumours were rife; while the Electoral Commission talked of running the election again on 14 August, Uche Chukwumerije, Secretary of Information, said that Beko Ransome-Kuti, the detained leader of the Campaign for Democracy, was still alive, and retired Major General Zamani Lekwot, found guilty of rioting, had not been executed.[8]

Abiola came to London on a private plane, was let in without a passport, and went on the BBC's *Newsnight* to denounce the annulment. He flew on to the US and met Vice-President Al Gore. Although some of the military said that they did not want him as their commander-in-chief because he was corrupt, he also knew many of their secrets. Wole Soyinka, who had received a Nobel Prize for Literature in 1986, remained a fearless public intellectual and gadfly of all Nigerian rulers. He sought to galvanise international support to recognise the Abiola election. He said, 'A tiny but powerful cabal is toying with the future of our nation. Any further delay in making the people's verdict official is a deliberate cultivation of chaos.' Abiola himself said, 'I won…I say categorically that this decision is unfair, unjust and consequently unacceptable.'[9]

International reaction helped to push Babangida off his throne but could not get Abiola into the newish presidential offices in Aso Rock, Abuja. Diplomats had been suspicious of Babangida's manoeuvring. On 15 June, ahead of the election, Michael O'Brien, director of the United States Information Service in Lagos, departed for home; he had been given 72 hours to leave the country after warning that suspension of the election would be unacceptable to the US. The government blamed the US for interference, a claim justified soon after the election when the US said its embassy was authorised 'to initiate high-level contacts with a variety of people who are opposed to the Babangida regime'.[10] The UK said that the elections had been orderly and had given Nigerians a fair opportunity to express their views; there was no reason why the results should not be announced. The UK followed up by withdrawing its military advice team and refusing visas for the Nigerian military. Chief Emeka Anyaoku, Secretary-General of the Commonwealth of Nations in 1990–2000, said the day after the formal annulment on 23 June that it was a 'severe setback to the cause of democracy, particularly at a time when all Commonwealth governments have pledged themselves to promote democratic rule in their countries'. It was a bitter disappointment to all those, including himself, who had looked forward to a democratically elected government in Nigeria.[11]

Was this another existential moment when 'Nigeria' could have come apart? Hostility to the annulment was strongest in the Yoruba southwest and Lagos, and it was not fully endorsed even in the east. But there was no machinery in the southwest that could have organised a secession comparable to the military rule of Ojukwu in the east prior to the breakaway of Biafra, and the controlling military at federal level and their business friends were committed to keeping Nigeria together. Looking back 21 years later, Soyinka said he thought there was much less risk of Nigeria's dissolution in 1993 than there had been in the 1960s.[12] There was, however, a hardening of the dangerous north–south fissures in the body politic, as high courts in Lagos, Benin City and Port Harcourt ordered the INEC to release results and declare the annulment illegal. There are still admirers of Abiola who regard the annulment of his election as one of Nigeria's lost opportunities. Kayode Soyinka, a prominent journalist unrelated to Wole, sees Abiola as a big man and a man of the world who could have helped restore Nigeria's reputation and economy after the failures of the Babangida years.[13]

Battered by internal opposition and international disapproval, Babangida gave way and transferred power to the Interim National Government (ING), led by Shonekan, on 26 August. Shonekan had little public support and was seen as a fall-guy by campaigners for Abiola and full democracy. Although the National Labour Congress strike was not a success, as the organisation had been weakened, there were many acts of resistance. Over a hundred demonstrators and rioters were killed by police and soldiers who were shooting on sight; newspapers, not only those in Abiola's *Concord* chain, were closed by the authorities. Underground opponents of a continuity regime, which was how the Shonekan government was viewed, were behind bombings and some terrorist acts. The most internationally significant of these involved the hijacking of a Nigeria Airways plane by a member of the Movement for the Advancement of Democracy. It was forced to fly to Niamey in the neighbouring Republic of Niger with 137 passengers and twelve crew on board.[14] To balance this opposition the government helped generate solidarity rallies in the north, including in Kaduna and the supposedly ethnically neutral capital, Abuja. Conservative politicians in the north, seeing the annulment as another military coup, thought that Shagari should be allowed to complete his second presidential term, which had been cut short by Buhari.

Shonekan lasted less than three months. He lost backing from SDP governors, who shunned him, and in the north where he was suspect as a Yoruba. An attempt to raise the petrol price by 700% met predictable opposition on the streets. The country seemed ungovernable, with strikes and rioting. The police had not been paid for months and were resorting to holding up citizens in the streets for money. Pay for the troops was becoming irregular and, embarrassingly, the Nigerian contingent with the UN peacekeeping operations in Somalia were not paid because Nigeria was not providing funds to the UN. On 10 November Abiola won a crucial judgement in the Lagos high court, which found that the ING was null and void because Babangida had lost his legislative authority to sign the decree empowering the ING by the time he did so.

Days later, the Minister of Defence, Sani Abacha, took power as Head of State. He was 50 years old, and was to rule from 1993 to his death in 1998. Born in Kano, he had been associated with all the successful military coups since 1966 and even announced the overthrow of both Shagari and Buhari in broadcasts. Unlike his contemporaries, he had not had a 'good war'. A second lieutenant in 1963, he was still only a major in 1969 and was jealous of those he had served under. Obasanjo, who had supported him when he had a breakdown, had had his dismissal papers on his desk during the war but did not sign them. Whether Obasanjo hesitated because he thought that Abacha might be useful to him in future, it was one of the greatest errors of judgement and nearly mortal for himself. Under Abacha's leadership, Nigeria entered the darkest period since its independence. Personal ambition and greed trumped any claims to be acting for the national good, and concepts of military honour and custodianship lost credibility.

Chapter 17

The disastrous Abacha years

Abacha may not have excelled in warfare, but he was extremely skilled at conspiracy. Wole Soyinka, who wore many hats to conceal his Afro hairstyle when he went underground in Lagos during the Abacha dictatorship, described him as 'a lizard'. The Interim National Government of August–November 1993, led by Ernest Shonekan, was obviously incapable of solving the economic and political crisis, and some in civil society saw a brief intervention by Abacha to restore Abiola's presumed victory of the November 1993 presidential elections as a sensible contribution. There was talk that Abacha had been 'invited' to take over. Abiola, who had been negotiating with the military, made a speech in Kaduna in September in which he praised Abacha. Abiola offered his running mate, Babagana Kingibe, the position of as Foreign Minister in Abacha's government, and it was said that half Abacha's initial group of ministers were in favour of Abiola's mandate. But others were worried; 67 senators wrote an open letter to Abacha opposing a continuation of military rule. The House of Representatives, in a resolution, condemned the self-seeking and undemocratic persons who were colluding with the army. Gani Fawehinmi, a lawyer who was a principled campaigner for human rights but was temporarily fooled by Abacha, reminded him in a letter that he had been in a succession of disastrous governments: 'The record of the Babangida regime, in which you were second in authority and influence, is one of dismal failure in every respect,' he wrote.[1]

Initially, Abacha made a number of populist gestures, reducing the petrol price increase, settling strikes, removing the ban on publication of the *Concord, Observer, Punch* and *Sketch* and bringing the publisher of the *Guardian* newspaper group into the government as Minister of Internal Affairs. By calling his government the Armed Forces Provisional Revolutionary Council he implied that it did not plan to hang around for long. It looked as though he wanted to soften the hated structural adjustment programme. He offered a constitutional conference. But before Christmas he had abolished all democratic structures, the two 'official' parties and elected state governments. Nigerians soon realised that even if it took steps to distance itself from the rule of Babangida and launched an attack on 'sacred cows' that had been battening off the state's resources, the regime would not be so different from its military predecessors. It rested on the Constitution (Modification and Suspension) Decree 107 of 1993, which stated that not only was the constitution suspended, but also that no Nigerian court could challenge any decree issued since the military takeover in December 1983.

The political crisis took several turns for the worse in 1994. Brigadier David Mark, one of the military clique around Babangida who was still chairing the Senate as a civilian some 20 years later, gave a revealing interview in *Newswatch* in April: he said that while the plotters in November had only planned to stay in power for one year, Abacha now wanted to rule for five years.[2] Problems in the Delta took on an international dimension when the human rights activist Ken Saro-Wiwa and others were put on trial for the murder of four conservative leaders of the Ogoni; Saro-Wiwa was being overtaken by growing radicalism in a youth wing of his Movement for the Survival of the Ogoni People. International concern brought together environmental campaigners, human rights activists, pro-democracy campaigners and those shocked by the defects in Nigerian military tribunals. Two leading human rights lawyers, Chief Gani Fawehinmi and Femi Falana, withdrew in protest from Saro-Wiwa's defence, and

Geoffrey Bindman, a well-known London lawyer who was observing the trial, dismissed it as a farce.

The constitutional conference that began in June was not the sovereign national conference called for in the southwest, and it was boycotted by many of Abiola's supporters. The day before the first anniversary of the presidential election, Abiola emerged in Lagos and declared himself president. Oil, gas and other unions went on strike, and refineries closed. Abiola had been criticised for lack of resolution: he was slow to see that Abacha had no intention of handing him power. He was now backed by a wider grouping, the National Democratic Coalition, which included compromised former politicians who were seen as suspect by Beko Ransome-Kuti's Campaign for Democracy, which had been formed in 1993 to oppose Abacha's dictatorship. Abiola addressed a large Lagos rally, drove through the city and was arrested for treason on 23 June.

The ferment around the anniversary of the election and annulment led to a clampdown with more arrests. Abacha dismissed more liberal ministers. Several pro-democracy campaigners went abroad in 1995–96 and, keen to show that sympathy extended beyond the US and UK, made strenuous efforts to enlist pressure from the newly democratic South Africa. Although Nigeria itself was still divided and much of the pro-democratic effort was seen as sectional in the north and east, the campaigners had successes on the international front. For example, although Nigeria had persuaded FIFA to allocate it the right to host the U-17 World Championship, the campaigners managed to get the event cancelled.

Chief Emeka Anyaoku, Nigeria's most prominent figure on the international stage as Commonwealth Secretary-General, had been pursuing a democratic and rights agenda with particular reference to his own continent, Africa. As ill luck would have it, Abacha's coup had coincided exactly with a successful conclusion to the long-running multi-party negotiations in South Africa that led to full democracy there in 1994. In July of 1994, Anyaoku visited Nigeria and issued a courageous and hard-hitting statement: 'By every index, Nigeria has become like a motor car with a capacity to run at 200 km per hour but which is moving only at 20 km per hour and showing signs of a possible total breakdown...There is therefore an urgent need to pull the country back from what seems to be an inexorable drift to national disaster...'[3]

Anyaoku saw Abacha, who let him visit Abiola in detention. Abiola gave him the names of people who could represent him, and Anyaoku suggested to Abacha that private talks could begin to resolve the crisis created by the 1993 annulment. Abacha did not respond, but Anyaoku did not give up. In a memorial lecture for Tafawa Balewa, who had been Prime Minister from 1960 until his assassination in 1966, on 19 December in Abuja he said that Nigerians 'will not want to wear dictatorship, whatever its stripe', that 'there are inherent problems with the very nature of a military government' and that military rule 'however benign or enlightened, is...rule by the big stick'. National television coverage was blacked out, and the Anyaoku family spent Christmas in Ghana, instead of as usual in Obosi, their home in the eastern state of Anambra.[4]

The following year, 1995, was when Abacha, never seen in public without looking sinister in dark glasses, achieved pariah status. There were three factors that came together: a so-called coup plot allegedly involving ex-generals Olusegun Obasanjo and Shehu Musa Yar'Adua; the execution of Saro-Wiwa and eight other MOSOP leaders for murders in Ogoniland; and the related suspension of Nigeria from the Commonwealth at a meeting in New Zealand.

The coup plot, under which 44 officers and retired officers were arrested, may have had reality beyond the paranoia of Abacha and his immediate coterie. But what was incredibly unlikely was that the former head of state, who had been trying unavailingly to bring about a unified approach to the crisis by the politicians and been roundly berated by the Yoruba for not insisting that Abiola be installed, was in any way involved. Arrested in March, he was tried by a military court in June that was presented with evidence that Obasanjo could show was faked, and he was sentenced to 25 years' imprisonment for concealing treason. Yar'Adua and 14 others were sentenced to death.

A huge international campaign, involving figures like former US president Jimmy Carter, Archbishop Desmond Tutu, former British prime minister James Callaghan, Anyaoku and Sonny Ramphal, achieved partial success. Obasanjo's sentence was cut to 15 years and the death sentences were commuted. US President Bill Clinton was alleged to have warned Abacha in three phone calls that his oil would be embargoed if the executions went ahead. The impact of all this was to spread negative publicity about Nigeria at a time when the world was celebrating freedom in South Africa and a reawakening of the continent. Obasanjo, who had been personally exposed to the frightfulness of prisons in Kirikiri, Lagos, Jos and Yola, remarked later that he would not wish it on his worst enemy and took consolation in Christianity and the Bible.[5] He was a tough character, and the experience hardened his sense of born-again providentialism. An attempt to poison him was foiled when he insisted on using his own doctor for blood tests.[6]

Shortly after it appeared that Abacha had backed down, his regime committed the folly of executing Saro-Wiwa and his eight Ogoni colleagues on the first day of a Commonwealth conference in Auckland in November. Abacha had actually shared an apartment with Saro-Wiwa at one point in the civil war, but he had no room for sentiment. Appeals for clemency from Nelson Mandela, John Major, the British prime minister, who denounced 'judicial execution', and Anyaoku counted for little.

The executions became a symbol of the barbarity of Abacha's rule. It is possible that even without them the Commonwealth, too easily dismissed as toothless, would have taken action against Nigeria. In the run-up to the Auckland summit, a Commonwealth non-governmental group led by Flora MacDonald, former Canadian Foreign Minister, had carried out a fact-finding tour. It produced a devastating report on the state of human rights, 'Nigeria: Stolen by Generals', with a cover picture of children kept behind barbed wire.[7] Simultaneously, the Commonwealth Secretariat and UK government had been working on plans to stiffen up the 1991 Harare Commonwealth Declaration on democracy and human rights. Following the executions President Mandela, who had become very hostile to the Abacha dictatorship, called for Nigeria to be expelled from the Commonwealth and withdrew the South African High Commissioner. But a compromise was agreed under which three west African military regimes were suspended: Nigeria, Sierra Leone and the Gambia. A new committee was set up to enforce the rules of membership, the Commonwealth Ministerial Action Group. This meant that Nigeria's international isolation increased, and a group of Foreign Ministers monitored Abacha's claimed transition to democracy.

A feature of the lobbying at this time was the interaction between Nigerian and international civil society activists. In Auckland, Commonwealth human rights activists were helped by the Body Shop Foundation, spun out of an ethical retail enterprise in the UK that took issues of the environment and human rights very seriously. The founder, Anita Roddick, had been shocked by accounts of environmental degradation in the oil-rich Delta and the suffering of the Ogoni who could no longer follow their traditional fishing culture.

Among those who were central to this interaction was Dr Beko Ransome-Kuti, who had helped the MacDonald mission. Along with several journalists he had been caught in the government dragnet after the supposed coup and given a long prison sentence. He was sent to Katsina prison in northern Nigeria, where his health was at risk and it was difficult for his Lagos-based family to bring him food. Within Nigeria his extensive, talented and unpredictable relations were well known, and it was a personal tragedy when his brother Fela, the irrepressible Afrobeat musician, died of complications from AIDS in 1997 and he could not attend the funeral. Another brother, Olikoye, who had become deputy director-general of the World Health Organisation in 1992, used the announcement of Fela's death to lambast the Nigerian government for not doing more to combat the epidemic.[8]

Even in Katsina jail Beko was not entirely cut off from his friends. A tiny radio was smuggled in to him inside a cake, so he knew what was going on in the wider world; a postcard of a London bus, addressed to him care of the prison governor, arrived to remind him that activists in the Commonwealth Human Rights Initiative had not forgotten him.

The international lobbying against the dictatorship dovetailed with increased insecurity at home. Osaghae has listed 14 major bombing incidents between January 1993 and June 1996, all attributed to opposition groups in different parts of the country; the crash of a presidential jet in January 1996 that killed a son of Abacha; and suspected political assassinations by the regime of a wife of Abiola and other opposition figures.[9] This unsettled state, combined with Abacha's dilatory talk of a return to democracy, raised the possibility of guerrilla warfare or insurrection at some point in the future. The kind of military regime he represented lacked long-term viability.

For Abacha's main strategy for democratic renewal was to promote five bogus parties, from praise-singers to those who profited from the government, all of which would nominate him for an elective presidency. It was a sham. But even this blinkered dictatorship made some changes with lasting significance. It increased by six the number of states to 36, one each for the six regions among which political leadership might be rotated in a democratic dispensation; this was a different and more even kind of regionalism than Nigeria had inherited at independence. It established a Human Rights Commission in response to international criticism. It did not execute military rebels and permitted appeals from military tribunals to the Supreme Court.

Long after Abacha's death in 1998, as controversy raged when his widow was awarded a centenary medal in 2014, a lengthy letter was published in *Weekly Trust*, a northern paper, defending his economic legacy.[10] Mohammed S. Dabai, who wrote it, claimed that Abacha had increased Nigerian foreign reserves from US$494M in 1993 to US$9.6bn in 1997; reduced Nigeria's external debt from US$36bn in 1993 to US$27bn in 1997; cut the inflation rate from 54% in 1993 to 8.5% in 1998; and introduced a Petroleum Trust Fund that invested in social services and infrastructure. At a time when further details were still emerging about funds corruptly salted away by the Abacha family around the world and it was authoritatively estimated that US$3–5bn of public assets had been looted over five years,[11] this was a challenge to conventional critiques and showed that Abacha still had his admirers.

In fact, while government receipts fluctuated with the international oil price, the overall picture for the economy was not good. Gross domestic product grew by only 2.3% on average, from 1993 to 2003, and there was negative GDP growth per head over the decade because of population increase. Consumer price inflation actually hit over 60% in 1994, international firms pulled out, teachers and public sector workers were owed large sums in arrears, unemployment rose and the Abacha regime dismissed numbers of those involved in oil contracting.

The regime responded to the economic crisis in two ways, launching a campaign against the 'sacred cows' of the rich and powerful and abandoning Babangida's strategy of liberalisation in favour of one of economic nationalism. A high point in Abacha's initial anti-corruption campaign was the report of a panel under Pius Okigbo that had examined the accounts of the Central Bank of Nigeria and found that US$12.4bn had been spent clandestinely by the Babangida administration between September 1988 and 30 June 1994 for no priority purposes. The Banks (Recovery of Debt) and Financial Malpractices in Banks Decree No. 18 of 1994 was aimed at the fraudulent practices of the banks and their borrowers during the structural adjustment era; the Sultan of Sokoto was one of the prominent persons brought before a tribunal, dethroned and detained. However Abacha, who was not afraid to imprison Obasanjo, shied away from tackling Babangida directly and the 'corrective' anti-corruption campaign, which had enjoyed some public support, ran out of steam.

A policy of economic nationalism involved pegging the Naira to an official rate of N22 to US$1 and abandoning the liberal market reforms supported by the International Monetary Fund and World Bank. But there was not enough foreign exchange, and the Naira dropped sharply on the black market. By 1995, as inflation shot up to over 150% – contradicting the official figures quoted by Dabai in his 2014 letter – the government returned to privatisation while still trying to reduce dependence on foreign loans. The introduction of Value Added Tax worsened price rises but helped the fiscal position. The presses printed more money. But there was little hope of real improvement in the economy. The political crisis was intertwined with the socioeconomic crisis.

Abacha's poor standing, which the regime tried to offset inter-nationally by appeals to African solidarity, made it hard for Nigeria to promote a coherent foreign policy.[12] Nonetheless there was a disparity between the way in which it was viewed globally and its status as a regional hegemon in west Africa. Canada, always the toughest proponent of human rights in the Commonwealth, broke relations with Nigeria after the Ogoni executions. Yet in July 1996 Abacha was elected chairman of the Economic Community of West African States and sought to broker a peace in the Liberian civil war. He maintained his support for the ECOWAS Monitoring Group (ECOMOG) forces there when other regional states were threatening to pull out, and in Sierra Leone it was Nigerian troops who managed to restore the ousted democratic president, Tejan Kabbah, in March 1998. Western states, in the van of criticism, grudgingly acknowledged Abacha's positive role in containing the instability in west Africa, fuelled by ethnic conflicts and profits from illegal diamonds. Though there were strains in relations with Francophone Benin and even with Sierra Leone, which had sometime voted against Nigeria, the long-term good neighbour policy of Nigeria with the smaller ECOWAS states served it well.

The arrival of a democratic South Africa on the African scene presented a different challenge. Nigeria's self-perception as the world's foremost black nation was in question. The Abacha years saw the start of a rivalry that would cast shadows well into the 21st century when Nkosazana Dlamini-Zuma, former Foreign Minister of South Africa, was chosen in 2012 to chair the African Union Commission with support from Anglophone and southern African states. She had beaten the incumbent, Jean Ping of Gabon, a long-running Francophone dictatorship, to what was perceived as the most powerful political job in Africa.

Initially, the Abacha regime seemed willing to listen to Mandela when he asked for clemency for Obasanjo and Yar'Adua, but Mandela felt let down when his appeal for Saro-Wiwa was ignored. High commissioners were withdrawn, and there was a period of friction when the government press in Nigeria was bad-mouthing South Africa as 'white' and a puppet of the West. As it became obvious that Mandela did not want a second term as president, and his successor Thabo Mbeki tightened his grip on policy, relations began to ease. Mbeki had spent some of his exile in Lagos and was on good terms with the Nigerian military. He did not share Mandela's commitment to human rights and was more concerned with building post-apartheid friendships with the mixed bag of African governments. He was hostile to the bossiness and hypocrisy of western governments.

In its own neighbourhood the Abacha government continued to wrestle with the issue of the Bakassi peninsula, a contested area on the eastern end of the Gulf of Guinea that was thought to contain oil and that was a cause of continuing friction with Cameroun. There had been a series of armed clashes in an area ruled by Nigeria. It had been part of the old Calabar Protectorate under the British, and the inhabitants were largely pro-Nigerian. However, Cameroun claimed that under a 1913 Anglo-German treaty, not abrogated when the Cameroons became mandated territories after the First World War, the peninsula belonged to the republic. Nigeria never ratified an agreement on maritime boundaries in 1975 that implied Cameroun sovereignty, and in 1994 Cameroun took the case to the International Court of Justice in The Hague. This was an issue calculated to stir nationalist sentiment on both sides of the border. In 1995, after a lengthy delay since its original application to join the Commonwealth, Cameroun was admitted at the same New Zealand summit that saw the Abacha regime suspended. Chief Anyaoku, still Secretary-General of the Commonwealth of Nations, may have felt that the organisation's vaunted 'healing touch' might help in future.[13]

Unexpectedly, on 8 June 1998, Nigerians learnt that their head of state, Abacha, was no more. Although some suspected poisoning, the story most widely believed was that his exertions with a couple of Indian prostitutes had proved too much for a weak heart. His Muslim funeral was rapid, and there was no post-mortem. In fact he had spent much of his final year indoors, at Aso Rock, with his relations with the outside world mediated through his head of security, Major Hamza al-Mustapha; his health was poor and outsiders were uncertain how much he was really in charge of the government.[14]

Abacha's death was a surprise. He had been expected to attend an Organisation of African Unity summit at Ougadougou, Burkina Faso, at which Mandela was present. Matthew Neuhaus, Australian High Commissioner, was one of the ambassadors and high commissioners in Nigeria who had gone to the meeting as observers and who dashed back to Lagos to find out what was going on. Even before official announcement of the death, a junior figure in a Lagos insurance firm who had a mental disability told his boss Professor J.O. Irukwu, 'The big fish is dead.' Professor Irukwu told the author that it was uncanny, and he was never sure whether the man had a sixth sense or was party to some grassroots network that spread the news.[15]

In the tension after Abacha's death, the army hierarchy moved to squash a potential coup attempt by junior officers, and General Abdulsalami Abubakar, the Chief of the Defence Staff, was sworn in on 9 June as Head of State. A Hausa Muslim, born in Minna like Babangida, Abubakar had started out in the air force and only joined the army when the civil war began. He seemed more of a professional than a conspirator, and he had trained as a soldier in Canada and commanded the UN force in the Lebanon. His wife was a judge and was one of those who counselled him to seek a constitutional solution to Nigeria's problems. Shortly after taking office he summoned six western ambassadors and high commissioners, who all urged him to move to elections, and he acted quickly to release Obasanjo and other prisoners. He had actually visited Obasanjo when he was held in Jos prison and arranged a private room for him with a refrigerator and air conditioner.[16] Meanwhile, the dictator's widow, Maryam Abacha, was stopped en route to the airport in Abuja with 38 suitcases, many loaded with cash. This was the start of a continuing effort by Nigerian authorities to retrieve the ill-gotten gains of the greediest head of state in the country's history.

Chapter 18
Democracy, and the return of Obasanjo

General Abubakar could see that military rule had reached a dead end. But he faced two problems. One was how to deal with Abiola, still in detention, and who vocal sectors of civil society thought should at last be installed as president. This elided with a more substantial issue of how best to move to a constitutional order with elected assemblies, governors and a president. Abubakar was aware of the clamour for elections, but could not forget that senior officers had been highly critical in the 1980s of what had been seen as a too-rapid transition under Obasanjo's administration in 1976–79.

The Abiola question was resolved unexpectedly on 7 July, when he died after drinking a cup of tea in the presence of two US diplomats. Days before he had been seen by Kofi Annan, former UN Secretary-General, and Chief Emeka Anyaoku, Commonwealth Secretary-General, who thought he was well and looking forward to imminent release. Abubakar had planned to free him on 9 July. Abiola had not abandoned hope of enjoying his presidential mandate, but his two prominent visitors had warned him that it would be difficult to insist on the presidency five years later in different circumstances.

There was immediate suspicion that this death was just too convenient. When Abubakar rang Anyaoku to tell him that Abiola had died suddenly of a heart attack, the Commonwealth Secretary-General suggested he request British and Canadian pathologists to conduct the post-mortem, as no Nigerian's verdict would be trusted. Anyaoku, who had had virtually no contact with Abacha towards the end, had been advising the interim head of state to move to elections and rebuild the country's international reputation. The pathologists reported that a heart attack had caused the death, and Anyaoku believed that excitement at impending release could have precipitated a seizure. But many Nigerians remain unsatisfied, and a heart attack can be stimulated. The Oputa Panel (Human Rights Violations Investigation Commission), which was established in 2000 to investigate human rights abuses after the return of democracy, concluded, after hearing from Major Hamza Mustapha, Abacha's head of security, that the brief Abubakar regime probably knew more than it revealed.[1]

Abubakar decided to move quickly to elections and a handover to civilians. Less than a fortnight after Abiola's death, on 20 July, he abolished Abacha's bogus parties and Abacha's scheduled presidential election on 1 August, at which he was to be the sole candidate. Instead, Abubakar proposed a sequence of elections to culminate in the inauguration of a civilian president on 29 May 1999. This was even more of a rush than Obasanjo's transition, but Abubakar had to take into account a need to rebuild Nigeria's shaky economy, the strong pressures for democracy that had an anti-northern as well as an anti-military bias, and the requirement to keep coup-hungry junior officers away from power.

The awesome challenge of making a secure transition to democracy in more transparent circumstances at the start of the 21st century was handled surprisingly deftly. While critics such as the prominent lawyer Gani Fawehinmi and the rights campaigners who had struggled against the military complained with justification of ballot rigging and the return of undesirable or second-rate civilian politicians, it was an achievement that, on 29 May 1999 – henceforth to be Democracy Day – Nigeria acquired an elected president. And, by the end of the first century of 'Nigeria' in 2014, the country had had an unbroken run of three elected presidents over an unprecedented period of 15 years.

How did the minor miracle happen? There were three elements: the choice of a tough personality, Obasanjo, to be the first president in the third republic; the creation of a nationwide party, the People's Democratic Party, as a vehicle for managing a polity that can sometimes seem ungovernable; and the philosophy of 'pacted transition', which involved compromise between rival beneficiaries of the military regime and their democratic opponents.[2]

Obasanjo, as in the 1970s, came to lead Nigeria as if by accident. In prison, the child brought up as a Baptist became a thorough-going born-again Christian, writing books on prayer and convinced of his special place in God's plan. Rather like Oliver Cromwell, England's Lord Protector in the seventeenth century, he saw himself as the recipient of a series of providences. But he was not easily persuaded to come to the nation's rescue by Abubakar and Babangida in discussions that began in Yola prison and continued after release at his Ota farm. In a generous act he wrote a letter of condolence to Abacha's widow.

In fact Obasanjo, who was greeted with joy by friends in Abeokuta on his release, said that he needed to rest and catch up with what had happened in the world during his imprisonment. His finances were poor, and he needed medical treatment.[3] But as early as 27 June, in a visit to Obasanjo at Ota, Babangida is said to have suggested to Obasanjo that he should seek the presidency. For power brokers in the military and north, the recent prisoner had many attractions. He remained respected in the army. As a Yoruba he would respond positively to the cry from the democratic opposition for a regional power shift from north to south. Yet he was not a tribalist but resolutely committed to the unity of the country. He had widespread appeal internationally and would help to rebuild Nigeria's battered reputation and tackle its debt problem; he was, for example, chair of the international advisory council of the anti-corruption campaign, Transparency International. He had also been trying to analyse weaknesses in Nigeria's governance since he left office in 1979, speaking out when he was still free to do so.

Not long after he had managed the transition in 1979, he had become disillusioned with civilian politicians, and his own reconversion to the democratic idea was hard won, as a result of his dislike of Babangida's procrastination and his imprisonment under the military kleptocracy of Abacha. Rather like Winston Churchill, he had concluded that democracy was the worst form of government, except for all the others.[4] But he had many criticisms of the system as it had been practised in Nigeria, including its venality, its tribalism, the atomisation that had given the federal government so much power over now 36 states, and a parochialism that gave local people advantages in education and employment over those born in other states. He did not rush to accept a request that he stand for the presidency.

On 28 October, however, he joined the PDP and put his hat in the ring to be its presidential candidate. The PDP was the most successful nationwide party to emerge from local government elections at the end of the year. It brought together many elements, allegedly including 280 organisations and 46 retired generals, with an umbrella as its symbol.[5] Nigerians had been deeply impressed by the success of the African National Congress in South Africa, which had bridged racial and tribal divisions to create a mass party that swept the polls in 1994. But unlike the ANC, with almost a century of history and a Freedom Charter adopted five years before Nigerian independence, the PDP was a hotch-potch organisationally and ideologically. It included Alex Ekwueme, Shehu Shagari's vice-president in 1979–83 who had been pushing Abacha to democratise, the party founded by Obasanjo's military deputy Shehu Yar'Adua, and many younger business people who had benefited during the military years. Former military figures, such as his colleague from the war Theophilus Danjuma and Babangida himself, fund-aised for Obasanjo as a candidate, and they got through to people like the young Kano tycoon Aliko Dangote, who donated N120M ($1.2M).

By the time of the PDP convention in February 1999, it was obvious that whoever won it would get elected as president. The PDP had been successful in elections for state governorships and the House of Representatives. Obasanjo faced a strong candidate, Alex Ekwueme, who was running as a civilian against an ex-general, a man painted as authoritarian. But the Obasanjo campaign outspent its opponent, and he won comfortably with 1,658 votes to 521 for Ekwueme. Obasanjo chose Atiku Abubakar, an early supporter who had headed Yar'Adua's party after his untimely death, to be his vice-presidential partner.

Twelve days after the convention, the country voted in a new president on 27 February 1999. Up against Obasanjo and the PDP was a rather incoherent alliance between the Alliance for Democracy, heir to Awolowo's Yoruba machine in the southwest, and the All Peoples' Party, a northern party that included friends of Abacha. Their presidential candidate was a Yoruba economist, Olu Falae, backed by a northern running mate. Notwithstanding, or possibly because of, a remarkable degree of rigging in the Delta states of Bayelsa and Rivers, the PDP slate claimed 63% of votes throughout the nation with victory in 26 of the 36 states. A brief attempt by Folae to challenge the results in court was dropped. Although Obasanjo failed to carry any of the states in the region from which he hailed, the southwest, he appeared to have an overwhelming mandate.

How far was this a 'pacted transition', the product of an overt or covert deal between powerful interests that had prospered in the two decades since the last transition and Obasanjo, the soldier turned civilian candidate? There was little doubt that Obasanjo was his own man, and there had been desperation in appeals for him to come to the rescue. He had suffered in prison and not forgotten. Within minutes of being sworn in as president he had fired the heads of the army, navy and air force, and he made it clear that he would go after corruption and seek to entrench human rights. His coming was not immediately welcomed by the US and UK, for the US remembered his support for the Marxist Movimento Popular de Libertação de Angola in the Angolan civil war and the British recalled his nationalisation of BP's Nigerian interests on the eve of the Commonwealth summit in Lusaka in 1977. Nonetheless, Obasanjo did benefit from financial and political assistance from those involved in the military regimes; he seemed a guarantee that the country would hold together, that the interests of the north would not be overlooked, and if he was 'coup-proof' in the new dispensation as a former military head of state, he would not decry the proper status of a professional, apolitical officer corps.

On arrival in Aso Rock, the presidential office in Abuja he had once thought of demolishing, Obasanjo faced three sets of problems. He needed to carry through a house cleaning after the excesses of the Abacha dictatorship and to embed a more viable democracy. He needed to turn round the economy that, in spite of China's growing interest in Africa's resources, still meant cutting a deal first with western institutions and investors to reduce the debt burden; and he needed to improve Nigeria's standing on the world stage.

On the democracy and anti-corruption front, the new president started well but then lost focus as the transition to a freer state unleashed social forces and violent disorder. He launched Democracy Day to celebrate democratic elections, cut back the military and told it to stay out of politics, and made it clear Nigeria had definitively put its era of coups and dictatorships behind it. After sacking the service chiefs he retired 200 other officers and had officers investigated who were apparently living beyond their means. But he lacked political subtlety and the building blocks of a united democratic Nigeria would be the work of generations to create. In his inaugural address he told citizens that they had been asked many times in the past to make sacrifices and be patient, and he too was asking for the same. Yet neither he nor Nigerians were good at patience when faced with poverty, ethnic and religious conflict, and the frustrations of daily life.

Within days of taking office Obasanjo presented an Anti-Corruption Bill that, after legislators watered down its provisions, led to the formation of the Independent Corrupt Practices and Other Related Offences Commission (ICPC) in September 2000 and an Economic and Financial Crimes Commission (EFCC) in 2003 when he grew dissatisfied with its ineffectiveness. He suspended all contracts and appointments made by the short-lived Abubakar government, which led to the cancellation of 1,684 contracts out of the 4,072 contracts it had signed. He launched a pursuit of Abacha's ill-gotten gains, involving 150 western banks, oil companies and even the Russian government, whose Soviet predecessor had loaned US$2.5bn to build the costly Ajaokuta steelworks, which had never produced steel at an economic price. Nuhu Ribadu, first chairman of the EFCC, has estimated that Abacha stole US$6bn, of which perhaps half was recovered by the Nigerian state in the following 15 years after a tortuous and expensive pursuit.[6]

The EFCC itself went after a wide range of targets, including state governors, corrupt businessmen and even Ribadu's theoretical boss, Inspector General of Police Mustafa Adebayo ('Tafa') Balogun, who was convicted and jailed, and who forfeited £150M under a plea bargain. Obasanjo thought well of Ribadu, who was reappointed when the president won a second term but ran into trouble after the second term ended, when he was dismissed from the police. Ribadu's institution made some dent in the prevailing atmosphere of corruption and enabled Nigeria to be taken off the intergovernmental Financial Action Task Force's list of Non-Cooperative Countries and Territories. He sought to crack down on financial fraudsters who had been using the Internet to offer get-rich-quick schemes to gullible Internet users throughout the world. But Ribadu was accused of chasing the president's opponents rather than his friends and of possibly not being squeaky clean himself, and his subsequent career as an opponent and then adherent of the People's Democratic Party found him mixing with politicians he had criticised for corruption.

Obasanjo also moved quickly to strengthen human rights. Abacha, responding to international opinion, had set up a National Human Rights Commission; but this body, as in some other countries that felt they had to respond to the mood after the end of the Cold War and the 1993 UN World Conference on Human Rights in Vienna, was dismissed as cosmetic by human rights activists in Nigeria. Election posters had linked Obasanjo with Mandela, as former prisoners who stood for human rights, and on 14 June 1999 the president set up a Human Rights Violation Investigation Commission.

This commission, known as the Oputa Panel because it was chaired by Justice Chudwudifu Oputa, worked for two years and its televised hearings were riveting. Its formal mandate was 'to establish the causes, nature and extent of human rights violations between 15 January 1966 and 28 May 1999, to identify perpetrators, determine the role of the state in the violations and to recommend means to pursue justice and prevent future abuses'. It was a tall order, and the president was also taking a risk by including the Muhammed/Obasanjo era in the late 1970s within the judge's mandate. In fact Oputa, by now aged 75, represented much of the best in a Nigerian judicial tradition that had not been entirely corroded by dictatorships and corruption.

Inspired in part by the South African Truth and Reconciliation Commission and by comparable South American exercises, the Oputa Panel produced a balanced and thoughtful report. It complained that three generals, Buhari, Babangida and Abubakar, had failed to give evidence, and each had cases to answer. Its public hearings helped to establish a public history and it brokered local acts of reconciliation in Ogoniland. It called for a presidential fund for compensation for victims, and renewed investigation into the deaths of Kudirat Abiola, a wife of M.K.O. Abiola, the assassinated editor Dele Giwa, Yar'Adua and even Abacha. It found that the Department of Military Intelligence and the feared State Security Service had carried out torture and that the state of prisons was disgraceful. It threatened the record of the Muhammed/Obasanjo military government when it sympathised with Igbo complaints about the Abandoned Property Act, 1979, relating to forfeiture of properties owned by Igbos before the war. But the impact of the Oputa report was disappointing.

The real challenges for Obasanjo on the home front lay in the economy and the governability of a restless country. In the 1970s he had been an economic nationalist, but by the early years of the new century he was converted to the need for privatisation of the 588 public enterprises inherited from the military era. It was reckoned that few were profitable, and that while they amounted to at least 40% of GDP and over 55% of the external debt, they were actually costing the country N200–300bn ($2–3bn) a year.[7] State control, underpinned by the rapacity of the executive, had been disastrous not only in the telephone monopoly, but also spectacularly in the robbed and underfunded electricity supply company, Nigerian Electricity Power Agency.

NEPA – 'Never Expect Power Always', as it was nicknamed – had built no new power stations for a decade and could only provide 30% of households with an intermittent supply, and the majority of businesses, like better-off families, relied on diesel generators. Customers who got any power did not pay bills; some tapped the cables illegally. Problems had not been solved by the second decade of the 21st century, when analysts compared Nigeria's modest power generation with the output available to homes and businesses in South Africa. But Obasanjo increased investment, opening new power stations and moving to a genuinely competitive market after the passage of the Electric Power Sector Reform Act, 2005. This set up an independent regulator and led to the sale of unbundled assets with the possibility of fresh investment over the following years. But it was a programme that moved too slowly both for the public and for genuine entrepreneurs.

Obasanjo, like his predecessors, got a bloody nose when he tried to cut fuel subsidies. In 2000 he thought he could sweeten the labour movement by doubling the minimum wage in May. He then raised the price of petrol from N20 to N30 a litre. The Nigerian Labour Congress called a general strike on 8 June, the PDP urged him to back down, and he threatened to resign. After a brief struggle the price was settled at N22 a litre. It was an important early lesson in the limitations on the power of a democratic president.

For although the oil price was kind to Obasanjo, tripling in price in his first year to US$37 a barrel due to crisis in the Middle East, it coincided with a surge in spending, a fall in the value of the Naira and a rise in inflation. The reality was that Nigeria, being ruled by a man in his 60s when half the population was 17 or under, was still a predominantly poor country. There was much frustration and pent-up anger. Gross national income per head in 2004 was only US$430, compared with US$507 for all low-income countries, US$606.54 for all sub-Saharan Africa and US$3,670 for South Africa.[8]

Initially Obasanjo was frustrated in his attempts to achieve the write-off of Nigerian debts. Chief Anyaoku, at the end of his term of office for the Commonwealth, instigated an investment conference in Abuja in 2000 organised by the Commonwealth Business Council that was designed to get fresh money into an ailing economy. But although Canada and the US were willing to cancel relatively small debts, the UK and international lenders were obdurate on the grounds that a major oil exporter did not deserve help comparable to the assistance provided under the Highly Indebted Poor Country agreements. There was a standoff with the IMF in 2002 after the National Assembly sought to inflate Obasanjo's capital budget by nearly 70%, and it was not until 2006, in his second term, that the government struck a deal with the Paris Club of 19 countries that drastically reduced annual interest payments. Obasanjo tried to offset the volatility of oil prices by establishing an Excess Crude Account to build up a reserve when the price was high, but this became an object of suspicion as a presidential slush fund.

A key element in starting to bring Nigeria's public finances under control was hard work by a group of technocrats, led by Dr Ngozi Okonjo-Iweala, who had been with the World Bank for 21 years, rising to be Vice-President and Corporate Secretary in 2002. Witty, intelligent and with high-level international experience, she represented that group of diasporic professionals that the government wanted to lure home to reconstruct Nigeria. She was appointed Minister of Finance in July 2003, having earlier advised Obasanjo at the suggestion of the British Prime Minister Tony Blair, and rejoiced in her Hausa nickname, Wahala, meaning 'trouble.'

Okonjo-Iweala and her economic team came up with a comprehensive reform plan that they argued would be quite as strong as anything the IMF could offer but would have the benefit of being home-grown and adjusted to Nigerian realities. This was called NEEDS, the National Economic Empowerment and Development Strategy, and in her words, 'It would stabilise the macroeconomy, fight corruption, bring transparency to government business, strengthen fiscal policy, improve the management of the budget, privatise inefficient state assets, liberalise certain essential sectors, and implement public service reform and financial-sector restructuring.'[9] Inevitably not all these aims were achieved, but Nigeria won plaudits for persuading the IMF to adopt a new monitoring approach, a Policy Support Instrument, and for persuading the Paris Club of donor states that debt servicing had to take account of Millennium Development Goals.

The economic reforms stretched into many aspects of life, from the congestion in the ports to the sclerosis in the civil service, and came up against vested interests everywhere. In 2006 Okonjo-Iweala and the president fell out when he abruptly switched her to be Foreign Minister, and she resigned, becoming managing director of the World Bank from 2007 to 2011. One of the toughest areas to change was the civil service; appointments had been made on political grounds, there were 'ghost workers', and the 'federal character' principle, designed to achieve ethnic balance, had been abused to recruit persons without qualification or merit. Basic salaries were low, fringe benefits too generous. In 2004 no one knew whether the federal civil service had 141,440 or 160,000 employees. Okonjo-Iweala was shocked to find that in her Ministry of Finance some 70% of the staff were lower-level, only 13% were graduates, and computer skills were in short supply.[10] About 40% of the permanent secretaries inherited from Abubakar were sacked, and in 2004 the president set up a Bureau of Public Sector Reforms to drive up standards.

Governability issues cropped up all over the country, not helped by the fact that some of the newly elected governors were helping themselves to state resources or using thugs and militias to intimidate opponents. One of the worst areas for conflict remained the Niger Delta. In 1999 at a town called Odi, an Ijaw district in the Delta state of Bayelsa, the army killed between 43 people, according to the government, and 2,483, according to Environmental Rights Action, a non-governmental body. Either way it was a massacre precipitated by the kidnap, torture and death of some police at the hands of party thugs known as the Asawana Boys. The army, with armoured personnel carriers, laid waste to the town, and, although Obasanjo said later that the deaths and destruction were 'regrettable', he never paid compensation.[11] The incident, so early in his presidency, tainted his commitment to human rights. It contrasted badly to the more fulsome apology of Yakubu Gowon, former head of state, to the people of Asaba for those killed during the civil war.

Obasanjo was ineffective in dealing with serious regional crises in the Delta and the north, and he was also confronted with fissiparous violence in the southwest and southeast. In the Delta the conditions that led to militancy – environmental destruction, pollution of rivers, gas flaring, youth unemployment, thuggery exploited by politicians and theft from oil pipelines justified as 'taking back what is ours' – did not alter with the coming of democracy. In 2003–04 there was fighting in Warri and Port Harcourt, and the president sent in a Joint Task Force to bring the cities under control. This was capped by the emergence of a well-armed group, the Movement for the Emancipation of the Niger Delta, based in the Gbaramatu kingdom, which was not mollified when the Niger Delta Development Commission produced a master plan estimated to cost US$50bn. MEND intended to block oil exports until resources were returned to the Delta. It launched a massive attack on the major Opobo pipeline in December 2005, and a campaign of sabotage, including assaults on offshore installations, led to a drop in output of 20% in a single day. Between January 2006 and March 2007, over 200 expatriate oil workers were taken hostage and big ransoms were paid.[12]

An astute former senator for the PDP in Rivers state, John Azuta-Mbata, told the author that he thought Obasanjo's rather slow reaction to the growth of militancy in the Delta rested on calculation. He implied that the president was happy to see some reduction in output because, at a time when Iraqi and Iranian oil were of reduced importance, it made Nigerian exports more valuable; it was at the height of militancy in the Delta that Nigeria first provided 25% of US oil imports.[13] When Obasanjo left Abuja at the end of his second term, it was reckoned that nearly a third of Nigeria's oil was unavailable due to militancy, Shell and other oil majors were still anathematised in the Delta and round the world for despoliation, and the demand for resource derivation, an increase in royalty payments to the oil states, was not assuaged.

The issues in the north were bound up with sharia. Ahmad Sani Yerima, elected by the opposition All People's Party to be Governor of Zamfara State (in office 1999–2007), decided to implement sharia for criminal as well as civil cases affecting Muslims. The overwhelming majority of Zamfara citizens were Muslim, but for Christians throughout the country the sight of Koranic punishments and Islamic vigilantes on patrol evoked horror. Alleged thieves had their hands amputated, alleged 'prostitutes' were whipped. Within two years another eleven northern states had extended sharia in this way, including religiously mixed states such as Kaduna, and some 3,000 died in different riots; when the bodies of Igbo victims were brought back to Aba and other towns in the southeast, vengeful locals murdered over 300 northerners.[14]

For Obasanjo, himself a Baptist and always a little suspect in the north, this episode must have brought back unhappy memories of the run-up to war in 1966. He was bitterly criticised in the south for tolerating a spread of sharia, which was questionable under the country's secular, federal constitution. For Wole Soyinka, it was at the top of his charge sheet against the government. There had been no real attempt to bring perpetrators to justice, either. The president sent in the army to regain control in Jos, where he installed a military government for six months, but his instinct that the disturbances would gradually fizzle out proved justified. Boko Haram ('Western Education Is Forbidden'), a potentially destabilising Islamic terror group, was already in obscure existence in the northeast in Obasanjo's time but did not attract prominence until 2009.

Compared with the Delta and the north, the problems in the southwest and southeast were of a lesser order. In Lagos and other southwestern towns, the ethnic violence was stimulated by a Yoruba identity group, the Odua People's Congress, which fought Hausa immigrants attracted to their greater prosperity. Obasanjo tried to ban the OPC but was stopped by the National Assembly, which thought he was being dictatorial. In the southeast the violence was led by a vigilante group, the Bakassi Boys, run by state governors who were also responding to traders who felt unprotected by the police. The Boys were brutal killers, and Obasanjo tried to break up their organisation. He also cracked down on Igbo revisionists who wanted to revive the old Biafra and created a Movement for the Actualisation of the Sovereign State of Biafra.

Obasanjo, with his army background and experience in running a military government in the 1970s, found that managing a more democratic polity some 20 years later was extremely challenging. Party management of the PDP, cobbled together from factions and local baronies but not yet a national party in the North American or European sense, was time-consuming but essential because the Senate and National Assembly could block the president's plans. The constitution also awarded significant powers to the states and their governors, although nearly all depended on revenues from the central government; a minority of states, in the southwest and north, were not run by the PDP and had an opposition agenda. In wealthy Lagos, for instance, the president tried to stop governor Bola Tinubu from more than doubling the number of local government areas. When the Supreme Court ruled against him in 2004, Obasanjo disobeyed. He won a reputation for intervening at all levels in the federal system and ignoring the courts when it suited him. Inevitably, although the president had first run for office on an anti-corruption ticket, opaque financial manipulations lay behind the PDP strategy for winning elections. Members of his own family became embroiled in corruption allegations.[15]

Most serious for Obasanjo was a continuing struggle with the National Assembly, which finally led the House of Representatives to call on him to resign in August 2002 or face impeachment. The battle had different aspects, involving the president's desire to limit the multiplication of parties in a new Electoral Act, and his dislike of representatives' pork barrel instincts and their impact on public finance. They had wanted constituency project budgets to be used to build up their own support bases.[16] The ringleader in the attempt to impeach the president, not long before he wanted to run for re-election in 2003, was Ghali Umar Na'Abba, Speaker of the House of Representatives. Na'Abba was an example of better-educated younger Nigerians whom Obasanjo found hard to handle. A Kano businessman who had been opposed as a student to Obasanjo in the 1970s, he had also been one of those who had taken risks in opposing Abacha. He complained that the president was riding roughshod over Senate and House and simply did not understand the need for compromise in a congressional system. But after a bitter fight, involving threats and lures by those running the PDP on the president's behalf, the impeachment campaign fizzled out in November. The power of incumbency was deployed to such effect that Na'Abba lost his seat.

In January 2003, after internal jockeying, a PDP congress over-whelmingly voted to support Obasanjo for a second term, putting aside criticisms of his dictatorial tendencies and a feeling in the north that he was now favouring the Yoruba who had not backed him in 1999. Once again the quality of Nigerian elections would be in question. There were deals for mutual support between the president and PDP governors; financial 'godfathers' helped politicians pay the enormous costs of an election; 26% of the electorate said two years later that they had been offered a bribe for their vote;[17] and the embattled and underfunded Independent National Election Commission, set up by Obasanjo but seriously lacking in capacity, failed to register significant numbers of voters.

But the PDP juggernaut and Obasanjo, running on his record and dismissing the 'Mandela option' of a one-term presidency, rolled on to success. At a federal level he had had little competition in what was seen as a battle of the generals. Official results gave him 61.94% of the votes to Muhammadu Buhari's 32.19% for the All Nigeria People's Party and Emeka Ojukwu's All Progressives Grand Alliance. The PDP won 213 out of the 346 seats in the House of Representatives. While Buhari was popular among the masses in the north, his stern attitude to corruption alienated the northern elites. Ojukwu, still an Igbo hero, was representing a justified feeling in the east that it was marginalised in federal politics and a suspicion that Obasanjo retained wartime attitudes of hostility. But this was a dirty election. European Union observers said that there had been no credible election in seven states of the southeast and Niger Delta and reported fraud in half a dozen elsewhere. In the Brass constituency in Bayelsa, in the Delta, there was a positively Stalinist achievement: 100% turnout and a 100% vote for the PDP. The exceptional corruption and fraud in the Delta stimulated militancy in the region.

Obasanjo was increasingly criticised in his second term for authoritarianism, and opinion polls showed him losing popularity. Nonetheless members of the presidential circle started pushing for constitutional change to enable him to run for a third term. This was bound up with his vicious dispute with his Vice-President, Atiku Abubakar, a successful northern businessman who would benefit from a presumed rotation to a PDP northern candidacy in 2007. Obasanjo saw Atiku as inadequate and possibly corrupt, and Atiku walked out of the PDP in 2006. Elsewhere in Africa there were running constitutional battles as two-term presidencies became standard in the upsurge of democracy. In Namibia and Mozambique, for example, two terms were retained, but in the neighbouring states of Chad and Togo the rules were changed in 2004 to permit longer terms, and notoriously in Zimbabwe, Angola, Uganda and Cameroun the 'big men' clung on to presidencies for life.

The third-term proposal for Obasanjo was endorsed by the PDP's national executive, and a change in tenure was tabled in a Constitution of the Federal Republic of Nigeria 1999 (Amendment) Bill 2006. He could have quashed the idea but did not. Then, in a remarkable display of civic and media pressure exerted on senators who were not always so responsive but had their own grouses against the president, the scheme was overwhelmingly defeated. The senate debate was broadcast live. When Ken Nnamani, president of the Senate, called for a voice vote at the end, the proposal was shouted down. This was an important decision and reflected the vitality of civil society and the press in an era of instant communications. Initially the return of democracy had seen a weakening in civil society, rather as had happened in South Africa, due to a loss of focus and co-option in freer politics among those who had fought the old regime. However, civil society was making a comeback: the press had also become more professional and, to his credit, the president had not tried to censor it.

Obasanjo, keen to keep a grip on Nigerian affairs, proclaimed the outcome as a victory for democracy and then worked hard to find a successor he could trust and potentially control. After the usual PDP manipulations and backstabbing a party convention in Abuja in December 2006 overwhelmingly endorsed Umaru Musa Yar'Adua, governor of Katsina State since 1999 as presidential candidate, with Goodluck Jonathan, governor of Bayelsa state in the Delta for less than two years, as his running-mate.

The little-known Yar'Adua was a brother to the well-known Shehu Yar'Adua, Obasanjo's former chief of staff and vice-president in the 1970s. A fellow prisoner under Abacha, Shehu had been poisoned and died in detention in 1997, but not before he had founded the People's Democratic Movement, a party that was one of the building blocks for the PDP. Umaru, a younger sibling and former chemistry professor, had nine children and had run an honest but not particularly dynamic administration in his far northern state. He was a Muslim but not aggressive in his implementation of sharia, and he was without international experience. Jonathan, a Christian and Ijaw, had hardly ventured outside his own state but might calm the militancy in the Delta.[18] Obasanjo, close to the centre of Nigerian affairs since the 1970s and an African elder statesman, could anticipate emeritus respect from both of them.

But there was a question over Yar'Adua's health. He was having kidney dialysis, and Obasanjo made a televised phone call to him in Germany, where he had gone for treatment during the presidential campaign, to show that he was still alive. When he died prematurely in 2010, aged 58, some thought that Obasanjo had chosen him because he would not last the course.

Many would say that, while his domestic performance was extremely mixed, Obasanjo deserved his nation's thanks for restoring its prestige in the world. This started with a reorganisation of the foreign service, led by an advisory council on foreign relations chaired by Chief Anyaoku. The challenge was twofold. During the military period the quality of Nigerian diplomacy – at its best in the past it had matched the reputations of countries like India and Brazil – had been corroded by the appointment of cronies, placemen and incompetents. Now the world and its trading patterns had changed: there were new economic powers in Asia and Latin America; the collapse of the Soviet Union and expansion of the European Union created new possibilities; and Africa, too, was showing political and economic dynamism. It was essential to adapt to a new era of instant communications, more international players and pushy and impatient civil society. It was unfortunate timing for Nigeria that the Group of Twenty developed and developing economies (G20), designed to replace the western

Group of Seven (G7), was set up in 1999 with South Africa as the only African member.

Obasanjo's personal contacts on the international stage gave him advantages. He established warm relationships with the United States and, after the 9/11 attacks on New York in 2001, supported US and NATO military action in Afghanistan, though this was unpopular in the north. US aid and military trainers were employed to modernise Nigerian forces. However, he was keen to reduce Nigeria's expensive military commitments as part of ECOMOG in Liberia and Sierra Leone, which had been a manifesto commitment when he was first elected, and he rejected calls to provide peacekeeping troops in Guinea-Bissau and Ivory Coast.

Within Africa he tried to build friendship with South Africa and its President Mbeki, who had worked in exile for the ANC out of a residential block in Lagos. A binational commission was set up to seek economic collaboration, and the two countries were allies in Obasanjo's successful campaign to replace the ineffectual Organisation of African Unity with a more ambitious African Union, modelled on the European Union. While Obasanjo and Mbeki rejected Libyan President Muammar Gaddafi's scheme for a United State of Africa with a single army, a constitutive act was agreed in 2000 and came into force the following year. In addition to bureaucratic apparatus it acquired a flag, an anthem and the ambition that an African team should win the FIFA World Cup as part of Agenda 2063, which laid out goals for the year 2063. This was a body not only with growing capacity involved in peacekeeping around the continent, but also capable of sending medical teams to Liberia to confront an Ebola epidemic.[19] Significantly, Obasanjo helped to write into its rules a ban on military regimes.[20] He was rewarded with the honour of chairing it during 2004–06, which involved him in crises like Darfur, where Nigeria was the largest military contributor to the AU peacekeepers, and in attempts to get member states to pay their dues.

However the Nigerian president ran into trouble in the backlash from the Liberian civil war, and also in his relations with Mbeki over the intractable problem of Zimbabwe. Charles Taylor, a deeply unpleasant figure who claimed 75% of the votes in a 1999 election in Liberia after winning power in an armed insurgency and intervening in Sierra Leone, claimed asylum in Nigeria in 2003 when his militia was on the brink of defeat. Human rights activists called for his transfer to a war crimes tribunal in The Hague. In rather murky circumstances, following a request from the new Liberian president and pressure from the US, Obasanjo had him handed over to the Netherlands in 2006.[21]

The issue of Zimbabwe and its ruler, Robert Mugabe, led to a breach with Mbeki at the 2003 Commonwealth Heads of Government Meeting in Abuja. The Zimbabwean government had been suspended from the Commonwealth following chaotic land invasions and human rights and electoral abuse. Obasanjo, with Mbeki and John Howard, the Australian Prime Minister, were tasked with finding a compromise. But Mbeki, who believed vainly in quiet diplomacy if not collusion with Mugabe, was poles apart from Howard, who was standing up for the Commonwealth's proclaimed post-1991 principles. Mugabe took Zimbabwe out of the association at the Abuja summit, Mbeki denounced an agreed and mollifying statements and an attempt by Zimbabwe and South Africa to prevent Secretary-General Don McKinnon from getting a second term was roundly defeated.[22] Obasanjo backed the Secretary-General, New Zealander Don McKinnon, and fought to prevent north/south and black/white divisions from damaging the Commonwealth.

While it was necessary for Nigeria to deal with America and Europe for debt relief and investment, it was also timely to cooperate with the emerging economic giants of Asia. Asian national oil companies were offered oil blocks: the Chinese proposed to rebuild the ancient Lagos–Kano railway, an Indian firm took over the benighted Ajaokuta steelworks and South Korean, Malaysian and Taiwanese companies were encouraged to join in the race to invest. In his second term Obasanjo seemed to revert to his 1970s affection for big infrastructure projects. His haste, Nigeria's administrative and managerial blockages and failures by the overseas contractors led to disappointing results. Bilateral trade with India was worth US$8.7bn in 2008, and it was over US$8bn with China, up from only US$384M a decade earlier. But after Obasanjo was replaced by Yar'Adua, the new president and the House of Representatives tore up nearly all Obasanjo's barter deals in which oil blocks were exchanged for promises to build infrastructure. They were too costly and not transparent.[23]

The continuing saga of the Bakassi peninsula was resolved deftly, though not entirely to the satisfaction of inhabitants who would have preferred to be Nigerian. Although theoretically bicultural, Cameroun was dominated by Francophones and ruled by a president, Paul Biya, who had been in power since 1982. The International Court of Justice awarded the region to Cameroun in 2002, and four years later Obasanjo signed an agreement to implement the court's decision and withdrew Nigerian troops. An area along the Nigerian side of the border was labelled 'Bakassi', so the Nigerian constitution was not impugned. At a farewell parade he proudly told the soldiers, 'We have set a lesson for Africa and the world. We have shown that it is possible to resolve a difficult border problem without war and unnecessary loss of lives and property.'[24]

The Obasanjo era will give rise to lasting controversy, with an autocratic president trying to relaunch democracy and an economic and political reformer trying to build a more coherent and honest state on the back of the mixed gallimaufry of the PDP, with its special interests and greed. He himself sought to continue calling the shots, embedding himself as an emeritus president of the PDP and intervening in the mandates of his successors. As an ex-general it seemed as though he had lifted the threat of military intervention by removing 'political' officers and promoting professionals, especially from minority tribes. Only a few years later, as ruthless Boko Haram guerrillas rampaged through northeastern states, questions would be asked about the real military capacity of an army that had kept Nigeria in thrall for so much of its independent life. For Wole Soyinka, Obasanjo was the worst of Nigeria's rulers – because he had had the opportunity to do so much.[25] Theophilus Danjuma, who had served with him in the war, had helped him to the presidency, and was Minister of Defence in his first government, remarked in 2008 that he was the most toxic leader that Nigeria had produced.[26]

Chapter 19
Yar'Adua, Jonathan and threats in the Delta and the northeast

Umaru Musa Yar'Adua took office as Head of State in May 2007 after what was generally thought to be an extremely dirty and rigged election. The presidential election was preceded by governorship elections in the states, dominated by the PDP. Yar'Adua was reported to have won 70% of the votes, as compared with 19% for Buhari and the northern-based All Nigeria People's Party, and 8% for the former Vice-President Atiku Abubakar. Stuart Mole, a Commonwealth election observer who arrived in Port Harcourt, capital of Rivers state, saw a large billboard for PDP governor Peter Odili that stated simply: 'It is settled.'[1] He soon realised that this meant that the election had been fixed, and the PDP claimed some 2.7M votes in Rivers state, a record in the country.[2] But the Independent National Electoral Commission, which had been set up at the return of democracy to see fair play but was now seen as hand in glove with the federal government, failed to challenge grotesque irregularities. Voters who had watched the manipulation of the state elections did not bother to turn out for the presidential ones, and critics compared the quality of the 2007 polls unfavourably with elections in nearby Sierra Leone and Liberia, which were struggling with the aftermath of war.

But Yar'Adua, who turned out not to be a puppet of Obasanjo, lasted scarcely two years before declining health knocked him out as an effective president. By November 2009 he was in hospital in Jeddah, and he was flown back in great secrecy in February 2010, with a military lockdown, to die in Abuja on 6 May 2010. He was a chain smoker, and the pressures of the presidency probably worsened his underlying kidney problems.

The last six months of his life saw a paralysis in government as a power struggle developed between the family of Yar'Adua and their northern supporters and those round his Vice-President Goodluck Jonathan, who wanted him declared Acting President and then Yar'Adua's successor under the constitution.

Was this another existential crisis for Nigeria? Was there a real possibility of another coup, at a time when the reputation of electoral democracy was so low, and there were Muslim–Christian clashes in Jos? There were senior officers in a Kano-based clique who were critical of political failures and the sense of drift;[3] and there was a justified fear in the northern elite that, if Jonathan came to power, it would be difficult to get rid of him because of the awesome benefits of incumbency. Underpinning these concerns was the argument for a rotational principle, to which the PDP was supposedly wedded, that after eight years of presidency for a southerner, Obasanjo, there should be an equivalent period in office for the north.

Civil society swung behind adherence to the constitution and was strongly opposed to the manipulations of Turai Yar'Adua, wife of the ailing president, with the result that Jonathan gradually won support as Acting President in the occult politics of Abuja. In part he was seen as a guarantee that an amnesty deal in the Delta, one of the key achievements in Yar'Adua's period of health, would not come to pieces. When Yar'Adua finally died, President Jonathan declared mourning and started campaigning to win his own mandate in 2011. Rather like the crisis over Obasanjo's try for a third term, this turned out to be a triumph for Nigeria's battered constitution. While some officers might briefly have been tempted to grab power, there was a recognition that the country and the world had moved on since the Abacha era of the 1990s.

Yar'Adua's term saw a serious attempt to deal with militancy in the Delta by a combination of amnesty and financial appeasement. He also oversaw Nigeria's strategy for dealing with the world economic crisis, triggered by ripples from the Lehman Brothers bankruptcy and toxic loans in the US housing market.

The Delta situation had got steadily worse in the new century, mixing violence, terrorism, environmental destruction that had wrecked agriculture and fishing, and loss of the oil income on which both federal government and states depended. Many gangs were linked to political factions and governors, and corruption was widespread. Amnesty International reported in 2009 that as many as 20,000–30,000 non-combatants were fleeing from crossfire as the Joint Task Force of troops and police tried to hunt down militants. Oil output dropped by a third between 2006 and 2009 due to warfare and illegal 'bunkering', and international companies pulled out or moved to extract oil offshore. Although derivation of federal oil revenue to the oil-producing states had risen from 1.3% to 13%, this did not deafen the cry that 'the oil is ours', and there was a walkout from Obasanjo's national convention by Delta delegates demanding 25%.

Early in 2009 the government launched an attack on militants in the western Delta with 3,000 troops, 2 warships and 14 smaller boats that could navigate the creeks, and several helicopter gunships. But within a couple of months this security strategy was amplified with an amnesty offer of around N50bn (US$332M), which would involve the retraining and reintegration of ex-militants and putting them on a government payroll. Each militant who surrendered got US$43 a month. Money was used to buy guns from militants, and more money was put into the Niger Delta Development Commission, the agency that was originally launched after the Willink Commission prior to independence. By 2014 the cost of the amnesty programme had ballooned to an estimated N266bn (US$1,622M).[4] While few would claim that the problems in the region had been solved, the programme put a cap on the issues and the presence of Jonathan in Aso Rock was seen as protection for a region that was producing so much of the country's wealth.

Yar'Adua's second major initiative was to clean up the banks in the aftermath of the global financial crisis. His key appointment was of Sanusi Lamido Sanusi as governor of the Central Bank of Nigeria in June 2009. Sanusi, of the royal house of Kano of which he would become Emir in 2014, was a tough central banker who dealt firmly with five of the largest Nigerian banks, bailing them out and firing their chief executives. Sanusi also started taking an interest in the mysterious disappearance of funds from the Nigerian National Petroleum Corporation. A National Assembly committee on the NNPC stated that billions of dollars had gone missing from foreign subsidiaries of the state oil firm. In February 2014 President Jonathan suspended him from the Central Bank after he complained that US$20bn had evaporated from the NNPC.

When Goodluck Jonathan became president on the death of his predecessor, he proclaimed loyalty to the dead man's strategy and a 'transformation agenda' that was to make Nigerians a wealthy people. In reality, behind his bowler hat, his smiles and his apparent meekness, was a determination to win the 2011 presidential election and as many as possible of the state governorships on behalf of the PDP. His wife Patience, against whom there had been corruption allegations that were withdrawn, was a tough lady, and so were others in his circle. The aims of Goodluck were to broaden his appeal outside the south-south, the Delta region beyond the Igbo states, and to win nationwide support. He got off to a strong start in January 2011 at a PDP convention, winning 70% of the votes and sidelining a northern opponent, Atiku Abubakar. He had promised all the first-term PDP governors that they would have his nomination for a second term, and governors control delegates.

But the results of the April elections, much cleaner than those of 2007 but still with elements of fraud and rigging,[5] were dangerous for Nigeria. The presidential poll, which Jonathan won with 59.6% of the votes to 32.3% for Muhammadu Buhari for the Congress for Progressive Change, showed a clearer north–south split than at any point since 1999. Jonathan won all the southern states and many in the middle belt, with the exception of Osun, a southwestern state that backed Nuhu Ribadu, the former head of the anti-corruption EFCC. Buhari swept twelve states in the north.

Not surprisingly there were riots in the north with an anti-southern, anti-Christian flavour, and Buhari tried to challenge the outcome. Emirs and traditional leaders were targeted by the unemployed and grassroots Buhari supporters. Not all the state and governorship results were predictable and, though Jonathan got at least 25% of the votes in 31 states to prove that the PDP was still a nationwide force, five of the southwestern states went to the opposition Action Congress of Nigeria. Olusegun Obasanjo, who had promised publicly that Jonathan would be a one-term president, could not deliver the Yoruba vote, and his daughter failed to win re-election as a senator. Two-thirds of members of the House of Assembly were new, there was a substantial turnover in the Senate, and the PDP lost four governorships, bringing the total down to 23. There was a sense that, in spite of a tradition that politics is business rather than public service, a burgeoning democracy was taking hold.

Jonathan had been lucky that the oil price was high as he went into an election, and after his win he tried to get a petroleum reform bill through parliament, to remove fuel subsidies and to overcome the country's chronic lack of modern refineries. In a signal to overseas investors that the government was determined to achieve more transparency and genuine development, he brought Dr Ngozi Okonjo-Iweala back from her job as managing director of the World Bank to be Coordinating Minister for the Economy in 2011.

The oil business was a narrow and unreliable basis for Nigeria's economy, with a world price dependent on sharp fluctuations in supply, demand and speculation. The government set up a sovereign wealth fund, but among the factors affecting Nigeria in Jonathan's term were the arrival of new supplies, from Brazil, Ghana and east Africa, the greater oil independence of the US as a result of the shale oil revolution, and the steady growth of energy substitutes in a decarbonising world. By the month of July 2014, Nigeria was not exporting a single barrel of oil to the US, to which it had been one of the top four suppliers only a year before. Exports to the US had declined from 1.3M barrels per day in 2006 to 500,000 barrels in 2012. The world price was down to US$92 a barrel (it had been US$145 in 2008), and an increasingly indigenous industry had reoriented its exports towards Asia.[6] The problem was getting worse. The price dropped further to US$60 in the second half of 2014, and Okonjo-Iweala had to tear up two forecasts for 2015 and warn that the budget would be the smallest for four years. In the oil-producing cartel, the Organisation of the Petroleum Exporting Countries, ministers could not agree to cut production.

But there were also problems at home, where subsidies were becoming unsustainable and there were serious rackets in fuel imports. Because of the country's lack of refineries, Nigeria was in the extraordinary position of having to import fuel for cars and for the diesel generators used for electricity. Bogus shipments were made. Fuel that attracted subsidy was actually re-exported. From 2010 on, both Jonathan and Okonjo-Iweala had been signalling that the subsidy, which had cost N3.655 trillion in the five years to September 2011, would be removed. On New Year's Day 2012 the retail price of petrol doubled in the expectation that the subsidy would go in April.

Given the history of attempts to reduce subsidies, it was predictable that there would be a hostile public reaction. But the government was taken unawares by the strikes and battering it received from anti-corruption and human rights campaigners throughout the country. Social media brought people out onto the streets. Mimicking mass protests in other countries, this was dubbed an 'Occupy' movement. Muslims and Christians protected each other from the security forces. In Lagos it was young professionals, some of whom had returned from the diaspora in hopes of better times at home, who were in the forefront of the demonstrations. In just over a fortnight the president was forced to compromise at a cost of an extra US$4bn.

One of the sources of public anger, backed by continuing exposés of corruption, was that government and international propaganda kept harping on about economic growth in Nigeria, said to have been 7% a year in the decade from 2003. In 2013 the total size of the economy outpaced that of South Africa, a country with less than a third of Nigeria's population.[7] Investors from Asia and the west were pouring money into the country. Yet many of the 170 million or so people were seeing little improvement in their standard of living.

Social cleavages were most dangerous in the north, where unemployment was high, politicians felt they risked exclusion from the Abuja gravy train as the Jonathan presidency dug in, and Muslims were influenced by radical jihadism in the Middle East, east Africa and the Sahel. A decayed form of Koranic education had left mendicant youths without employable skills and open to gangsterism with a religious twist. Emirs and traditional leaders were losing respect. Communities with proud memories of the Sokoto Caliphate in the nineteenth century were worried by penetration by pentecostal Christians. And instability in the Sahel was growing, with weaponry and fighters on the move after Muammar Gaddafi was assassinated in the Libyan civil war in October 2011, while a civil war in Mali broke out the following year.

It was out of this combustible material that Boko Haram, an Islamic fundamentalist sect not that different from its predecessors, came into existence at the start of the new century and grew to be a subject of international concern. Initially non-violent, it was founded by a charismatic preacher, Mohammed Yusuf. It is widely believed that in around 2002 Yusuf was co-opted by Ali Modu Sheriff, a then gubernatorial candidate for Borno state. Yusuf's large youth movement would support Sheriff in return for full implementation of sharia and jobs for his followers. Sheriff has denied that there was a deal. However Boko Haram, literally 'Western Education Is Forbidden',[8] complained of official corruption and spread to the neighbouring states of Bauchi, Yobe and Kano. Yusuf received funds from abroad, possibly including from Osama bin Laden, which he used for a microcredit scheme and relief for refugees and unemployed youth.

In 2009 there were a series of clashes between Boko Haram and police. The group launched an uprising that was crushed by troops, resulting in hundreds dead, the destruction of their principal mosque, and the extra-judicial killing of Yusuf. A year later Boko Haram launched revenge attacks on the police and military barracks, and this evolved into a terror campaign led by the wild and violent Abubakar Shekau. In August 2011, bombs went off in the UN building in Abuja. In 2013 Nigeria began to realise the seriousness of the insurgency when motorbike assassins killed the driver and two bodyguards of the elderly Emir of Kano, wounding him, and President Jonathan declared a state of emergency in three northeastern states: Borno, Yobe and Adamawa.

While the federal government oscillated between negotiation and a security crackdown, not eased by lack of coordination with opposition governors in the states concerned, Boko Haram's power was spreading. A listing of 133 deaths on 8 March 2014 recorded 18 incidents in Borno state alone,[9] many in and around Gwoza, which was declared as a Boko Haram 'caliphate' later in the year, and refugees fled to the state capital of Maiduguri, ironically described as 'the home of peace' in the past. Altogether 3,000 people lost their lives in less than five months. Hundreds of schools and government buildings were destroyed in the northeast, and around half a million people were displaced.

The struggle came to international attention with Boko Haram's capture of 276 secondary schoolgirls at Chibok, in Adamawa, who had gone to a boarding school to take exams. Although over 50 managed to escape, the rest, mostly Christian, were taken into the extensive Sambisa Forest, and a gloating and erratic Abubakar Shekau released videos claiming that the Christian girls had been converted to Islam and married off, and that government announcements of deals and truces were lies.

This outrage ignited opinion in southern Nigeria especially and internationally, with an online hashtag campaign to 'BringBackOurGirls' and demonstrations in Abuja, Lagos and elsewhere. Even Michelle Obama tweeted her support. The Nigerian women's association in Spain, where the widow of General Ojukwu was ambassador, protested publicly. A group of Nigerian fans watching their team play Bosnia and Herzogovina at Cuiába, Brazil, in the World Cup, unfurled a banner. The US, UK, China and Israel were among states offering military and other assistance to retrieve the captives. But the reaction of the presidency was disastrous. Patience Jonathan accused the mothers of the girls of being part of an opposition campaign. Goodluck Jonathan, who had sent condolences to the British government within 48 hours of the murder of Fusilier Lee Rigby by two Muslim fanatics of Nigerian heritage, waited nearly three weeks before showing sympathy to his compatriots who had lost their daughters.

Meanwhile the insurgency shone a harsh light on the deficiencies of the army, from which senior officers were fired; 97 soldiers (including 16 officers) were court-martialled for refusing to fight, and a dozen were sentenced to death in May 2014 for shooting at their commander. Another 54 were court-martialled later in the year, and reports emerged of cowardice in senior officers and of ordinary soldiers wearing civilian clothes underneath their uniforms so that they might run away undiscovered.

Troops complained that funds for weapons and equipment had been stolen and that they were less well armed than Boko Haram, which had anti-aircraft guns and captured tanks. The credibility of the armed forces was damaged when its official claims that Shekau had been killed were disproved when he released videos of himself. Its heavy-handed security measures in the villages and countryside, with civilian deaths and the arrest of the wives and children of militants, were denounced by human rights bodies. By late 2014 Boko Haram was moving from its hit-and-run terror campaign to an attempt to raise flags and hold territory, proclaiming a caliphate in Gwoza, an Adamawa town of 300,000 close to the Cameroun border. It killed people ruthlessly, with fellow Muslims among the dead, and nearly assassinated the new Emir of Kano and former central banker Sanusi Lamido Sanusi, who spoke out against it and encouraged self-defence forces. Although the army claimed victory at the town of Konduga, seeing off a threat to Maiduguri, and the National Assembly in Abuja voted for US$1bn to purchase arms, the situation was out of control.

The war against Boko Haram had regional consequences. Nigeria's borders are long and porous, offering to the militants opportunities for recruitment, safe havens and mischief. The group recruited in Niger, fired rockets at and raided into Cameroun villages, and embarrassed two governments when the wife of Amadou Ali, the Vice-Prime Minister of Cameroun, was abducted from the town of Kolofata.

As the Jonathan presidency ran on, this war weakened the status in foreign affairs of the government, which had gained credit earlier by backing Alassane Ouatarra to be president of the Ivory Coast in 2010, and the National Transitional Council in the civil war in Libya in 2011–12.[10] Since independence, Nigeria had stood proudly for Africa while contributing more than its share to

UN peacekeeping around the world.[11] In 2013 Nigeria sent 1,400 troops to support France's intervention in Mali, designed to prevent Islamists winning a civil war. But this intervention was not popular at home, and there was a feeling that the government, which had a rotating place on the UN Security Council but was not obviously playing a role in international crises from Ukraine to the Middle East, was becoming dependent on outside powers. France called a conference on west African security in Paris in May 2014, which aimed to improve security cooperation between Nigeria and its Francophone neighbours, the US promised a major programme to control Nigeria's borders, and the UK beefed up its aid to Nigeria's war college. President Jonathan said after the Paris meeting, 'Boko Haram is no longer a terrorist group, it is operating clearly as an al-Qaeda operation, it is an al-Qaeda of West Africa.'[12]

Poverty and prejudice continued to depress social indicators, with wide variations around Nigeria. Estimates for the levels of HIV/AIDS were between 3–4% of the population, with some 40% of new infections coming from the police and military, and a lack of coordination between federal, state, international and non-governmental agencies. In the north, where half of girls were married by the age of 15, lack of awareness remained a major problem. While anti-retrovirals were gradually improving life expectancy, a worker with the Bill, Hillary and Chelsea Clinton Foundation told the author in May 2013 that 100 tons of anti-retrovirals had to be destroyed in 2012 because they were past their expiry date. Early in 2014 the criminalisation of gay sex, already illegal, was strengthened when Jonathan signed a law banning same-sex marriage, gay organisations and public shows of same-sex affection. In spite of the aims of the Millennium Development Goals, the under-five mortality rate worsened from 138 per thousand live births in 2007 to 158 in 2011.[13] Lack of vaccination and poor household hygiene were to blame.

The educational deficits, particularly at primary and secondary level in the north, were linked to unemployment and the growth of Boko Haram. They were particularly grievous for girls, though unemployed males with a secondary education provided pools of anger for militants to fish in. In Zamfara in the northwest, the first state to adopt sharia, only 5% of girls between five and 16 could read and write. Borno state, in the northeast, closed all its high schools prior to the Chibok attack because of the murderous impact of Boko Haram. Yet even before these recent rampages, it was estimated that 10.5M school-age Nigerians were not attending, mostly in the north. In 2012 the attendance at primary schools was only 42% in the northeast and 47.8% in the northwest, compared with a national figure of 71%, which had actually gone up by 10% in only four years. The effect of Boko Haram was to promote a vicious circle with bigger disparities between south and north and between boys and girls. History, which could be a subject of understanding as well as contention, was removed from state school curricula. In Rivers state in the Delta, in contrast to the north, Governor Rotimi Amaechi built 200 new schools and hired 13,000 new teachers.

The politics of the Jonathan presidency saw a crumbling of the PDP, where the defection of Amaechi was crucial, followed by a fight back from the president's supporters and a realisation that the opposition was finding it hard to put together a coherent alternative. In the background was annoyance among some of his erstwhile friends, like Olusegun Obasanjo, who was playing a mischievous role, that Jonathan had gone back on his promise not to contest the 2015 elections. Security threats from the north (Boko Haram) and the Delta (from the Movement for the Emancipation of the Niger Delta and others) were seen as political weapons from the regions concerned.

The north/south cleavage, demonstrated in the 2011 elections, frightened more dispassionate Nigerians and led to pessimistic talk once again about the capacity of the country to stay united. An Igbo informant in Kano told the author in March 2014 that he would make sure to be not only out of the city in February 2015, when presidential and state elections were due, but out of Nigeria altogether. The fear was that, with Jonathan hoping to be in power for ten years consecutively, there would be trouble whether he won or lost. Northerners, who had lost power and patronage with Yar'Adua's untimely death, could foresee that the south would be ruling for 18 out of 20 years running.

The crisis within the PDP, caused primarily by Jonathan's rejection of the regional rotation principle but also by other issues, came to a head in 2013. Initially seven PDP state governors rebelled and set up a 'new PDP'; by November five of them had joined a new combined opposition, the All Progressives Congress. The APC had been put together earlier in the year in an alliance between Buhari's northern-based Congress for Progressive Change, the Action Congress for Nigeria, which was masterminded by Bola Tinubu, wealthy former governor of Lagos whose party had captured nearly all the southwestern states in 2011, and two smaller parties.[14] Along the way Jonathan's PDP lost control of the National Governors' Forum, of which the rebel governor Amaechi was elected chairman, and found increasing difficulty in getting legislation, like the petroleum reform bill, through the National Assembly.

Public criticism in late 2013, when critical letters were leaked from Obasanjo and Sanusi Lamido Sanusi, the outgoing Governor of the Central Bank of Nigeria, did not make it easier for Jonathan. But his fightback had already begun. Two of the governors who had defected to the 'new PDP' did not join the opposition; former Delta militants, who became well-paid security guards for oil installations, announced with an implied threat that they were backing Jonathan;[15] and the presidency launched another national conference to take place in the first half of 2014 to review all aspects of Nigeria's constitution and current problems. Although this conference could be seen as a diversionary tactic, it could be expected to occupy the attention of the media and political class with potentially long-term impacts.

In January 2014 the PDP won the key Igbo state of Anambra. In March the president appointed former General Aliyu Mohammed Gusau as Minister of Defence. Gusau, now over 70 and from Zamfara, was one of the civil war veterans who went on to play a role in both military and civilian dispensations. He helped Muhammadu Buhari to overthrow Shehu Shagari in 1983 and Babangida to overthrow Buhari in 1985, being rewarded with the post of director of Military Intelligence by Babangida. Out of favour in the Abacha years, he was brought back by Obasanjo to be his National Security Adviser until he fell out with the president in 2006. He was a classic insider from the northern military establishment, recipient of many secrets, and he joined Jonathan on his own terms.

Having strengthened his hand in the southeast and with the military, Jonathan launched a successful counter-punch in Ekiti in the southwest in June. Governor Kayode Fayemi had been running an enlightened state administration on behalf of the ACN that had become the All Progressives Congress. Backed by the Bola Tinubu machine, he had won an exhausting legal battle to become governor. He was providing laptops for schools, insisting on higher standards of transparency in the administration and better performance by teachers and civil servants. Like Governor Babatunde Fashola in Lagos, he was an advertisement for the better governance demanded by an educated middle class.

But he was trounced by Ayo Fayose, the PDP candidate, by 203,090 votes to 120,433 after a violent campaign and conceded straightaway. What happened? Fayose had been impeached for corruption in a previous spell as governor, but he was an effective rabble-rouser and street performer. He campaigned on 'stomach issues', suggesting that Fayemi was an elitist who did not understand the people and his civil service reforms would lead to sackings. He was powerfully backed by Jonathan's PDP war chest and security forces. Subsequent revelations showed that there was a well-conceived master plan for intimidation by the security services, on authority stemming back to the presidency. Both Kayode and his wife Bisi had taken doctorates abroad and been active in the civil society opposition to Abacha, in which Kayode had founded the Centre for Democracy and Development. The PDP victory was not only a defeat for the opposition, but also a shot across the bows of diasporan professionals who had returned to Nigeria in hopes that they could help make it more modern and progressive.

In the following month, however, an opposition governor was comfortably re-elected in Osun, another southwestern state. But the chieftains of the APC, Buhari and Tinubu, had much to think about as they planned for the 2015 elections. One possibility that was discounted, given the greater salience of religion in Nigerian politics, was that the two could stand together as presidential and vice-presidential candidates, for Tinubu like Buhari was Muslim. When Abiola and Kingibe won the aborted election in 1993, it was on a Muslim-Muslim ticket. This was no longer politically feasible over 20 years later.

In December 2014 an APC convention in Abuja chose Buhari as presidential candidate with Professor Yemi Osinbajo, a former Attorney-General of Lagos and a Christian, as his running mate. The calculation was that Buhari's tough anti-corruption reputation and his willingness as a former general to crack down on Boko Haram and the Delta militias would win votes across the country; his alliance with Tinubu's Yoruba machine would guarantee funding and southwestern support. With properly managed and fair elections it looked as if, for the first time since 1999, the opposition had a good chance of defeating a lacklustre PDP president. But with the potential for election rigging and the occult powers available to a president, it was not clear that even a strong challenge could presage a democratic change of government at the end of Nigeria's first century.

Section 5

Reflections

Chinua Achebe, one of the world's great writers, once remarked that people in Nigeria talk of the country's troubles much as people in England talk of the weather – an everyday topic of conversation that will never end. In his book published in 1983, which was dedicated to the children of Nigeria, he argued that 'The trouble with Nigeria is simply and squarely a failure of leadership. There is nothing basically wrong with the Nigerian character...The Nigerian problem is the unwillingness or inability of its leaders to rise to the responsibility, to the challenge of personal example that are the hallmarks of true leadership.' He remarked on the miraculous way in which Lagos public servants started work at 7.30 in the morning the day after Murtala Muhammed seized power in 1975 but added gloomily, 'We have lost the twentieth century; are we bent on seeing that our children also lose the twenty-first? God forbid!'[1]

Several informants have commented to the author that this is a country that periodically looks over a precipice but that, except during the civil war, has never been in the most serious danger of falling. Others might challenge this view. But a century in the life of any state is an opportunity for reflection. The increasingly powerful United States of 1876, expanding from ocean to ocean, was not the country born of 13 rebellious colonies in 1776; the Germany that Otto von Bismarck had unified in 1871 after defeating France in the Franco-Prussian War was a key player in the European community a century later, but had been divided again following defeat in the second of two world wars.

Some Nigerians in early 2014 were uncomfortable with celebrating the centenary of what had started as a colonial construct. It was perhaps telling that the Federal Government, which had awarded 50 gold medallions to celebrate the jubilee of independence in 2010, awarded in 2014 a hundred medallions in silver to a mixed bag of people who themselves or whose ancestors had played a part in a tumultuous history – including General Abacha's widow, former leaders, the Lugard family and Queen Elizabeth II. But Nigeria is far from unique in inheriting boundaries created by external force, and for most of the century it is Nigerians who have been responsible for their country's destiny.

Much centenary discussion has focused on the insecure amalgamation of north and south in 1914 and the continuing north/south socioeconomic and religious differences that can make talk of 'One Nigeria' seem an exaggeration. Preference for indigenes in many of the 36 states can make a non-indigene seem an outsider and the product of an inter-tribal union a local misfit rather than a more authentic 'Nigerian'.[2] Hausas can still be the object of opprobrium in the south; one effect of Boko Haram was to make southerners in the *sabon garis* feel less safe in northern cities. But it is simplistic to see the issue as just one of north/south, and the map contains a mosaic of ethnicities and traditions. Underlying the weakness of the federation is a felt lack of ownership by citizens and a competitive drive for federal resources among the politicians who run the 36 states. Arguably there are only two, Lagos with its commercial wealth and the rich agricultural state of Sokoto, which have fiscal autonomy. Delta states, like Rivers and Bayelsa, are benefiting from revenue derivation from Abuja.

Eghosa Osaghae has argued that this want of ownership originates in the forced creation of a postcolonial state, which was not the product of a free choice by the peoples living in what is now Nigeria.[3] However street demonstrations elsewhere in the world in the

21st century, such as the Occupy movements and the 'Arab Spring', have shown that dissatisfaction with governance and even claimed democracy is widespread. Instant communications have mobilised anger, particularly among the young and better-educated, against rulers, injustice and unemployment. In Nigeria there are proximate causes in distrust of elections that have been rigged and of elites that have illegitimate riches.

In taking a long view of this rich history, it is possible to look at many factors, and the following are an arbitrary selection.

Politics as business

Prior to independence there was already a close association between politics and business, which was seen in the regional banks that were used to fund political parties, the association of business people with politicians for their mutual benefit, a willingness to see prominence in politics as a route to wealth, and a corresponding demand among voters for tangible rewards for their support. Other 'democratic' countries are exposed to similar pressures, and there was a strong vein of idealistic nationalism in the generation of Awo, Zik and the Sardauna. But the boundaries between public service and personal enrichment became dangerously blurred during the military era of the late 1960s and 1970s and positively brazen in the second republic of Shagari. Key military figures in governments of the 1980s and 1990s, and not only the Abacha family, have since been reported with wealth that could not be explained by the size of army salaries. Babangida, now seriously rich, has been accused of making off with US$12 billion following the oil price rise in the 1992 Gulf War and assisting favoured entrepreneurs. Dr Mike Adenuga, a Nigerian tycoon with oil and telecom interests, was one of those awarded oil blocks during the

Babangida era that helped his rise in business. While 'rich lists' are hard to verify, *Forbes* in the US has estimated that former general Theophilus Danjuma, who has set up a philanthropic foundation, has a fortune of US$700M.[4] Private soldiers sent to the Congo in the 1960s as UN peacekeepers earned 'Dag's Dash' in valuable dollar salaries: their seniors who captured power later, able to rule with few checks and balances, were in a position to award licences to their friends and directly or indirectly to themselves. One close observer told the author that the manipulation of corrupt payments and opportunities by Babangida was part of a strategy to assuage or pay off different factions.

The arrival of democracy in 1999 did not remove military godfathers from civilian politics or end the connection between business and politics that had been a bane of the second republic. Indeed, it opened up the opportunity for moneymaking to a wider circle. Nigerian politics, from the winning of support to become a candidate to the winning of an election, are extremely expensive. A knowledgeable insider, commenting on Bola Tinubu, the former governor of Lagos state and key strategist in the Yoruba states, told the author, 'Tinubu has a big war chest.' In Tinubu's case he has combined his activity as a politician with construction enterprises and a role in the outsourcing of revenue collection in Lagos. Nuhu Ribadu, when chairman of the anti-corruption body, the Economic and Financial Crimes Commission, said in 2007 that 23 of the 36 state governors were wanted on corruption charges and that he was taking steps to prevent them leaving the country.

Ever since the return to elective democracy, there has been a steady drip of political corruption cases that, with the rigging of elections and the lack of economic benefit to so many, have eroded faith in the system. It is worth instancing a few examples. James Ibori, former governor of Delta state and principal financial backer of President Yar'Adua, was found guilty of US$50M worth of

money laundering and fraud in a British court in 2012. He had been
extradited from Dubai after Yar'Adua's death ended his political cover.
Judge Anthony Pitts said he might have stolen up to US$200M and
sentenced him to 13 years in jail. Three years earlier, a federal court in
Asaba had dismissed 170 charges against him.[5]

Peter Odili, People's Democratic Party Governor of Rivers state,
was singled out by Ribadu and the EFCC in 2007 for extensive fraud
and corruption and was spending less on education in the state than
on his own security. Indeed security votes for governors, rarely subject
to public audit, are a common source of abuse as well as payments to
thugs; these security budgets theoretically pay to protect the governor
and his closest collaborators. Where corruption is proven, the political
interests of the presidency can forestall legal action. In March 2013
President Jonathan suddenly offered a pardon to his predecessor as
Governor of Bayelsa state, Diepreye Alamieyeseigha, who had been
charged with money laundering in 2005 in London, where he was
believed to hold US$13.5M in stolen funds. He skipped bail in the
UK and in Nigeria he was found guilty in one of the first successful
prosecutions by the EFCC. He was pardoned along with the former
head of the Bank of the North, who was found guilty of stealing
millions of Naira from his customers. Bill Gates cancelled a visit to
Nigeria in protest, where he was supporting child health projects, and
there were threats of US sanctions.

It is wrong to suppose that all politicians or all business people
are necessarily corrupt, but it is hard to maintain a reputation for
probity in politics where so much money is required and alliances have
to be built. For instance, Ribadu, who had made his name as a scourge
of corruption, was in mixed company in 2011 when he fought the
presidential election for the opposition. He subsequently defected to
the PDP in hopes of securing the party's nomination for governor of
the northeastern state of Adamawa. However several business people

have told the author how they resisted attempts to extract bribes, either by informing other government officials or threatening to inform media and civil society. Nonetheless, corruption is still endemic and often linked to an obstructive bureaucracy; Nigeria was ranked 144 out of 177 countries in Transparency International's Corruption Perceptions Index in 2013 and 147 in the World Bank's 'ease of doing business' survey in the same year, in which South Africa came in at 41 and Ghana at 67. An active independent media has helped publicise scandals even where the judicial process was unreliable, but a weary public often shrugs its shoulders.

Nigeria's heavy dependence on oil revenue has led to an elaborate gavotte involving foreign and Nigerian oil companies, politicians and administrators with substantial losses to the public purse. There are scams involving the import of refined fuel, the award of oil blocks on a non-competitive basis and the skimming of monies belonging to the Nigerian National Petroleum Corporation. In 2010 the federal government took Halliburton, the US oil services firm, to court for bribes to secure contracts for the US$6bn liquefied natural gas plant at Bonny over a decade between 1995, in the Abacha era, and 2005 during the presidency of Obasanjo. In 2014, Italian public prosecutors sought UK government support in pursuing ENI, the Italian energy firm, accused of using the Nigerian government as a route for bribes to obtain Oil Prospecting Licence 245.[6]

Although the oil-producing states have their own opportunities for corruption, the grandest larceny is available to the federal government using the state-owned NNPC as an instrument. Sanusi Lamido Sanusi, Governor of the Central Bank of Nigeria during 2009–14, raised a storm when he said that US$20bn had gone missing from the NNPC accounts and been taken by the president's associates.[7] He was suspended by President Jonathan in February 2014 but left the bank in June, when he was elected to the prominent spiritual and cultural position as Emir of Kano following the death of his elderly great-uncle. Sanusi is respected internationally as a banker and as a scholar in the Islamic world. His allegations of theft from the NNPC have never been satisfactorily refuted.

To be a senator or a member of the House of Representatives is to be incredibly well paid by world standards, and that helps explain the bitterness, rigging and financial manipulation underlying Nigerian politics. With a range of allowances, from motor vehicles to the cost of furniture, the basic pay of elected representatives is wildly inflated and little advertised to electors. It is reckoned that in 2013, each one of the 109 senators was taking home approximately US$1.7M (N240M) a year in salary and allowances, while each one of the 360 members of the House of Representatives received US$1.45M (N204M).[8]

Given the merry-go-round of money for favours among prominent politicians and state governors and the cost of winning elections, it is not surprising that officials also seek financial advantage. An informant in Abuja in 2013 recalled visiting an auditor who was a friend at a leading ministry in the capital. In the course of a four-hour conversation, the auditor was passed five brown envelopes by contractors seeking work. He passed them across to the informant who saw that in all they were worth some US$1,600. With gifts of this kind, the auditor had been able to buy a plot of land in and around the capital every fortnight and now owned 200 plots. He planned to sell them when he left the civil service, treating them as his pension.

This corruption of officialdom can have an impact on citizens at an immediate level, especially where the officials concerned are not being properly paid. Travelling by car with Morenike Ransome-Kuti not long after the return of democracy, we observed firemen in Lagos selling water from their appliances to those who were not getting a regular water supply and an attempt by police to get a bribe after stopping us on the Lagos–Abeokuta road, an all too common event for Nigerians. Richard Uku, director of communications at the Commonwealth Secretariat until 2014, recounts his experience at a border crossing into Nigeria where traders were being asked for bribes. When he argued on behalf of the women concerned, the money was returned, but he feared that the system would be reintroduced after he left.[9] Low-level corruption of this kind remains systemic and is hard to combat.

Ethnicity and religion

Some of the most intractable issues in the world are caused by a toxic mixture of ethnic and religious difference, fed by a sense of victimhood. In the Middle East, Israelis feel threatened by more numerous Arabs surrounding them; in Sri Lanka the Tamils have felt threatened by a Sinhala Buddhist majority, which in turn has been aware of the massive population of India to the north; in Northern Ireland the sense of double victimhood has been mortal, with republicans and Roman Catholics in the north as one minority, living alongside a Protestant and unionist population that is a minority on the island of Ireland.

In Nigeria, where no ethnicity has a majority and it is a mistake to dwell too much even on the larger groupings such as Hausa-Fulani, Yoruba and Igbo, the sense of victimhood as entitlement is a rallying cry for politicians and a reason why the three states at independence have multiplied twelvefold to create the 36 states today. Some are doubtfully viable and all compete for federal largesse. A key debate in the national conference of 2014 turned on the allocation of resources between the federal government, the states and the local government. No binding decisions would be taken until after the 2015 presidential election, but there was a widespread cry for 'true federalism', a devolution of power from Abuja, which currently controls the national budget and central bank, rich parastatals like the NNPC, and the military and police. Behind this cry lies a desire for greater self-government for local communities and ethnicities. The heritage of victory in the civil war and lengthy terms of military control has created a top-heavy system of government carried forward into the democratic era.

People sometimes ask why, in a Nigeria where religiosity is paraded, compassionate Islam and Christian charity seem in short supply and corruption and political thuggery can flourish. The federal government not only assists pilgrims to make the Haj to Mecca, but also supports Christians who wish to make a pilgrimage to Jerusalem and the holy places in the Palestinian territories. With cheaper air travel the numbers making the Haj have risen rapidly, and in 2013 the Saudi government had to impose quotas. It is beyond the remit of this history to delve into the complexity of religious belief and observance in a Nigeria where traditional religions continue to survive alongside Islam and Christianity. President Jonathan, listed as an Anglican, found it convenient to worship at a church of the Redeemed Church of Christ, one of the most successful of the pentecostal churches that has now built large congregations in the United Kingdom; the Christian Association of Nigeria was part of his support base.

What is clear is that the eastward-looking and Sahara-facing Islam of the north, with its recurring and militant fundamentalisms most recently appearing in the form of Boko Haram, is different from the Islam of Lagos. In Lagos it is common for families to contain both Christians and Muslims, living together without friction and converting in both directions; in one case, for instance, the only relic of Islam in a person who had switched to Christianity was an unwillingness to eat pork.[10]

But the situation in northern Nigeria is often tense, especially in religiously mixed towns, with fights, church and mosque burnings, and murders. A combination of religion and ethnicity among northerners, with the historic separation of *sabon garis*, have exposed southerners to hostility. The large size of Muslim families, and high levels of unemployment and lower levels of education have led to jealousy and a reservoir of resentful youths who hold an anti-modernity worldview. Southerners become surrogate westerners and convenient targets for multiple dissatisfactions. Although there are now successful northern businessmen like Aliko Dangote – 23rd in the *Forbes* rich list of global billionaires in 2014[11] – and the Ahmadu Bello University, Zaria, founded in 1962, claims to be the second-largest university in Africa, there is a radical Islam that taps into earlier critiques of the emirs and feudals championed by Aminu Kano.

These attitudes go beyond Boko Haram, which itself is linked by modern communications to other radical Islamist movements like al-Qaeda, al-Shabaab in Somalia and the Islamic State of Iraq and Syria. Where Christianity has been making gains in the north, it has brought with it a commitment to girls' education and been met with hostility. Educated women are less likely to put up with the patriarchy of fundamentalist Islam. It was significant, in Boko Haram's capture of the Chibok secondary schoolgirls, that the majority were Christians who wanted to take exams to advance their prospects. Religion has become more of an issue in Nigeria in the 21st century, so that former President Obasanjo was not alone in warning both the PDP and the APC opposition against choosing a Muslim and a Muslim, or a Christian and a Christian, as presidential and vice-presidential candidates for the 2015 elections.

Nigerian Christianity is severely scriptural, so that a homophobic reading of the Bible was used to support a law of January 2014 against gay marriage and membership in gay rights organisations. It is also strong, well funded and seeks converts. Devotees can spend many hours in church on a Sunday. Pastors set up their own churches. Nigerian

Anglicans in the Church of Nigeria now claim 18M baptised members, the second-largest national group in the Anglican Communion, and have fought liberal tendencies among British and US Anglicans. The traditional Anglican and Catholic churches, expanding themselves, are complemented by faster-growing pentecostals, supported by tithing and prosperity theology. Leaders of these sects may advertise their own wealth and imply that godliness leads to riches on earth, an attractive gospel to the poor. As in Latin America their followers may become vote banks, directed to support politicians favoured by the preacher.

Nonetheless, even while recognising the ethnic and religious complexities in both northern and southern Nigeria, the north/south division is still a shorthand used both inside and outside the country to analyse politics, demography and family structures, differences of wealth, social services and educational attainment. With all that has passed since independence, it has been hard to escape the legacy of a British rule that kept the north separate for 46 years, with Islam and social structures protected, while the more westernised and Christianised south was divided between the southwest and southeast. Northern states look northwards across the Sahara to Cairo and Muslim north Africa and eastwards to Khartoum and Mecca. Southern states traditionally look to Europe and North America.

Since the civil war there have been several strategies designed to bind 'one Nigeria' together: an insistence on rules of 'federal character' intended to balance employment for persons of different ethnicity; promotion of understanding and togetherness in the elite through the National Youth Service Corps that sends young students to internships around the country; a multiplication of states aimed at giving recognition to more ethnicities within the federal umbrella; and promotion of six combinations of six states each, three in the north and three in the south, which are supposed to facilitate a rotation of power in the presidency.

Many consider these strategies to be faulty or insufficient. The federal character approach to appointments in the public sphere has led to jobs for second-raters or cronies and mediocrity. Insecurity in the northeast and Delta has frightened off middle-class youngsters from getting a first-hand experience of different and less stable parts of their country; some NYSC youngsters have been murdered. Counter-intuitively, efforts at affirmative action have increased resentment and complaints of marginalisation by those who have not benefited.[12] The multiplication of states has stimulated ethnic competition and identity politics, which can veer into corruption. And, in the view of northerners, the democratic era since 1999 has seen a six-year rule from the southwest followed only by the brief Yar'Adua interregnum, and then a threat of 13 years of south-south presidency with Goodluck Jonathan. Rotation within the PDP and Nigeria has broken down.

Population movements and faster communications are impacting on the ethnic and religious face of the country. Boko Haram's savagery has caused refugee flows to safer towns in Borno state. Greater Lagos, which Professor Utomi argues now amounts to 70% of Nigeria's non-oil economy, is not only a magnet for investment from the north and east, but has also attracted migrants from throughout the country and from west African neighbours. Census figures remain unreliable in Nigeria, but he believes that Yorubas may now be in a minority in the city region, with up to 40% of Lagosians being Igbo.[13]

There is also a diaspora factor. While Nigerians abroad may use their own languages and keep in daily contact with their families and communities, they are perceived as Nigerians and are reminded, often in English, of how others see Nigerians. In Johannesburg, Nigerians have been stereotyped as drug-dealers and criminals. In London, they are recognised as professionals, artists and high achievers, who are also helping to keep public services going, from nursing to street cleaning. Significant numbers of Nigerians, not only of the middle class, now have connections outside the country, sometimes with dual nationality. This applies in the United Kingdom and in the United States, where Nigerian scientists have played a role in the US space programme and where women travel so that their babies can be born as US citizens. It also applies in the Islamic world, where some 9 million Nigerians now live in the Sudan and Nigerian doctors work in Saudi hospitals. In 2014 the national convention recommended that Nigerians in the diaspora be able to vote.

Does an external perspective soften or harden the ethnic and religious lines? It depends where the individual or family comes from. For those with a southern background, it can promote a weary cynicism and criticism of Nigerian Islam. Noo Saro-Wiwa, daughter of the executed campaigner Ken Saro-Wiwa, was educated outside the country and wrote a rather bitter and disappointed travel book, *Looking for Transwonderland: Travels in Nigeria* (2012).[14] She commented on the low-level gangsterism of Area Boys in Lagos, the fact that too many attractions she had remembered as a child had been allowed to run down, and that white Zimbabwean farmers, invited to Kwara state in 2004, had difficulty managing Muslim workers who disappeared unpredictably on Fridays.[15] Others can find an overseas education confuses their identity. Mukhtar Balewa, son of the assassinated prime minister, says that his English education left him 'a scrambled egg' and that he needed to spend time in Saudi Arabia and Egypt to learn Arabic and rediscover his spiritual roots.[16]

Continuing religious and ethnic differences lead to students going in different directions. While many southerners go to universities in the English-speaking world, northerners go to Cairo, Khartoum or Riyadh. Aliko Dangote, a tycoon and entrepreneur born in Kano in 1957, went to Al-Azhar University, Cairo. This university, founded around 970, is famous for its Koranic learning and libraries, and it only started to include secular subjects in 1961. Coming back to Nigeria,

Dangote was armed with finance by an uncle and launched a spectacular career that now extends across cement, sugar, flour, tomato processing, rice growing, rice milling, an oil refinery and a petrochemical project. But his main office is in Lagos, where his philanthropic foundation is also based, and his vision is both Nigeria-wide and international.

In addition to the returning students, many others who have served in international organisations or for firms outside the country have returned with a stronger sense of 'Nigeria'. But inside the country the institution that has claimed most vociferously to represent the national interest is the military. It has used its national mission as a justification for coups and claimed that its continuing casualties, in Joint Task Force losses in internal security warfare against Boko Haram and the Delta militias, demonstrate its patriotism in blood. But how far has the military been an ethnically and religiously blind institution? Or has it, as alleged by opponents of the dictatorships, been a default defence mechanism for the interests of the Muslim north?

Here, too, there is a colonial legacy. The British, throughout their empire, had a racist view that some tribes and peoples were warriors while others were more pacific, agricultural or commercial. In Nigeria, as seen earlier, Lugard respected the soldierly qualities of the feudal armies of the north, even though he deprecated and suppressed their habit of slave-raiding among the 'pagan' tribes. It was not surprising that, after the northern emirs were defeated, Lugard would recruit members of the Nigeria Regiment in the Royal West Africa Frontier Force from among the Hausa and Fulani. In the 1930s Margery Perham reported that Yoruba were being weeded out.

By the time of independence the small Nigerian army was truly battle-hardened, with warfare experience in the first and second world wars and its first tricky exposure to UN peacekeeping in the Congo. Although many ethnicities were represented, and Igbo and middle-belt officers were prominent in the upper ranks as a result of their better education, much of the army came from the north. From their large families the emirs would encourage a son to join the army as a respectable career. Hausa peasants, knowing that pay was assured and illiteracy not a barrier, were willing to join up, too.

The Biafran War of 1967–70 effectively knocked out the Igbo element, and the Yoruba were outnumbered by northerners. It was not until the 21st century that Igbos were again selected for the most senior positions. It was President Obasanjo, many of whose economy team were also Igbo, who made Thomas Aguiyi-Ironsi, son of the first military head of state, Minister of Defence. He also promoted Air Marshal Paul Dike as Chief of the Air Staff in 2006, and two years later President Yar'Adua made him Chief of the Defence Staff. The picture of the reintegration of the Igbo was completed in 2010 when Goodluck Jonathan made Lieutenant General Azubuike Ihejirika the Chief of Army Staff.

Although neither Gowon nor Obasanjo came from the north, it was a fact that from 1975 to 1999 there were five military rulers of Nigeria who did; four of them came to power as a result of successful conspiracies. Opponents of dictatorship, most vocal in the south, were right to point out that the army in power could not be regarded as a neutral institution, although northerners would say that it was inevitable that victors in the war would be dominant over two decades later. Clearly, one of the successes of the democratic era from 1999 was the reduction of the significance of ethnicity in the military, while new issues of professional competence have arisen as troops have struggled to put down rebellions in the northeast and Delta. The United States refused to sell arms to Nigeria as the Boko Haram insurgency worsened, in protest at the army's human rights abuses. Human rights training is lacking, the soldiers are poorly equipped, and they complain that military funds have been stolen. Local self-defence groups have appeared to protect towns in the northeast, with the encouragement of the Emir of Kano, because of the inadequacy and occasional cowardice of regular troops. There is a big difference between peacekeeping for the UN abroad and internal security work at home, where soldiers may have to occupy their own villages, and they may share sympathy with those they have to shoot. The failings of the army have been brutally exposed in its inability to combat Boko Haram.

Oil, inequity and poverty

At independence the new government must have felt blessed by a good fairy. Nigeria's oil began to flow in increasing quantities. But by 1967, when the civil war broke out, oil riches were already seen as a curse. International critics of the federal government denounced 'a war for oil' much as critics of George W. Bush and Tony Blair were to attack their Iraqi invasion in 2003. In fact the oil reserves then being exploited lay outside the Biafran heartland, but two Middle Eastern wars enormously increased the value of the 'sweet' low-sulphur crude extracted from the Niger Delta. Both the United States and western Europe came to depend on this supply and, notoriously, General Gowon said in the 1970s that the only problem for Nigeria was how to spend the money. In an era of the Festival of Black Arts and Culture and hubris, a Nigerian elite acted like oil sheikhs, driving a hundred metres when they could have walked, ignoring agriculture and importing food, adopting a rentier lifestyle and living for the day. Yet as early as 1953 in Kuwait the Kuwait Investment Authority was born, designed to invest oil royalties to guarantee the state's future when the oil ran out. In the Shetlands, small islands off the north of Scotland, canny negotiating in the 1970s ensured that the islands retained a bounty for every barrel of oil landed at the Sullom Voe terminal as the North Sea fields came on stream.

Although its significance has slightly altered over the last 40 years with the vagaries of the oil price, the Nigerian embassy in Washington was still able to say in 2014 that 'oil constitutes about 95% of generated revenue'.[17] Whereas the US was taking 40% of Nigerian output in the noughties, it was taking none by that year and the big export markets were then in India and elsewhere. Nonetheless, Nigeria has had an oil economy for a long time, and its damaging impact goes far wider than the corruption and environmental destruction that are most immediately obvious. Piracy and oil theft in the Gulf of Guinea, emanating from the creeks of the Delta, became worse than piracy off the Horn of Africa in 2013, according to the International Maritime Bureau's Piracy Reporting Centre.[18] Only in the last few years has the federal government established an excess crude account designed to even the flows into public coffers and a sovereign wealth fund to safeguard the future. It is quite possible that the global campaign for decarbonisation, to inhibit climate change, will devalue all oil reserves before Nigeria reaches its peak production.

In the Delta itself there is continuing lawlessness and 'bunkering'. Inemo Samiamo, a human rights and environmental campaigner in Port Harcourt, says 'it is impossible to stop it'. Pipelines from smallish wells crisscross a wide area and are hard to police. Periodically the army raids illegal refineries. A Royal Dutch Shell employee told the author that these refineries are obvious from the air, and most people assume they are corruptly tolerated. The stealing and refining of fuel is on an industrial scale, with an open-air market for illegal fuel in the so-called 'Togo triangle', transhipped to larger tankers. Until recently nearly all the gas associated with oil was wastefully flared, adding to the environmental blight of four oil spills a day and fires.

The *Sunday Times* of London, describing an explosion near Port Harcourt when Shell contractors blew up a pipeline in the course of stealing fuel themselves, stated in 2014:

The blast led to the shutdown of the trans-Niger pipeline, which carries crude worth £200M (£120M) every day and is one of the key arteries in Nigeria, Africa's biggest oil producer…An estimated US$1.7bn of Nigeria's oil is stolen monthly in what amounts to one of the largest organised crime operations. It involves a broad range of players, from politicians and the armed forces to foreign oil traders and small-time pirates. The spoils beat the US$13bn a year that Mexico's notorious drug cartels are estimated to make.[19]

Natural gas reserves are estimated to be three times as big as the oil reserves. A king of half a million Okrika people in the Delta told the author that he thought the fundamental problem was the lack of respect shown by successive governments to local communities. Serious allegations of environmental abuse have also been made against the big international companies, such as Shell and the Chevron Corporation, working in the region.

In the colonial era the Royal Dutch Shell group had a virtual monopoly, but that was broken at independence as other oil majors, including Italy's ENI, were brought in on a royalty-share basis. The nationalisation of BP, as part of the Obasanjo military government's effort to pressurise the Thatcher government in the UK on Rhodesia, reflected a more forthright attitude to economic sovereignty. By the 21st century, with stronger national oil firms like Oando, the multinationals were selling their onshore acreages and moving to offshore and deep-water oil. They thought that they would be safer there, but are now exposed to piracy in the Gulf of Guinea and Bight of Bonny.

All being well, local companies will also increase the supply of refined petrol and end the scandal of imports of a product that originates in Nigeria. Among refineries coming on stream are a large-scale Dangote Group enterprise, and a rather smaller refinery in

Anambra state owned by the Orient Petroleum Refinery Company, a firm that has Chief Anyaoku as chairman and the former Vice-President Alex Ekwueme on its board. Orient has made a point of insisting on probity in its relations with the federal and state government.

But what has happened to the enormous wealth generated by hydrocarbons over such a long period? The paradox of oil in Nigeria is that it has damaged other industries and done too little to alleviate poverty or to improve public services. While most agree that the economy has grown by 6–7% a year from 2006, leading the economist Jim O'Neill to describe Nigeria as one of the MINT countries of rapid growth (Mexico, Indonesia, Nigeria and Turkey), the Nigerian Bureau of Statistics reported that 61% of citizens lived on less than a dollar a day in 2010, up from 52% in 2004.[20] John Litwack, Lead Economist for Nigeria for the World Bank since 2010, argued in 2014 that poverty rates had declined significantly over the previous four years but remained stubbornly high in rural areas, and in the north; he said that there were 58M poor Nigerians, more than half of whom lived in the northeast and northwest. In the 21st century the growth in oil, telecoms and banking has been jobless.

Seeing the shiny new buildings on Victoria Island in Lagos, it would be easy to imagine that the economy is indeed taking off and that President Jonathan's Nigeria Industrial Revolution Plan of February 2013 was having a substantial impact. But in a country where over 60% of the people are under 25, some 45% under 15, 80% of graduates are unemployed and underemployment is rife, any paid job can be fatally precious. This was brought home vividly in a series of tragedies in March 2014, when the Immigration Service invited youngsters to aptitude tests to fill 3,000 positions. In Abuja around 68,000 turned up at the national stadium, and eight were killed in a stampede; in Port Harcourt, another 20,000 came for the same jobs, and four were killed in another stampede. Three pregnant young women and three young men were killed in similar crushes in Benin City in Edo state, and Minna in Niger state. As the commentator Femi Fani-Kayode wrote, 'The only crime that these children…had committed was to try to get a job to secure their future.'[21]

Attempts to combat poverty have been rather like trying to make water flow uphill, especially in northern Nigeria where UNESCO estimated that 10.5M children were out of school even before the Boko Haram insurgency was so widespread. In addition to cultural and religious doubts about 'western' education, the parents face uniform and other costs in spite of the Universal Basic Education Act, 2004, which was supposed to guarantee compulsory free schooling. There is a gender gap in schools of one girl to three boys in some northern states, and throughout the country 30% of primary schoolchildren drop out before completing their studies. Early marriage for teenage girls has been used to justify their lack of education. Rural primary schools are often unwelcoming, lacking water, electricity and toilet facilities. The federal government's National Poverty Eradication Programme has been working with the UK's aid agency, the Department for International Development, in a North East Transformation Initiative, a brave attempt to stem the tide of poverty in an insecure region where up to half of all girls under 15 enter polygamous marriages and a decayed form of Koranic instruction sees young Almajiri men begging on the streets. Nigeria as a whole still has a high birthrate: an estimated 5.25 children born to each woman, compared to 4.09 in Ghana and 2.23 in South Africa.[22]

Oil wealth has not given Nigeria, unlike some Middle Eastern oil states, a world-class health service. It is estimated that malaria, with around 100M cases a year, causes over 300,000 deaths a year, which compares with around 215,000 caused by HIV/AIDS. Malaria is implicated in 11% of maternal mortality. Although Dr Olikoye Ransome-Kuti's far-sighted plans in the 1980s for a reliable basic health service were set back by corruption and under-funding, there are still dedicated doctors and nurses who are exemplary.

A noteworthy story emerged in July 2014, when the quick thinking of a doctor in a Lagos hospital stemmed what could have been a serious Ebola outbreak. Ameyo Adadevoh, an endocrinologist, realised that a Liberian-American official, Patrick Sawyer, who was feverish and vomiting, might actually be suffering from the potentially deadly disease. Adadevoh put him in an isolation ward, set up aggressive barrier nursing, organised the disinfection of the hospital and downloaded and distributed Ebola factsheets. Some of her colleagues did not visit the ward, but she did and succumbed to the disease herself. The authorities, using a polio surveillance system, tracked 900 people to check the temperature of Sawyer's possible contacts. What could have been an epidemic on the scale of Liberia, Sierra Leone and Guinea was kept to a handful of deaths.[23]

But while oil wealth could be put to better public uses, and has been in other countries that have managed to prevent a natural resource from being a curse, a serious critique is that it has damaged the economy. The rewards have been kept too narrowly, the trickle-down effect has been too limited, and the availability of oil wealth has squeezed out other types of investment that might generate more employment, especially in agriculture. In February 2013 Dr John Isemede, director general of the Nigerian Association of Chambers of Commerce, Industry, Mines and Agriculture, said that the oil sector was killing the economy by failing to add value, especially in building agricultural exports. Ironically, therefore, Dr Akin Adesina, Minister of Agriculture and *Forbes* African Person of the Year for 2013, claimed that 'In Nigeria, we're making agriculture the new oil.' Yet whereas Nigeria attracted pipeline investments of US$59bn in 2011–14, it was only spending 1.6% of the national budget on agriculture, which employs 70% of the labour force.[24]

Nigeria still faces a critical shortage of electricity, with estimates that it has a tenth of the supply of South Africa, with companies and the better-off reliant on diesel generators.[25] With plentiful reserves of natural gas as well as sunshine, this is perverse. Countries in northern Europe, with much less sunshine than Nigeria, make more use of solar power. But an entrepreneur who had been offered a concession for solar panels for west Africa told the author that he had turned down the chance because he knew he would be driven out of business by the generator cartel.

Successive governments in the military and democratic eras have sought to boost agricultural self-sufficiency. Ex-president Obasanjo, himself a farmer and a major producer of chickens at his Ota farms, argued in *Forbes* magazine that the latest agricultural transformation agenda was having an impact;[26] annual rice output, for instance, had gone up from 2.2M tons to 3.1M tons in five years, but his claim that the country would be self-sufficient in 2015 seemed optimistic. The Jonathan government had a strategy that involved reducing the lending risk to farmers; attracting private sector agribusiness to set up processing plants; promoting commodity marketing corporations, for the scrapping of marketing boards during structural adjustment had left farmers exposed to greater price volatility; and stimulating production. By virtue of soil and climate, Nigeria should be agriculturally wealthy and a food exporter, but this is not yet the case.

Oil-related corruption is, as has been seen, not the only type of corruption. But one informant suggested an unexpected result of the increased effectiveness of global crackdowns on money laundering: the appearance of a new development model in Nigeria. Rich Nigerians, less able to take their ill-gotten gains to the safety of London, Zurich or New York, were actually forced to invest in Nigeria. The growth of a stronger domestic capitalism was the outcome.

One Nigeria?

Globalisation, with all its financial and psychic insecurities, has promoted identity politics. The collapse of the Soviet Union in 1991 unleashed significant new states on the United Nations. Yugoslavia, a much smaller entity, broke into six smaller sovereignties. The Kurds, a people unrecognised in the Anglo-French Sykes-Picot Agreement of 1916 that carved up the Ottoman empire, had achieved autonomous status in Iraq in the 21st century. Even the Scots, part of a union with England, Wales and a reluctant Ireland since 1707, came within 10% of independent statehood in a referendum after 307 years of togetherness in 2015. It has never been easier to break up a nation state, and even in Africa, so wedded to old colonial boundaries, Eritrea and South Sudan have joined the African Union, and unrecognised Somaliland is effectively autonomous. What are the chances of Nigeria staying as one?

Unlike Tanzania, where Julius Nyerere welded many ethnicities and a religiously divided country into a united nationalist movement before and during his presidency, Nigeria never had a united nationalist movement. It is not clear even today that the PDP or APC are truly national parties rather than rival coalitions. Zik's dream as a young idealist foundered on the obdurate regional interests of the southwest and north. As in Pakistan, and with equally disastrous results, it was left to the military to claim the mantle of the national interest.

Fissiparous tendencies have existed throughout the Nigerian century and are unlikely to disappear. The writ of the federal government in Abuja does not run in areas controlled by Boko Haram in the northeast and by militias and criminals in the Delta. But that is far from saying that the Lugardian polity, as modified by independent Nigerians, is past its sell-by date. There are many reasons why this geographical bloc, containing so many ethnicities and with a population number still controversial,[27] seems unlikely now to break up or even to dissolve into the weak confederation proposed by Ojukwu at Aburi. Maitama Sule, octogenarian survivor of the first government after independence, stated clearly in 2014 that the merger of north and south in 1914 was not a mistake and that a Nigeria that fractured Yugoslav-style would be much less than the sum of its parts.[28] The unanimous report of the 2014 national convention recommended a structure in which the states are federating units, deciding on the number of local government councils, with less finance for Abuja. It did not suggest the break-up of Nigeria. The existence of a strong African nation, which can represent the continent on the world stage and pay its global dues in peacekeeping, remains a source of pride.

The elements that make for a sense of 'Nigerianness' are powerful, combining communications and economics and even the Nollywood film industry. Civil society is vibrant and played decisive roles in killing Obasanjo's stratagem for a third term and in insisting that Vice-President Jonathan should take over from the ailing Yar'Adua. The constitution dropped on the country by the last military government, while not produced in a democratic way, has been made to work to strengthen democracy. It can be amended. Whether civil society can break through the corruptions that surround politics – corruptions from which some voters themselves may benefit – to establish a more responsive and effective democracy is a challenge for the 21st century. Newer media and online enterprises, such as Sahara Reporters and Channels TV, are continuing the tradition of anti-establishment guerrilla journalism, which kept democratic sentiments alive during the dictatorships.

In the meantime it is arguable that Nigerians are becoming more intertwined economically. It has been suggested that Igbos own 70% of the land in Abuja, that the wealthier northerners are heavily invested in Lagos state and that oil riches have been ploughed into real estate in Lagos as well as high-end properties in London and Manhattan. And cultural and intellectual drives from the Yorubas and Igbos have lit up the music and literature of all Nigerians. While internal stereotypes will persist, there is a recognition that some communities are simply better than others at some activities. The popular national football team, the Super Eagles, is overwhelmingly composed of southerners, but one of its star players at the 2014 World Cup in Brazil was Ahmed Musa, born in Jos.

A major weakness remains an unwillingness to confront and make use of Nigeria's past. This shows up in different ways, not only in the absence of history from the school curriculum. Poor maintenance of historic buildings – although Governor Babatunde Fashola sought to make Lagos and its marina more green – is one index. The abandonment of the grandiose National Theatre in Lagos, built from a Bulgarian design in soft soil for FESTAC, is a symptom of both waste and disrespect. An attempt to mount a large-scale history of Nigeria since the 1914 amalgamation, which was to be coordinated by a respected Ibadan professor, Tekena Tamuno, was written off by the federal government prior to the anniversary.[29]

It is not as though Nigerians have failed to analyse what has gone wrong and recommend improvements. But it was left to civil society and media to publish both the Oputa Panel report in 2005, and the national convention report in 2014.[30] Successive governments have been shy of advertising defects and recommendations, which could educate the public and lead to reform. It is pointless to invest in such inquiries if so little use is to be made of them.

The Oputa Panel, for instance, was forthright in criticising 'the scourge of military rule' and 'the cult of the Head of State'. In the first section of its report it stated:

1.2 For much the greater part of the period covered by this Report, Nigeria was under military rule. During this period,

most of our rulers' prime motivation and preoccupation
was not service to country but the accumulation of wealth
and personal gratification.

1.3 This personal accumulation of wealth led to the decay
of our society. Public and private morality reached its nadir;
and the casualties included human dignity, human rights
and our basic freedoms. We also experienced institutional
and structural decay.

The national conference of 2014, whose payments to members
who had been selected by the government were criticised for
extravagance, was remarkably comprehensive in its recommendations.
Among many it proposed a Political Parties Regulation and Electoral
Offences Commission, a strategy to reduce the power of money in
politics and corruption more broadly. It had a nationalist bias in the
economic field, proposing, for instance, that government and its agencies
be required to buy Nigerian products and services and that a country
with growing power should develop a military-industrial complex.
Intriguingly it also wanted to scrap Obasanjo's Democracy Day, 29
May, which recalled the handover of power to a civilian president.

How far has an independent Nigeria retained a relationship
with its former colonial power, and will a friendship persist? Visitors
to the country, seeing the common law and a critical media, let alone
an expensive part of Lagos named for the great white Queen, will
be struck by continuing connections. But Nigeria has many other
associations in the world, and if its population expands as has been
predicted and its governance and economy benefit, it is possible to
imagine a Nigeria in 2100 having the same big brother relationship
to the United Kingdom that the United States enjoyed by 2000. *Le
Monde*, in a report on the 2015 presidential election, forecast that

Nigeria will have 450M inhabitants in 2050, by which time it will be the world's third most populous state.[31]

Nigeria never had a British settler population, but many British people have lived there for business and other purposes, just as many Nigerians have studied and worked in the UK. Sir John Major, British Prime Minister in the 1990s, went to Jos as an executive for the Standard Chartered Bank in 1967. He had a serious car accident there, which put paid to his cricketing but not to his love of the sport. These exchanges can have lasting effects; in Major this experience, allied to growing up in Brixton as Caribbean migrants arrived, led to a lasting hostility to racism. There are many other examples. When Sir David Hunt, who had chaired the governors of the then Commonwealth Institute, retired in the 1980s, the Institute organised a farewell gift; many High Commissions donated £20, but the Nigerian High Commissioner contributed £1,000. He had not forgotten that Hunt had been UK High Commissioner in Lagos during the civil war and was seen as a firm friend of the republic.[32]

Nigeria's role in the world, though less significant under President Jonathan than under Obasanjo, is nevertheless part of the glue that keeps the state together. It dwarfs its neighbours, though it continues to show solidarity with other west African members of the Commonwealth; there was a certain irony when Abacha sent troops to Sierra Leone to restore a democratically elected President Ahmad Tejan Kabbah. It is a big player in the African Union and, if the Commonwealth is to survive as a serious international body, it will be because Nigeria is fully engaged in its activities. It has shown consistent commitment to the United Nations.

The existential question for Nigeria may never entirely disappear while ethnicities remain dissatisfied with their position in the federation, while disparities in education and wealth remain sharp and while religion is a tool for anger rather than harmony. More politicians have to join with journalists and civil society in pushing for greater probity in public life, and progress is bound to be slow. But given its manifold riches, in human and physical resources, Nigeria's second century could surprise the world, and Nigerians themselves, with a success story.

Afterword

Nigerians woke up at the end of March 2015 to find they had done something unprecedented in their country: they had voted out a sitting president and put an end to 16 years of rule by the People's Democratic Party. The victory for Muhammadu Buhari of the All Progressives Congress was comfortable, by 15.4M votes to 12.8M for Goodluck Jonathan, but not overwhelming; Jonathan retained 15 states along with Abuja, compared with 21 for Buhari. However, the two most populous cities, Lagos and Kano, voted strongly for Buhari, and he won five states in the south, having won none at all there only four years earlier. When state elections for governors took place a fortnight later the pattern was repeated: the PDP was largely confined to the Igbo and Delta states of the southeast and south-south.

Just over a century after Frederick Lugard's amalgamation of the protectorates into the Colony of Nigeria on 1 January 1914, this democratic achievement marked an important victory for Nigerians' ownership of their own state. The old cry for change, resonant throughout the democratic world, is always 'throw the rascals out'. When electors take charge it is a reminder to their rulers that, even though they may be blinded by giveaways and gimmicks for much of the time, they are ultimately more powerful than politicians. In Africa, although countries as varied as Ghana, Zambia and Mauritius have changed governments in elections, Nigeria now put itself in a vanguard. States where liberation movements have ruled for many decades after liberation, particularly in southern Africa,[1] could only look on with admiration.

Given the power of incumbency in Nigerian politics, how had the APC managed to break the PDP stranglehold? Furthermore, how had the change been achieved without the rioting and deaths that had been feared, for some 800 had died in violence in 2011 and Boko Haram had threatened to disrupt the polls four years later?

There were several factors that came together, some of which would be important for the future: the character of Buhari as compared with Jonathan; the erosion of the PDP and the effectiveness of the APC, which was based on a rebuilt alliance of the southwest and north – an alliance that had won the civil war, but had been overshadowed by an alliance of the north with the southeast during much of civilian politics; the courage and improved efficiency of the Independent National Election Commission and its Chairman, Attahiru Jega; and the vigilance and monitoring of civil society, which offset much of the big money spending on the campaigns with potential for rigging. A young electorate, familiar with social media, successfully challenged the control of information by the state and traditional media barons.

Buhari's win, at the age of 72 and his fourth attempt on the presidency, reflected a trust that he would challenge corruption, that he would defeat Boko Haram and rebuild the capacity and honour of the armed forces, and that he would build infrastructure and create jobs in spite of the downturn in oil prices. Some of the 'ex-dictator' jibes from non-Nigerians – that he had made civil servants do frog jumps and used soldiers under military rule to whip queues into shape – were memories that went down well with voters fed up with corruption and lazy officials.

Speaking at London's Chatham House in February 2015, he said he did not apologise for his actions during his 20 months of military rule in the 1980s, but that he was a born-again democrat.[2] In fact he had plainly learnt much during his sequence of election campaigns, including the importance of overcoming religious divisions. This religious tolerance was reflected in other elections. For example, in the northern state of Niger the Christian senatorial candidate, David Umaru of the APC, defeated a Muslim PDP candidate in a district that was over 90% Muslim; in Taraba state, overwhelmingly Christian, a Muslim woman, who was APC candidate to be governor, forced a rerun of the poll.

Buhari had the advantage of hailing from the north – he was born in Daura in the northwestern state of Katsina – and could be expected to be a more effective combatant against Boko Haram. But there was a question mark against him, as there had been against Obasanjo when he was elected. Would an elderly ex-general have the flexibility to handle the expectations of a youthful population, many of whom are at home in a digital world and extremely dissatisfied with the country they live in? Nonetheless, he made a sharp contrast to Jonathan, whose government seemed adrift in 2014–15, unable to respond to the oil price collapse or the outrages of Boko Haram, and concerned only with winning re-election.

For Jonathan had gradually lost control of the PDP from 2013 onward, when the Rivers governor, Rotimi Amaechi, led a breakaway faction in the party. Ironically, in the elections of 2015, the PDP in Rivers defeated Amaechi's candidate with inflated votes in campaigns in which it was alleged that the president's wife, Patience Jonathan, had played a part. Although the APC won convincingly throughout most of the country, much was unclear about the policies of the new government that would take control at the end of May; younger technocrats, some inspired by the social democracy of the Awolowo era, were likely to have a major role, determined to tackle the recidivist development problems of water, health, electricity, education, housing and food. Yet vested interests remain strong, and some are represented in the APC coalition.

The Boko Haram threat had been contained so that by the time of the elections it was in control of only one local government district in the northeast, although there was still no release for the bulk of the secondary girl students who had been captured at Chibok. Shekau was unable to disrupt the polls, and Boko Haram's affiliation to the Islamic State of Iraq and Syria looked like empty propaganda. Yet the Boko Haram issue had played a role in the election, for INEC was prevailed on to postpone the polls for six weeks. The justification given was that the security forces would be so busy defeating Boko Haram, still causing mayhem in early 2015, that they would be unable to protect polling stations throughout the country. The APC called foul, and some suspected that the reference to the security services meant that they might be employed to rig the elections as had happened in Ekiti state.

But the upshot was different. The extra time enabled more voters to get the biometric voting cards that were an ingredient in a cleaner election; more voters in the northeastern states were free to vote and the great majority voted for Buhari; and a combination of Nigerian bombing and military action by Chad, Niger, Cameroun with South African 'contractors' enabled the Nigerian commanders to claim military success. This rapid defeat for Boko Haram supported the view of many that the Nigerian government could have dealt with the insurgency much faster if it had had the political will.

For another victory for Nigeria lay in the enhanced respect for INEC and civil society's monitoring and vigilance that emerged from the elections. Serious concerns about the quality of the voting, intimidation and reported results were largely restricted to just two states, Rivers and Akwa Ibom, both in the south-south. There had been rumours that President Jonathan was plotting to remove Attahiru

Jega, an academic who had been opposed to the military and who appeared to the government to be placing too much weight on the independence of his mandate. But his steadiness throughout the campaign and his reading of the results through heckling that led some digital enthusiasts to conjure a new verb 'to jega' from his performance gave pride to those who saw the country as emerging into a more transparent polity. This was underpinned by grassroots monitoring by many civil society organisations. An account by the Sahara Reporters website that Jonathan had tried to rig the results at the last moment suggested that cool action by Jega plus strict adherence to the constitution by senior police had kept the election on course.[3]

There was also international support for a peaceful outcome to what all were aware was a hotly contested campaign. Kofi Annan brought Jonathan and Buhari together in a pledge for peace and John Kerry, US Secretary of State, and Philip Hammond, Foreign Secretary of the UK, made a joint appeal for calm. Within Nigeria, too, there were religious leaders and elder statesmen who were seeking to calm the passions. These efforts were vindicated shortly after the election when Jonathan went on nationwide television to congratulate his opponent. This was designed to take the wind out of angry supporters and marked a new stage of civility in national politics.

With so many problems to be solved, it was unrealistic to suppose that a change of government alone would have magical results. What Nigerians had shown, however, was impressive resilience, with more confidence in the future of themselves and their state.

April 2015

Notes

CHAPTER 1

1 Oba Dosunmu, transcribed as Docemo in the British document of cession, reigned in Lagos 1853–85.

2 The treaty of cession is published in K. Whiteman, *Lagos* (Oxford: Signal Books, 2012), pp. 25–56. Lugard lived from 1858 to 1945.

3 She lived from 1852 to 1929 and married Lugard in 1902. A skilled propagandist for the British Empire and a pioneering journalist, she travelled widely in southern Africa, Canada and Australia. She was a friend of Cecil Rhodes, and she joined Lugard in Hong Kong in 1907–12 when he was governor of the colony.

4 George Bradshaw launched a series of railway timetables that made sense of competing company services for nineteenth-century passengers.

5 The full speech is published in appendix B to R. Olaniyan, ed., *The Amalgamation and Its Enemies* (Ile-Ile: Obafemi Awolowo University Press, 2003), pp 232–36.

6 The definition and number of indigenous ethnicities are disputed; up to 350 are quoted.

7 M. Uhomoibhi, interview with the author, Abuja, 30 May 2013.

8 Slavery was still a way of life in Brazil and the southern states of the United States, although the Royal Navy's West Africa Squadron sought to intercept ships carrying enslaved Africans across the Atlantic.

9 Information from Freedom Park, Lagos, a cultural and recreational area recently opened in the building and grounds of the former prison.

10 So called apparently because they came back via Sierra Leone. Lagos's fine architecture in the late nineteenth century is indebted to the group of these Christian nationalist pioneers who were known as 'Brazilians'.

11 For a brilliant and racy account of the Berlin conference and Leopold's 'philanthropy', see T. Pakenham, *The Scramble for Africa, 1876–1912* (London: Abacus, 1991), pp. 239–55.

12 See M.F. Perham, *Lugard: The Years of Adventure, 1858–1898* (London: Collins, 1956); Ibid., *Lugard: The Years of Authority, 1898–1945* (London: Collins, 1960); Ibid., *West African Passage: A Journey through Nigeria, Chad, and the Cameroons, 1931–1932*, ed. A.H.M. Kirk-Greene (London: Peter Owen, 1983). She also edited his diaries in conjunction with Mary Bull.

13 Perham, *Years of Authority*, p. 26.

14 Ibid, p. 27.

15 Ibid, p. 152.

16 T. Pakenham, *Scramble for Africa*, p. 652; Churchill pointed out the inconsistency between British concern over the executions of Africans in Natal following a trial and the 'extermination of an unarmed rabble' in Nigeria. Lord Elgin was Colonial Secretary, and Churchill represented the department in the Commons.

17 The key player in the Oil Rivers was Major MacDonald, later Sir Claude MacDonald; he was hostile to the Royal Niger Company.

18 Research for the centenary of Port Harcourt found that the harbour was identified in January 1913 and its land controversially 'bought' from chiefs in May 1913; J. Nwondu, interview with the author, Port Harcourt, 12 March 2014.

19 Lugard said there had been a rapid rise in liquor duties in the South, amounting to £1,138,000 in 1913 in F. Lugard, 'Report by Sir F.D. Lugard on the Amalgamation of Northern and Southern Nigeria and Administration 1912–1919', presented to Parliament December 1919, Cmnd 468, rpt. in A.H.M. Kirk-Greene, *Lugard and the Amalgation of Nigeria* (London: Frank Cass, 1968).

20 F. Lugard, *The Dual Mandate in British Tropical Africa* (London: Frank Cass, 1965).

21 F. Lugard to Flora Lugard, 10 October 1912, qtd. in Perham, *Years of Authority*, p. 390.

22 Perham, *Years of Authority*, p. 138.

23 Lugard, 'Report', p. 12.

24 Ibid., p.12.

CHAPTER 2

1 See A. Osuntokun, *Nigeria in the First World War* (Atlantic Highlands, NJ: Humanities Press, 1979), pp. 169–71.

2 In office 1910–24.

3 See the darkly comic novel By W. Boyd, *An Ice-Cream War* (London: Hamish Hamilton, 1982).

4 F. Lugard to Colonial Office, 17 May 1916, qtd. in Osuntokun, *First World War*, p. 241.

5 In fact von Lettow-Vorbeck did not surrender until two days after the armistice; by that stage he was in Northern Rhodesia (Zambia), having crossed the Rovuma river into Portuguese East Africa (Mozambique) in November 1917, continuing his guerrilla war against one of the weaker Allies there.

6 The report of an inquiry into the killings was never published; Osuntokun, *First World War*, p. 109.

7 Lugard, 'Report', p. 13.

8 In fact the annual contribution rose to £51,000 by 1917; Osuntokun, *First World War*, p. 142, note 10.

9 According to popular Muslim beliefs the Mahdi was to appear to end the troubles confronting Muslims, cleanse society, and prepare for a second coming of the Prophet. In 1916 a local Mahdi rose up in the middle Benue to fight against the British, but his supporters were defeated at Nukko and he was tried and executed in 1917; S. Abubakar, 'The Northern Provinces under Colonial Rule: 1900–1959', in *Groundwork of Nigerian History*, ed. O. Ikime (Ibadan: HEBN Publishers, 1980), pp. 471–72.

10 20,601 pilgrims left Northern Nigeria between 1913 and 1918, and over 4,000 more returned; Osuntokun, *First World War*, p. 153.

CHAPTER 3

1 R.A. Olaniyan and A. Alao, 'The Amalgamation, Colonial Politics and Nationalism, 1914–1960', in *The Amalgamation and Its Enemies*, ed. R.A. Olaniyan (Ife-Ife: Obafemi Awolowo University Press, 2003), p. 9.

2 *Daily Times Nigeria* (Lagos), 15–19 February 1916, qtd. in Osuntokun, *First World War*, p. 82.

3 Widely quoted but rarely referenced, this statement satirising the claims of the colonial authorities to have the best interests of Nigerians at heart probably appeared first in Macaulay's *Times of Nigeria*.

4 This aim echoed a famous passage in Abraham Lincoln's Gettysburg Address, 1863.

5   Margery Perham's diaries held at Rhodes House (MP 48/1, 48) were subsequently published; Papers of Dame Margery Freda Perham, [1844]–1980, MSS. Perham. Rhodes House, Oxford; M. Perham, *West African Passage: A Journey through Nigeria, Chad and the Cameroons, 1931–32*, ed. A.H.M. Kirk-Greene (London: P. Owen, 1983).

6   The 'Brazilians' were descendants of slaves taken to Brazil who had returned in freedom to Lagos bearing Portuguese names.

7   Margery Perham remarked drily, 'Surely three hundred and sixty five would have sufficed'. Perham, MP 48/1.

CHAPTER 4

1   T.N. Tamuno, 'British Colonial Administration in the Twentieth Century', in O. Ikime, ed., *Groundwork of Nigerian History*, 393–410 (Ibadan: HEBN Publishers, 1980), p. 471.

2   Liberia was also part of Casely Hayford's dream for an English-speaking federation in west Africa.

3   Churchill was Colonial Secretary from 1921 to 1922.

4   Qtd. in M. Crowder, *The Story of Nigeria* (London: Faber and Faber, 1966), p. 255; events rather earlier than the year 2000, in the European Union and ECOWAS, could be prayed in aid of this forecast.

5   Qtd. in T. Clark, *A Right Honourable Gentleman: Abubakar from the Black Rock* (London: Edward Arnold, 1991), p. 18.

6   This closed in 1936, by which time a centre at Yalwa was serving the north.

7   Perham, MP 48/1.

8   Clark, *Right Honourable Gentleman*, p. 16.

9   Papers of Dame Margery Freda Perham, MP 48/1, 69.

10 Papers of Dame Margery Freda Perham, MP 48/1, 43.

CHAPTER 5

1   This economic section rests heavily on R.J. Gavin and W. Oyemakinde, 'Economic Development in Nigeria since 1800', in *Groundwork of Nigerian History*, ed. O. Ikime, 482–517 (Ibadan: HEBN Publishers, 1980), especially pp. 503–511.

2   Toyin Falola and Matthew Heaton, *A History of Nigeria* (Cambridge University Press), 2008, p. 141.

3   Papers of Dame Margery Freda Perham, MP 48/2, 13.

4   Gavin and Oyemakinde, 'Economic Development', p. 512.

CHAPTER 6

1   The founder of the West African Students Union was Ladipo Solanke, a Nigerian lawyer; membership was drawn from the four west African colonies.

2   Founded in 1878, it was the second-oldest secondary school in Nigeria.

3   N. Azikiwe, *My Odyssey: An Autobiography* (London: Christopher Hurst, 1970), p. 161.

4   This account of Azikiwe in the Gold Coast is largely taken from Ibid.

5   *The Morning Post* was swallowed up by the more successful *Daily Telegraph*, but three decades later the author's great-aunt would still refer affectionately to the *Telegraph* as her *Morning Post*.

6   O. Awolowo, *Awo: Autobiography of Chief Obafemi Awolowo* (Cambridge: Cambridge University Press, 1960), p. 69; Ibid., *Adventures in Power: My March through Prison, Book 1* (Ibadan: Macmillan Nigerian Publishers, 1985). Much of this account of Awo's early career is taken from his autobiography.

7   *West Africa* (30 December 1939): p. 1,715.

8   This list is taken from G.O. Olusanya, 'The Nationalist Movement in Nigeria', in *Groundwork of Nigerian History*, ed. O. Ikime (Ibadan: HEBN Publishers, 1980), p. 558.

9   See G.O. Olusanya, *The Second World War and Politics in Nigeria 1939–1945* (Ibadan: University of Lago and Evans Brothers, 1973), p. 22.

10 The status of slaves and ex-slaves was still an issue in the south, too. Perham remarked that the Alafin of Oyo had 'an attendant wife or slave (the status is, it seems, tactfully blurred by our administration) holding over his kingly head and figure, a prosaic black English umbrella'; Perham, MP 48/1, 23.

11 S. Abubakar, 'Northern Provinces', p. 475.

12 Clark, *Right Honourable Gentleman*, p. 37.

13 There is now a grammar school named for the Rev. I.O. Ransome-Kuti in Abeokuta.

14 See C. Johnson-Odim and N. Emma Mba, *For Women and the Nation: Funmilayo Ransome-Kuti of Nigeria* (Urbana, IL: University of Illinois Press, 1997), pp. 28–37. Further material was supplied to the author by the Ransome-Kuti family.

15 Information given to the author by the late Beko Ransome-Kuti.

16 Malcolm McDonald, son of Ramsay McDonald, the former Labour Prime Minister, joined the Conservatives in a national government like his father and was Colonial Secretary for a second spell from 1938 to 1940; after the Second World War he played a significant role in decolonisation.

17 Quoted in full in *West Africa* (9 September 1939).

CHAPTER 7

1 When Churchill became Prime Minister again in 1951, the Lagos *West African Pilot* commented (17 November 1951): 'Winston Churchill, who is an incarnation of British imperialism, is now destined to wield political power once more. If that should be the case, then good-night to colonial freedom.'

2 *West Africa* (16 March 1940).

3 D. Killingray and R. Rathbone, eds., *Africa and the Second World War* (London: Macmillan, 1986), p. 13.

4 Qtd. in G.O. Olusanya, *The Second World War and Politics in Nigeria, 1939–1945* (Ibadan: University of Lagos and Evans Brothers, 1973), p. 52.

5 D. Killingray, 'Labour Mobilisation in British Colonial Africa for the War Effort, 1939–46', in *Africa and the Second World War*, ed. D. Killingray and R. Rathbone (London: Macmillan, 1986), p. 69.

6 Olusanya, *Second World War*, p. 51.

7 Qtd. in Ibid, p. 56.

8 The wartime Squadron Leader Ulric Cross of Trinidad, who died in 2013 after a distinguished legal career that included chairing the Commonwealth Foundation in the 1980s, was merely one of many Caribbean volunteers who risked their lives in the skies and went on to important post-war careers in politics and the professions.

9 These numbers are drawn from D. Killingray and M. Plaut, *Fighting for Britain: African Soldiers in the Second World War* (Woodbridge: James Currey, 2010).

10 A. Mockler, *Haile Selassie's War* (Oxford: Oxford University Press, 1984), pp. 367–68, qtd. in Killingray and Plaut, *Fighting for Britain.*, p. 147.

11 IWM recording 8245/03/01–02. Interview with Brigadier G.H. Cree. It is not clear whether the 'Abyssinian' was a captured soldier who had been fighting with the Italians or a 'Patriot' who had been fighting against them.

12 S. Woodburn Kirby, *History of the Second World War: The War against Japan*, vol. 3: *The Decisive Battles* (London: HMSO, 1961), appendix.

13 A good example of this affection was recorded by Brigadier R.H.M. Hill, writing about the 82nd (West African) divisional artillery at the conclusion of the Arakan campaign, December 1944–May 1945: 'Finally I would say this. You gunners of 82 Div have given me much cause for pride. I greatly appreciate your efforts and your achievements. I look to you to profit by your experiences, and to pass the lessons on to the newcomers; to foster the team spirit of our division; to surpass your past successes, and to contribute handsomely to the ultimate damnation of the Jap. Good luck and good shooting in the adventures that lie ahead. Vive le sport'; H.B. Heath, 'The Arakan Campaign, December 1944 to May 1945', ed. R.H.M. Hill, undated, Imperial War Museum, London.

14 These benefactors would have come from the Muslim Rohingya minority, much persecuted more recently by the majority Buddhist population of Burma.

15 B. Phillips, 'Al-Jazeera Correspondent', 2 November 2011.

16 The 82nd division had crossed spears as its motif.

17 In fact Ghana, independent in 1957, emerged from colonial status in less than 15 years from this memo; Nigeria won its independence in 1960, exactly 15 years after the end of the war.

18 N. Azikiwe, *My Odyssey: An Autobiography* (London: Christopher Hurst, 1970), p. 368.

19 W. Soyinka, *Aké: The Years of Childhood* (London: Rex Collings, 1981), pp. 199–200, qtd. in Johnson-Odim and Mba, *Women and the Nation*, p. 66. Johnson-Odim and Mba explained that the ALC lobbied in conjunction with the Nigerian Union of Teachers, the body founded by the Rev. I.O. Ransome-Kuti.

20 In fact Zik ran a chain of papers in southern Nigeria that also included the *Eastern Nigerian Guardian* of Port Harcourt (1940), the *Nigerian Spokesman* of Onitsha (1943), and the *Southern Nigerian Defender* of Warri then Ibadan (1943).

21 G.O. Olusanya, 'Nationalist Movement', p. 562.

22 Earlier one of Zik's editors, Anthony Enahoro, was given a nine-month sentence for libelling Governor Bourdillon.

23 Clark, *Right Honourable Gentleman*, p. 72.

CHAPTER 8

1　There were exceptions to this generalisation. In 1948 the Eastern House of Assembly passed a Port Harcourt Bill, which enabled citizens there to elect a town council.

2　*West Africa* (7 August 1948).

3　These issues are discussed further in G. Olusanya, 'Constitutional Developments in Nigeria 1861–1960', in *Groundwork of Nigerian History*, ed. O. Ikime (Ibadan: HEBN Publishers, 1980), pp. 524–28.

4　Clark, *Right Honourable Gentleman*, pp. 70–71.

5　Hugh Foot, later Sir Hugh and then Lord Caradon, had a distinguished career. He was governor of Cyprus and later the UK ambassador to the United Nations, appointed by the Wilson Labour government. His father was Isaac Foot, a Liberal MP; his younger brother was Michael Foot, who was to be leader of the Labour Party; another brother was Dingle Foot, a barrister, latterly a Labour minister but retained by the United Gold Coast Convention after the 1948 riots in Accra and refused entry to Nigeria to defend Anthony Enahoro in the Awolowo treason trial; Hugh's son, Paul Foot, was a radical investigative journalist, best known for his work for *Private Eye*.

6　The bitterness among Zik's more radical followers was illustrated by the stoning, in a Lagos church, of a barrister who had resigned from the NCNC after Zik's return from London and who gave evidence for the Crown in the sedition case.

7　Olusanya, 'Nationalist Movement', pp. 563–64.

8　*West Africa* (4 March 1950).

9　'Nigeria is not a nation, it is a mere geographical expression. There are no "Nigerians" in the same sense as there are "English" or "Welsh" or "French"; the word Nigeria is merely a distinctive appellation to distinguish those who live within the boundaries of Nigeria from those who do not'; O. Awolowo, *Path to Nigerian Freedom* (London: Faber and Faber, 1947), p. 48.

10　*West Africa* (1 September 1951).

11　For comparison, a British Member of Parliament was paid £1,000 a year in 1946.

12　*West Africa* (5 January 1951).

13　See G.O. Dawodu, *Awo or Zik: Who Won the 1951 Western Nigerian Elections?* (Ibadan: Aika Books, 1998).

14 Qtd. in R. Olaniyan, *Amalgamation and Its Enemies*, p. 34.

15 *West Africa* (7 June 1952).

16 *West Africa* (26 January 1952).

CHAPTER 9

1 E.A. Ifidon, 'A Review of Studies of Disamalgamation in Nigeria', in *The Amalgamation and Its Enemies: An Interpretive History of Modern Nigeria*, ed. R. Olaniyan (Ile-Ife: Obafemi Awolowo University Press, 2003), p. 24.

2 J. Macpherson to Colonial Secretary, Report, 31 May 1953, FCO 141/13462, National Archives, Kew.

3 Qtd. in J.N. Paden, *Ahmadu Bello, Sardauna of Sokoto: Values and Leadership in Nigeria* (London: Hodder & Stoughton, 1986), p. 135. Paden states that the Sardauna's 'autobiography' was written for him by Sir Rex Niven, who had been a British official in Northern Nigeria and who told Paden the Sardauna 'was not the slightest bit interested in what was in or out of the book'.

4 Maitama Sule said that it was not a mistake. He thought the British had helped to preserve the religion and culture of the north, by means of indirect rule. Sule was a survivor of the first government at independence, for which he was minister for minerals and oil. M. Sule, interview with the author, Kano, 6 March 2014.

5 The riots were precipitated by a visit to the north by the Action Group's Samuel Akintola, trying to explain the case and build support for early self-government, and involved clashes between thuggish supporters loosely linked to the competing political parties. Igbos suffered particularly, and there was an exodus to the East that foreshadowed the build-up to the civil war in the 1960s.

6 P. Johnson, *Eye of Fire: A Biography of Chief Emeka Anyaoku, Commonwealth Secretary-general* (Trenton, NJ, and London, Africa World Press and Turnaround, 2000), p. 202.

7 Colonial Office: Nigeria, *Reports of the Commission Appointed to Inquire into the Fears of Minorities and the Means of Allaying Them*, Cmnd 505 (London: HMSO, 1958), p. 88.

8 Ibid., p. 88.

9 Ibid,. p. 89.

10 R. Grey, January 1956, and C. Pleass, October 1956, notes, FCO 141/13462, National Archives, Kew. These private comments related to constitutional talks in 1956; both Ralph Grey and Clem Pleass received knighthoods.

11 Brief prepared for Harold Macmillan, British Prime Minister, whose African tour included his 'wind of change' speech to the South African parliament. National Archive, December 1959/January 1960, FCO 141/1359.

12 These business connections are analysed in T. Falola and A.G. Adebayo, 'The Context: The Political Economy of Colonial Nigeria', in *Obafemi Awolowo: The End of an Era?*, ed. T. Falola *et al.* (Ile-Ife: Obafemi Awolowo University, 1988).

13 *West Africa* (14 February 1953).

CHAPTER 10

1 Other states that became independent in 1960 were Cameroun, Togo, Senegal, Mali, the Malagasy Republic, Somalia, Congo/Leopoldville, Congo/Brazzaville, Dahomey, Ivory Coast, Upper Volta, Niger, Chad, Gabon, Central African Republic and Mauretania.

2 In May 2013 *Kakadu, the Musical* was performed by the Playhouse Initiative at the Muson Centre, Lagos; it was a melancholy look back at a happier time in the former capital, before military coups and the civil war.

3 Johnson-Odim and Mba, *Women and the Nation*, p. 147.

4 *West Africa* (8 October 1960).

5 Ibid.

6 Harold Smith worked in the labour department in Lagos in 1955–60. The controversy is kept alive on the Internet, where Smith's claims with regard to the 1959 election, regional elections and census figures are both supported and debunked.

7 *Respect for Human Dignity*, printed by the Government Printer, Enugu, an inaugural address delivered by Dr Nnamdi Azikiwe, Governor-General and Commander in Chief, Federation of Nigeria, 16 November 1960. In 1947 he had quoted Buchman's call for a 'hate-free, fear-free, greed-free world'; see *My Odyssey*, p. 160.

8 *West Africa* (15 October 1960).

CHAPTER 11

1 Wazobia is now the name of a string of Nigerian radio stations, which broadcast in pidgin, and a restaurant in south London.

2 This anthem was replaced in 1978 with 'Arise, O Compatriots', the product of a competition in Nigeria, but President Jonathan's government awarded a centenary medal to Miss Williams in 2014 to acknowledge her contribution.

3   M. Sule, interview with the author, Kano, 6 March 2014.

4   E. Anyaoku, interview with the author, Lagos, 14 March 2014. There was a sequel, in that Aguiyi-Ironsi asked Anyaoku to be his principal private secretary in January 1966 after the coup which made him head of state; Anyaoku was en route from a diplomatic post in the United States to join the new Commonwealth Secretariat in London and declined the offer; had he accepted he would probably have been murdered in the 1966 counter-coup.

5   See W. Schwarz, *Nigeria* (London: Pall Mall Press, 1968), pp. 138–47.

6   For a fuller discussion, see E.E. Osaghae, *Crippled Giant: Nigeria since Independence* (London: C. Hurst & Co., 1998), pp. 38–41.

7   Chief Anyaoku told the author that he was one of only six persons who saw the 1962 figures, accurately leaked to the two papers.

8   Prime Minister Tafawa Balewa.

9   Ahmadu Bello, Sardauna of Sokoto.

10 Schwarz, *Nigeria*, p. 37.

11 M. Sule, interview with the author.

12 O. Teriba, 'Development Strategy, Investment Decision and Expenditure Patterns of a Public Development Institution: The Case of the Western Nigerian Development Corporation, 1949–1962', *Nigerian Journal of Economic and Social Studies* 8/2 (1966): pp. 256–58, cited in T. Forrest, *Politics and Economic Development in Nigeria* (Boulder, CO: Westview Press, 1993), p. 37.

13 Schwarz, *Nigeria*, p. 157.

CHAPTER 12

1   Osaghae, *Crippled Giant*, p. 46.

2   See Schwarz, *Nigeria*, p. 187.

3   R. Bourne, *Catastrophe: What Went Wrong in Zimbabwe?* (London: Zed Books, 2011). In his *The Labour Government 1964–70* (Harmondsworth: Penguin Books, 1974), Harold Wilson states that 'Britain was in the dock' and that he heard gunfire on the way into Lagos and on the way back to the airport. At the airport entrance at departure Abubakar told Wilson, 'You have a great future as Prime Minister of our mother country. You are fortunate. One thing only I wish for you, that you never have to become Prime Minister of a federal and divided country', pp. 25–56.

4 Schwarz, *Nigeria*, p. 194.

5 Y. Gowon, interview with the author, Abuja, 5 March 2014.

6 *West Africa* (January 1966).

7 Osaghae, *Crippled Giant*, p. 57, note 2, suggests that Aguiyi-Ironsi moved commanders of the five army battalions just before the coup to ensure that the four outside the East were controlled by Igbo officers. In an interview with the author, Maitama Sule said that he had been informed by a credible source that the president's ill-health that had kept him at Nsukka and then taken him to the UK for 'convalescence' was spurious; Zik wanted to be out of the way when the coup took place.

8 C. Ikeazor, *Nigeria 1966: The Turning Point* (London: New Millenium, 1997), p. 65.

9 E. Anyaoku, interview with the author, Lagos, 15 March 2014.

10 General Gowon, as head of state at the start of the war, pardoned Boro and his two lieutenants, Sam Owonaro and Dick Nottingham, and they enlisted with the Federals; Boro was killed in May 1968 and given the posthumous award of the Order of Nigeria.

11 K. Soyinka, interview with the author, Abuja, 16 March 2014.

12 *West Africa* (6 August 1966).

13 Osaghae, *Crippled Giant*, p. 61, gives more importance to the intervention of Francis Cumming-Bruce, UK High Commissioner and Elbert Matthews, US Ambassador; Kayode Soyinka stated, 'Ademola and the British High Commissioner saved Gowon and Nigeria by meeting with the northern leaders and successfully arguing that since the northerners had taken political control and were now in government, they had no reason to leave Nigeria'; K. Soyinka, obituary of Sir Adetokunbo Ademola, *Independent*, 12 February 1993.

14 Schwarz, *Nigeria*, p. 211.

15 This Petroleum Act replaced the Mineral Oil Ordinance, 1937, which had reserved oil rights for British companies in the colonial era.

16 M. Gould, *The Biafran War* (London: I.B. Tauris, 2012), p. 142 *et passim*.

17 Ibid., p. 72.

18 Ibid, p. 114.

19 Osaghae, *Crippled Giant*, p. 70.

20 It is relevant that Wilson, an instinctive humanitarian himself, had also defied strong pressure from the United States to send British troops to Vietnam.

21 Gowon, interview with author. By the time of his apology, following publication of a book about Asaba, Gowon was known for his Christian evangelism in Nigeria.

22 B. Bloom, *West Africa* (24 January 1970); it first appeared in the *Financial Times*.

23 Osaghae, *Crippled Giant*, p. 69; T. Falola and M.M. Heaton, *A History of Nigeria* (Cambridge: Cambridge University Press, 2008), p. 180.

24 An account of the role of Wole Soyinka in transmitting proposals for an anti-Northern alliance led by Biafra to Obasanjo, appears in M. Gould, *Biafran War*, p. 64. Soyinka was subsequently imprisoned without trial by the Gowon regime and wrote *The Man Died: Prison Notes of Wole Soyinka* (London: Rex Collings, 1972) after this experience. In an interview with the author, 8 May 2014, Soyinka said Obasanjo had cynically betrayed him.

25 I thank Eghosa Osaghae and Kaye Whiteman for this information. E. Osaghae and K. Whiteman, interview with the author, 24 March 2014.

26 For example Mrs. Maryam Babangida, wife of General and then President Ibrahim Babangida, was from Asaba. Such family alliances underpinned political relationships between the north and east after the war. During the crisis surrounding President Yar'Adua's death in 2011 it was possible to discover some of the military manoeuvring via these wives' networks.

CHAPTER 13

1 Gowon, interview with author.

2 See Osaghae, *Crippled Giant*, pp. 70–71. Zik had sent a congratulatory message to Gowon after Biafra's surrender urging him to feed the hungry, heal the sick, 'forgive the misguided ones', remember the dead and temper justice with mercy; *West Africa* (January 1970).

3 A. Diete-Spiff, interview with the author, Port Harcourt, 10 March 2014.

4 *West Africa* (16 February 1976).

5 There had been an early complaint by the Muhammed regime when a photo of Gowon carrying his tray of food as a student was published in the Nigerian press; this was thought to reflect badly on the dignity of a former Head of State, and Lieutenant General T.Y. Danjuma was sent to London to remonstrate with Gowon over such 'schoolboyish behaviour'; after Nigeria cut off its grant to Gowon he was able to continue his studies with help from

the Lonrho magnate 'Tiny' Rowland, who helped others, such as the cheap flights pioneer Freddie Laker, when they were down.

6   Forrest, *Politics and Economic Development*, p. 134, table 7.1.

7   *West Africa* (12 April 1976).

8   Forrest, *Politics and Economic Development*, pp. 143–44.

9   *West Africa* (12 April 1976). Nigeria borrowed; Forrest, *Politics and Economic Development*, p. 145.

10 Forrest, *Politics and Economic Development*, p. 141.

11 *West Africa* (31 May 1976).

12 Forrest, *Politics and Economic Development*, p. 142.

CHAPTER 14

1   Osaghae, *Crippled Giant*, p. 120.

2   K. Srinivasan (Indian High Commissioner in Nigeria, 1980–83), interview with the author, London, summer 2013.

3   On the impact of these loans on ensuing corruption, see K. Soyinka, *Diplomatic Baggage and MOSSAD and Nigeria, the Dikko Story* (Lagos: Newswatch Books, 1994), esp. Ch. 7 (on the Fougerolle Affair), pp. 90–111.

4   Osaghae, *Crippled Giant*, p. 155.

5   Rice imports grew from 5,000 metric tons in 1974 to 50,000 metric tons in 1976 and to 761,000 metric tons in 1978; Forrest, *Politics and Economic Development*, p. 187, table 9.1.

6   See analysis of this debate in Ibid., especially Ch. 9: 'The State and Agriculture in the 1980s', pp. 181–205.

7   Anonymous, interview with the author, Abuja, May 2013.

8   Forrest, *Politics and Economic Development*, p. 177, quoting a World Bank report of 1988.

9   Visiting Nigeria in 1983, the author came across districts where teachers had not received a salary for more than six months.

10 Sule, interview with the author, Kano, 6 March 2014.

11 Uhomoibhi, interview with the author, Abuja, 30 May 2013.

12 Speech reported in *West Africa* (9 January 1984); the final words were not identical to Muhammed's.

13 Robert Mugabe in Zimbabwe, who had cause to be grateful to Nigeria but was always hostile to military takeovers, cautiously remarked that the change of government was a matter for the Nigerians.

14 Osaghae, *Crippled Giant*, p. 145.

15 Forrest uses this nickname; Forrest, *Politics and Economic Development*, p. 74.

16 Soyinka, *Diplomatic Baggage*, p. 17.

17 P. Slawson, interview with the author, Nutbourne (Sussex, UK), 26 May 2014.

18 Osaghae, *Crippled Giant*, p. 166.

19 Forrest, *Politics and Economic Development*, p. 171, quoting D. Bevan, P. Collier, and J. Gunning, *Nigeria: Policy Responses to Shocks, 1970–1990* (San Francisco: International Center for Economic Growth, 1992).

20 Diete-Spiff, the naval officer who was running Rivers state for Gowon, faced hardship after Gowon's overthrow and opened a sports shop.

CHAPTER 15

1 UN Economic Commission for Africa, qtd. in *West Africa* (9 January 1989).

2 The full story is told in Soyinka, *Diplomatic Baggage*.

3 Soyinka wrote, 'Dikko was very lucky indeed. He was so sedated by the drug that he may not have survived the flight to Lagos had the kidnap not been foiled'; ibid., p. 32. Ironically the Nigerian government had been talking with the British about a legal extradition of Dikko prior to the kidnap.

4 In 1989 the Nigerian government failed in legal attempts to extradite Chief Akinloye, former chairman of the NPN, and Malam Ali Makele, former Minister of Steel Development; one of the defending barristers was Colin Nicholls QC, for many years chairman of the Commonwealth Lawyers' Association; as such he was present in Abuja in 2003 when a Commonwealth summit approved the 'Latimer House guidelines' for the proper spheres of executive, judiciary and legislature.

5 Dr Ashiwaju himself arranged for a Nigerian textile exhibition and other contributions in the summer festival included a Nigerian cast in a play by Wole Soyinka, although he was out of favour with the military, and musicians who took part in an African Music Village in Holland Park. The Institute in Kensington, which closed in 2000, was largely funded by the British government but included all High Commissioners as governors.

6 I.B. Dambazau, interview with the author, Kano, 8 March 2014.

7 *West Africa* (2 September 1985).

8 See Osaghae, *Crippled Giant*, pp. 193–94.

9 J. Iliffe, *Obasanjo, Nigeria and the World* (London: James Currey, 2011), p. 116.

10 If the real exchange rate was 100 in 1980, it had risen to 185 in 1984 and had fallen to 29 in 1987; Forrest, *Politics and Economic Development*, p. 214, table 10.1.

11 Osaghae, *Crippled Giant*, p. 204.

12 Beko's full name in Yoruba was Bekololari, which means 'rich but not in material wealth'.

13 Soyinka had earlier chaired a road safety agency in Oyo state.

14 See Osaghae, *Crippled Giant*, pp. 194–5.

15 O. Obasanjo, *My Command: An Account of the Nigerian Civil War, 1967–1970* (London: Heinemann, 1981).

16 *West Africa* (26 August 1985).

17 Spectrum Books, Ibadan, 1987.

18 Iliffe, *Obasanjo*, p. 111, quoting Obasanjo.

19 Iliffe, *Obasanjo*, p. 112.

20 See S. Adejumobi and A. Momoh, eds. *The Political Economy of Nigeria under Military Rule (1984–1993)* (Harare: SAPES Books, 1995).

21 Kayode Soyinka, prominent Nigerian journalist, was in the room with Dele Giwa when the bomb went off and was lucky to survive.

22 The Oputa Panel, set up after the return to democracy in 1999, concluded that two security chiefs, Brigadier Haliku Akilu and Colonel A. K. Togun, were accountable for Giwa's death, but Babangida was complicit.

23 Civilian governments had also tried to lean on the press; Bethel Njoku, who had been a director of the *Daily Times Nigeria* (Lagos) under Shagari, recalled being interviewed by security officials who complained that news about the president was not on the front page all the time.

24 The other joint chairman was Malcolm Fraser, former Prime Minister of Australia.

25 See Osaghae, *Crippled Giant*, p. 268, note; Nigeria funded a road linking Sierra Leone and Liberia, and a US$2M Babangida school of international studies at the University of Liberia.

26 *West Africa* (27 February 1989).

CHAPTER 16

1   See Iliffe, *Obasanjo*, p. 138.

2   *West Africa* (11–17 January 1993).

3   Ibid.

4   For a long time this reparations campaign made little progress. But in the second decade of the 21st century, it acquired diplomatic momentum when in March 2014 the heads of government of 15 Caribbean states (CARICOM) ratified a plan to seek compensation from the UK, France, Spain, Portugal, the Netherlands, Norway, Sweden and Denmark for 'native genocide and slavery'. Committees were set up in eight countries to prepare detailed cases, a London law firm was engaged, and CARICOM threatened to appeal to the International Court of Justice if necessary.

5   Abiola, a brilliant student, had been one year ahead of Obasanjo at the Baptist Boys High School, Abeokuta; although a Muslim he attended chapel, led services and could quote the Bible. Ernest Shonekan was also from Abeokuta.

6   *West Africa* (8–14 March 1993).

7   See Osaghae, *Crippled Giant*, p. 240, table 6.6; details of state votes not released by the NEC were published in *African Concord*.

8   *West Africa* (2–8 August 1993).

9   *West Africa* (5-11 July 1993).

10 Ibid.

11 Johnson, *Eye of Fire*, pp. 253–54. Anyaoku said Babangida had told him that there was no hidden agenda, and Nigeria was going to return to civilian rule; after the annulment Anyaoku was concerned that Nigeria had lost credibility abroad.

12 W. Soyinka, interview with the author, 7 May 2014.

13 K. Soyinka, interview with the author, 16 March 2014.

14 The hijack took place on 25 October, the last day of a Commonwealth summit in Cyprus; the hijackers demanded the installation of Abiola as president; disclosure of details of a 1992 air force crash in which 200 military officers died; that Babangida be put on trial and newspapers he had closed be reopened; and that Dele Giwa's death be investigated properly.

CHAPTER 17

1 *West Africa* (29 November–3 December 1993).

2 Qtd. in Osaghae, *Crippled Giant*, p. 247.

3 See Johnson, *Eye of Fire*, for a full discussion of Anyaoku's relationship with the Abacha regime.

4 Ibid., pp. 25–59.

5 Iliffe, *Obasanjo*, p. 155.

6 Family informant, personal communication to the author, May 2013.

7 Flora MacDonald was accompanied by Dr Enoch Dumbutshena of Zimbabwe and Dr Neville Linton of Trinidad and Tobago in a group organised by the Commonwealth Human Rights Initiative. Their report is available at www.humanrightsinitiative.org/publications.

8 Recently Femi Kuti, a bandleader like his father Fela, has been fronting an anti-AIDS poster campaign in pidgin, which points out that it is impossible to tell whether someone has AIDS simply by looking at them.

9 Osaghae, *Crippled Giant*, p. 302.

10 M.S. Dabai, 'Why There's Nothing Wrong about Honouring Abacha', *Weekly Trust* (Abuja), 8 March 2014, p. 38.

11 See N. Okonjo-Iweala, *Reforming the Unreformable: Lessons from Nigeria* (Cambridge, MA: MIT Press, 2012), p. 84.

12 Shortly after the Commonwealth voted to suspend Nigeria's membership, for example, an attempt to get the International Labour Organisation to censure the government was defeated by the African bloc.

13 It was Prime Minister Nehru who referred to the 'healing touch' of the Commonwealth. Cameroun, already ruled by President Paul Biya, was allowed to join the Commonwealth after a visit from a team led by Dr Kamal Hossain, former Foreign Minister of Bangladesh; human rights advocates were doubtful that Cameroun met the minimum requirements set out in the Commonwealth's Harare Declaration, 1991.

14 After Abacha's death Major Mustapha was arrested and initially found guilty of the murder of Kudirat Abiola, a wife of M.K.O. Abiola, but subsequently acquitted. General Dembazau believes that he amassed power in the name of the head of state as Abacha's health was failing; interview with the author.

15 Personal communication from Professor J.O. Irukwu.

16 Iliffe, *Obasanjo*, p. 155.

CHAPTER 18

1 See Iliffe, *Obasanjo*, p. 164; interview with Chief Anyaoku, *The Guardian Sunday Magazine* (Nigeria), 13 January 2013.

2 The explanatory concept of 'pacted transition' has been developed by Professor Sylvester Odion Akhaine, to whom I am indebted; he was Secretary of the Campaign for Democracy when it was headed by Beko Ransome-Kuti.

3 See Iliffe, *Obasanjo*, pp. 164–5.

4 Churchill made this remark in the British House of Commons on 11 November 1947, attributing it to an anonymous source.

5 Iliffe, *Obasanjo*, p. 165.

6 Ribadu made this estimate of theft on US TV in 2009: L. Bergmen, 'Corruption Case Exposes Scope of Bribery in Nigeria', *PBS Newshour*, broadcast on PBS, 24 April 2009, www.pbs.org/newshour/bb/africa-jan-june-09-nigeria_04-24/. Okonjo-Iweala, *Reforming the Unreformable*, pp. 84–85, pointed out that the loot of public assets was equivalent to up to 4.3% of GDP and 34.4% of the federal budget in 2006: 'More than US$2.2bn was carted away from the Central Bank of Nigeria in truckloads of cash in the form of foreign currency and travellers' cheques.'

7 Iliffe, *Obasanjo*, p. 207.

8 See Okonjo-Iweala, *Reforming the Unreformable*, p. 152, appendix table A2.1, quoting World Bank Development Indicators.

9 Ibid., p. 99.

10 Ibid., p. 52.

11 See Iliffe, *Obasanjo*, pp. 193–94.

12 E. Odoemene, 'Development without Borders: Engagement of a Catholic Faith-based Organization for the Common Good in the Post-Military Period'. PhD thesis (University of London, 2014).

13 J. Azuta-Mbata, interview with the author, Port Harcourt, 12 March 2014.

14 Iliffe, *Obasanjo*, pp. 190–91, *ThisDay* (Lagos), 2 November 1999, 21 December 1999, 1 March 2000, 6 October 2001._

15 Iliffe, *Obasanjo*, pp. 255–58, examines some cases of favours relating to Obasanjo directly, while acknowledging the difficulty of finding proof.

16 Such constituency project budgets are not unusual in African countries, allowing politicians to bestow schools and clinics for example, to cement voter loyalty.

17 Iliffe, *Obasanjo*, p. 243.

18 Jonathan had limited political experience; although he never used it one of his names was Azikiwe, in honour of the nationalist leader.

19 African Commission Directorate of Information and Communication, 'AUC Delegation to Attend the 69th UN General Assembly', press release, 20 September 2014.

20 The Commonwealth had initiated such bans in 1995, and both the South Pacific and Africa followed suit.

21 In April 2012 Taylor was found guilty by the special court on eleven counts, including terror, murder and rape, and was sentenced to 50 years in prison. He is serving his sentence in the United Kingdom.

22 See D. McKinnon, *In the Ring: A Commonwealth Memoir* (London: Elliot & Thompson, 2013) for an account by the then Secretary-General, a New Zealander.

23 *Africa-Asia Confidential* (Cambridge, UK), April 2009.

24 Obasanjo, qtd. in Iliffe, *Obasanjo*, p. 285.

25 Interview with the author.

26 *The Guardian* (Nigeria), 17 February 2008, qtd. in Iliffe, *Obasanjo*, p. 1.

CHAPTER 19

1 Personal communication from Stuart Mole.

2 See Iliffe, *Obasanjo*, p. 298.

3 *Africa Confidential* (Cambridge, UK), 8 January 2010, reported 'A khaki option on the table'.

4 Azuta-Mbata, interview with the author, Port Harcourt, 12 March 2014.

5 Roman Catholic grassroots election monitors reported a variety of abuses, but the hierarchy gave the election a clean bill of health (information from Emmanuel Odoemene); Professor Bola Akinterinwa, returning officer in Lagos state in 2011, told the author he was satisfied that there was no rigging in the state then.

6 *Financial Times* (London), 3 October 2014.

7 International Crisis Group, *AfricaReport* 216, April 2014.

8 The original self-described name was either, in Arabic, *Jama'atu Ahlis Sunna Lidda'Awati Wal-Jihad* ('Group of the People of Sunnah for Preaching and Jihad') or *Wilayat al Sudan al Gharbi* ('West Africa (Black People's Land) Province').

9 *Weekly Trust* (Abjua), 8 March 2014.

10 These decisions by Nigeria were flagged up as examples of Nigerian support for democracy in Africa by Martin Uhomoibhi, Permanent Secretary in the Foreign Ministry, in a paper titled 'History of Nigeria's Foreign Policy: Continuity and Change', February 2012.

11 Professor Bola Akinterinwa, director-general, Nigerian Institute of International Affairs, Lagos made this 'Africanist' point strongly to the author at an interview in May 2013.

12 Reuters, 17 May 2014.

13 UNICEF figures, qtd. in *Punch*, 14 August 2013.

14 These were the All Nigeria People's Party, and the All Progressives Grand Alliance.

15 *Africa Confidential* (Cambridge, UK), 20 September 2013.

REFLECTIONS

1 C. Achebe, *The Trouble with Nigeria* (London: Heinemann, 1983).

2 In 2014 Sokoto, for example, specifically declared that non-indigenes could have all the opportunities for schooling of indigenes. 'Indigene' is the common usage to describe a resident of a state.

3 Eghosa Osaghae made this case in delivering 'A State of Our Own: Second Independence, Federalism and the Decolonisation of the State in Africa', his inaugural Anyaoku lecture at the Institute of Commonwealth Studies, University of London, 9 April 2014.

4 *Sunday Times* (London), 19 October 2014, quoted this sum in the context of a potential takeover of the Afren oil company by SAPetro, a Nigerian exploration firm founded by Danjuma.

5 *Africa Confidential* (Cambridge, UK), 27 April 2012.

6 *Africa Confidential* (Cambridge, UK), 10 October 2014.

7 Rich state oil companies, and their suspected role in financing governing parties, have led to controversies in other emerging democracies; President Dilma Rousseff of Brazil nearly lost her re-election bid in 2014 after exposure of a scandal in Petrobras.

8 *Vanguard*, 25 August 2013.

9 Personal communication from Richard Uku.

10 Personal communication from a family informant.

11 Forbes Rich List, 2014; Dangote is far and away the richest African in this list, although on one day in November 2014 he slipped from 23rd to 37th place;

The Guardian (London), 14 November 2014, said he was worth US$25.7bn in 2014, a year in which Nigeria had 23 dollar billionaires.

12 Personal communication from Pat Utomi, May 2013.

13 Ibid.

14 N. Saro-Wiwa, *Looking for Transwonderland: Travels in Nigeria* (London: Granta, 2012).

15 Ibid., pp. 258–65.

16 Interview with the author, Abuja, May 2013.

17 Embassy of the Federal Republic of Nigeria, Washington, DC.

18 *Africa Confidential* (Cambridge, UK), 5 December 2014.

19 *Sunday Times* (London), 16 February 2014.

20 Jim O'Neill coined the acronym BRICS for Brazil, Russia, India, China and South Africa; MINT represents Mexico, Indonesia, Nigeria and Turkey; statistics from the National Bureau of Statistics, www.nigerianstat.gov.ng.

21 F. Fani-Kayode, a former Minister of Aviation, in *ThisDay* (Lagos), 18 March 2014; he argued that the tests were a shameless money-making scam as around 100,000 youngsters were having to pay N1,000 each for the test forms.

22 2014 estimates from the Central Intelligence Agency, *World Fact Book*, accessed 27 June 2015, https://www.cia.gov/library/publications/the-world-factbook.

23 The story was widely reported, for instance in Mark, 'High Price', *The Guardian* (London).

24 O. Obasanjo, 'In Nigeria, Agriculture is 'The New Oil'', *Forbes*, 14 May 2014.

25 *Africa Confidential* (Cambridge, UK), 21 November 2014, stated that President Jonathan's aim to see a total of 10,000 megawatts installed would bring Nigeria up to a fifth of South Africa's capacity.

26 Obasanjo, 'Agriculture'.

27 Western reporting of the 2015 presidential election variously described the population as numbering 170M or 180M, though the actual number of votes counted was only just over 28M.

28 M. Sule, interview with the author, Kano, 6 March 2014.

29 T. Tamuno, private communication to the author, Ibadan, 24 May 2013.

30 The Oputa Panel report was jointly published by the Civil Society Forum, Nigeria and the Nigerian Democratic Movement, Washington DC on 13 January 2005; the national convention report was made available by thewillnigeria.com.

31 *Le Monde* (Paris), 27 March 2015, forecast that India would have 1.7M and China 1.2M at the same date.

32 Hunt, a brilliant diplomat, had been private secretary to both Churchill and Attlee; in retirement he won *Mastermind* on British television; his successor as chair of governors at the Institute, Sir John Williams, had also been at the Lagos High Commission and remarked that he only won the respect of Yoruba negotiators when he learnt to argue as fiercely as they did.

AFTERWORD

1 States with long-running ruling parties include Tanzania, Zimbabwe, Mozambique, South Africa and Namibia.

2 Buhari spoke to a crowded hall on 26 February 2015.

3 'How Jonathan Plotted to Rig Polls', investigation by Sahara Reporters, 17 April 2015, www.saharaReporters.com.

Bibliography

UNPUBLISHED SOURCES

Akinterinwa, Bola. Interview with the author. Lagos, May 2013.

Anyaoku, Emeka. Interview with the author. Lagos, 14–15 March 2014.

Azuta-Mbata, John. Interview with the author. Port Harcourt, 12 March 2014.

Balewa, Mukhtar. Interview with the author. Abuja, May 2013.

Dambazau, Idris Bello. Interview with the author. Kano, 8 March 2014.

Diete-Spiff, Alfred. Interview with the author. Port Harcourt, 10 March 2014.

Gowon, Yakubu. Interview with the author. Abuja, 5 March 2014.

Grey, Ralph. Notes. January 1956. FCO 141/13462, National Archives, Kew.

Heath, H.B. 'The Arakan Campaign, December 1944 to May 1945'. Ed. R.H.M. Hill. Undated memoir. Imperial War Museum, London.

Interview with Brigadier G.H. Cree. 8245/03/01–02, Imperial War Museum, London.

Macpherson, John to Colonial Secretary. Report. 31 May 1953. FCO 141/13462. National Archives, Kew.

Nwondu, Judith. Interview with the author. Port Harcourt, 12 March 2014.

Odoemene, Emmanuel. 'Development without Borders: Engagement of a Catholic Faith-based Organization for the Common Good in the Post-Military Period'. PhD thesis. University of London, 2014.

Osaghae, Eghosa. Interview with the author. 24 March 2014.

——'A State of Our Own: Second Independence, Federalism and the Decolonisation of the State in Africa'. Inaugural Anyaoku lecture. Institute of Commonwealth Studies, University of London, 9 April 2014.

Papers of Dame Margery Freda Perham, [1844]–1980. MSS. Perham. Rhodes House, Oxford.

Pleass, Clem. Notes. January 1956. FCO 141/13462, National Archives, Kew.

Slawson, Paul. Interview with the author. Nutbourne (Sussex, UK), 26 May 2014.

Soyinka, Kayode. Interview with the author. Abuja, 16 March 2014.

Soyinka, Wole. Interview with the author. London, 7 May 2014.

Srinivasan, Krishan. Interview with the author. London, summer 2013.

Sule, Maitama. Interview with the author. Kano, 6 March 2014.

Uhomoibhi, Martin. 'History of Nigeria's Foreign Policy: Continuity and Change'. February 2012.

——Interview with the author. Abuja, 30 May 2013.

Whiteman, Kaye. Interview with the author. 24 March 2014.

PUBLISHED SOURCES

Aborisade, Oladimeji and Robert J. Mundt. *Politics in Nigeria*. New York: Longman, 1998.

Abubakar, Sa'ad. 'The Northern Provinces under Colonial Rule: 1900–1959'. In *Groundwork of Nigerian History*, ed. Obaro Ikime. 447–481. Ibadan: HEBN Publishers, 1980.

Achebe, Chinua. *There Was A Country*. New York: Penguin Press, 2012.

——*The Trouble with Nigeria*. London: Heinemann, 1983.

——*Things Fall Apart*. London: Heinemann, 1958.

Adejumobi, Said, and Abubakar Momoh. *The Political Economy of Nigeria under Military Rule (1984–1993)*. Harare: SAPES Books, 1995.

African Commission Directorate of Information and Communication. 'AUC Delegation to Attend the 69th UN General Assembly'. Press release. 20 September 2014. http://www.au.int/fr/sites/default/files/Press%20 Release%20-En_77.pdf.

Ajayi, J.F. Ade. *Milestones in Nigerian History*. Ibadan and London: Ibadan University Press and Longman, 1982.

Ajayi, J.F. Ade, and Michael Crowder, eds. *History of West Africa*. 2 vols. 2nd edn. London: Longman, 1976.

Akinterinwa, Bola. *Nigeria and the Challenge of Nation-Building*. Lagos: Nigerian Institute of International Affairs, 2013.

Alagoa, E.J. ed. *Conflict Management and Resolution in Nigeria: The Niger Delta Perspective*. Port Harcourt: Pearl Publishers, 2010.

Alden, Chris. *China in Africa.* London: Zed Books, 2007.

Anene, Joseph C. *The International Boundaries of Nigeria 1885–1960: The Framework of an Emergent African Nation.* New York: Humanities Press, 1970.

Arnold, Guy. *Africa: A Modern History.* London: Atlantic Books, 2005.

Ashiwaju, Garba, and Olusegun Areola. *Nigeria: The First 25 Years.* Ibadan: Ibadan University Press, 1975.

Awolowo, Obafemi. *Path to Nigerian Freedom.* London: Faber and Faber, 1947.

——*Awo: Autobiography of Chief Obafemi Awolowo.* Cambridge: Cambridge University Press, 1960.

——*Adventures in Power: My March through Prison, Book 1.* Ibadan: Macmillan Nigerian Publishers, 1985.

Azikiwe, Nnamdi. *Political Blueprint of Nigeria.* Lagos: African Book Co., 1943.

——*Nigeria in World Politics.* London: Office of the Commissioner for the Eastern Region of Nigeria in the United Kingdom, 1959.

——*Zik: A Selection from the Speeches of Nnamdi Azikiwe.* Cambridge: Cambridge University Press, 1961.

——*My Odyssey: An Autobiography.* London: Christopher Hurst, 1970.

——*Ideology for Nigeria: Capitalism, Socialism, or Welfarism?* Yaba, Lagos: Macmillan Nigeria, 1980 (© 1979).

Beckett, Paul, and Crawford Young, eds. *Dilemmas of Democracy in Nigeria.* Rochester, NY: University of Rochester Press, 1997.

Bello, Ahmadu. *My Life.* Cambridge: Cambridge University Press, 1962.

Bergmen, Lowell. 'Corruption Case Exposes Scope of Bribery in Nigeria'. *PBS Newshour.* Broadcast on PBS, 24 April 2009. www.pbs.org/newshour/bb/africa-jan-june-09-nigeria_04-24/.

Bevan, David, Paul Collier and Jan Willem Gunning. *Nigeria: Policy Responses to Shocks, 1970–1990.* San Francisco: International Center for Economic Growth, 1992.

Bloom, Bridget. *West Africa* (24 January 1970).

Bourne, Richard. *Catastrophe: What Went Wrong in Zimbabwe?* London: Zed Books, 2011.

Boyd, William. *An Ice-Cream War.* London: Hamish Hamilton, 1982.

Burns, Alan. *History of Nigeria.* London: Allen and Unwin, 1972.

Campbell, John. *Nigeria: Dancing on the Brink.* Lanham, MD: Rowman & Littlefield Publishers, 2011.

Central Intelligence Agency. *World Fact Book.* Accessed 27 June 2015. https:// www.cia.gov/library/publications/the-world-factbook.

Civil Society Forum, Nigeria and Nigerian Democratic Movement, Washington DC. Truth Commission: Human Rights Violations Investigation Commission [Oputa Panel Report]. 13 January 2005. www.segundawodu.com.

Clark, Trevor. *A Right Honourable Gentleman: Abubakar from the Black Rock, A Narrative Chronicle of the Life and Times of Nigeria's Alhaji Sir Abubakar Tafawa Balewa.* London: Edward Arnold, 1991.

Coleman, James Smoot. *Nigeria: Background to Nationalism.* Berkeley, CA: University of California Press, 1958.

Colonial Office: Nigeria. *Reports of the Commission Appointed to Inquire into the Fears of Minorities and the Means of Allaying Them.* London: HMSO, 1958.

Comolli, Virginia. *Boko Haram: Nigeria's Islamist Insurgency.* London: Hurst & Company, 2015.

Commonwealth Secretariat. *The National Assembly and Presidential Elections in Nigeria, 12 and 19 April, 2003.* London: Commonwealth Secretariat, 2006.

——*Report of the Commonwealth Observer Group: Nigeria State and Federal Elections, 14 and 21 April 2007.* London: Commonwealth Secretariat, 2007.

Crowder, Michael. *The Story of Nigeria.* London: Faber and Faber, 1966.

Cunliffe-Jones, Peter. *My Nigeria: Five Decades of Independence.* New York: Palgrave Macmillan, 2010.

Dabai, Mohammed S. 'Why There's Nothing Wrong with Honouring Abacha'. *Weekly Trust,* 8 March 2014: 38.

Dawodu, Ganiyu Olawale. *Awo or Zik: Who Won the 1951 Western Nigerian Elections?* Ibadan: Aika Books, 1998.

Diamond, Larry Jay, A.H.M. Kirk-Greene, and Oyeleye Oyediran. *Transition without End: Nigerian Politics and Civil Society under Babangida.* Boulder, CO: Lynne Rienner Publishers, 1997.

Dike, K. Onwuka. *Trade and Politics in the Niger Delta 1830–1885: An Introduction to the Economic and Political History of Nigeria.* Oxford: Clarendon Press, 1956.

Dike, Victor E. *Nigeria and the Politics of Unreason: A Study of the Obasanjo Regime.* London: Adonis & Abbey, 2003.

Ekeh, Peter Palmer, and Eghosa E. Osaghae, eds. *Federal Character and Federalism in Nigeria.* Ibadan: Heinemann Educational Books (Nigeria), 1989.

Elaigwu, J. Isawa. *The Politics of Federalism in Nigeria*. London: Adonis & Abbey, 2007.

Embassy of the Federal Republic of Nigeria, Washington, DC. *United States Diplomatic Mission to Nigeria*. http://nigeria.usembassy.gov.

Falola, Toyin, and A.G. Adebayo. 'The Context: The Political Economy of Colonial Nigeria'. In *Obafemi Awolowo: The End of an Era?*, ed. Toyan Falola *et al.*, AIle-Ife: University of Ife Press, 1988.

Falola, Toyin, and Matthew M. Heaton. *A History of Nigeria*. Cambridge: Cambridge University Press, 2008.

Falola, Toyin, and Julius Omozuanvbo Ihonvbere. *The Rise and Fall of Nigeria's Second Republic, 1979–84*. London: Zed Books, 1985.

Fani-Kayode, Femi. *ThisDay*, 18 March 2014.

Faught, C. Brad. *Into Africa: The Imperial Life of Margery Perham*. London: I.B. Tauris, 2012.

Forrest, Tom. *Politics and Economic Development in Nigeria*. Boulder, CO: Westview Press, 1993.

Forsyth, F. *The Making of an African Legend: The Story of Biafra*. London: Penguin, 1969.

Gavin, R.J., and Wale Oyemakinde, 'Economic Development in Nigeria since 1800'. In *Groundwork of Nigerian History*, ed. Obaro Ikime, 482–517. Ibadan: HEBN Publishers, 1980.

Gott, Richard. *Britain's Empire: Resistance, Repression and Revolt*. London: Verso Books, 2011.

Gould, Michael. *The Biafran War: The Struggle for Modern Nigeria*. London: I.B. Tauris, 2012.

Gowon, Yakubu. *Faith in Unity*. Lagos: Federal Ministry of Information, 1970.

Graf, William D. *The Nigerian State: Political Economy, State Class, and Political System in the Post-Colonial Era*. London: James Currey, 1988.

Hatchard, John. *Combating Corruption: Legal Approaches to Supporting Good Governance and Integrity in Africa*. Cheltenham: Edward Elgar, 2014.

Hill, J.N.C. *Nigeria since Independence: Forever Fragile?* Houndsmills, Basingstoke: Palgrave Macmillan, 2012.

Hodgkin, Thomas ed. *Nigerian Perspectives: An Historical Anthology*. London: Oxford University Press, 1960.

Ifidon, Ehimika A. 'A Review of Studies of Disamalgamation in Nigeria'. In *The Amalgamation and Its Enemies: An Interpretive History of Modern Nigeria*, ed. Richard Olaniyan, 23–45. Ile-Ife: Obafemi Awolowo University Press, 2003.

Ihonvbere, Julius Omozuanvbo. *Nigeria: The Politics of Adjustment and Democracy*. New Brunswick, NJ: Transaction Books, 1994.

Ihonvbere, Julius Omozuanvbo, and Timothy M. Shaw. *Towards a Political Economy of Nigeria: Petroleum and Politics at the (Semi-)Periphery*. Aldershot: Avebury, 1999.

Ikeazor, Chukwudum. *Nigeria 1966: The Turning Point*. London: New Millenium, 1997.

Ikime, Obaro. *The Fall of Nigeria: The British Conquest*. London: Heinemann, 1977.

——, ed. *Groundwork of Nigerian History*. Ibadan: HEBN Publishers, 1980.

Iliffe, John. *Obasanjo, Nigeria and the World*. Woodbridge: Boydell & Brewer, 2011.

International Crisis Group, 'Curbing Violence in Nigeria (II): The Boko Haram Insurgency'. *AfricaReport* 216, 3 April 2014. http://www.crisisgroup.org/en/regions/africa/west-africa/nigeria/216-curbing-violence-in-nigeria-ii-the-boko-haram-insurgency.aspx.

Irukwu, J.O. *Nigeria at the Crossroads: A Nation in Transition*. London: Witherby, 1983.

——*Nigeria: The Last Chance*. Ibadan: Spectrum Books, 2005.

Isichei, Elizabeth Allo. *A History of Nigeria*. London: Longman, 1983.

Iyayi, Festus. *Heroes*. Harlow: Longman, 1986.

Johnson, Phyllis. *Eye of Fire: A Biography of Chief Emeka Anyaoku, Commonwealth Secretary-General*. Trenton, NJ, and Africa World Press and Turnaround, 2000.

Johnson-Odim, Cheryl and Nina Emma Mba. *For Women and the Nation: Funmilayo Ransome-Kuti of Nigeria*. Urbana, IL: University of Illinois Press, 1997.

Kerslake, R.T. *Time and the Hour: Nigeria, East Africa and the Second World War*. London: Radcliffe Press, 1997.

Killingray, David. 'Labour Mobilisation in British Colonial Africa for the War Effort, 1939–46'. In *Africa and the Second World War*, ed. David Killingray and Richard Rathbone, 68–96. London: Macmillan, 1986.

Killingray, David, and Martin Plaut. *Fighting for Britain: African Soldiers in the Second World War*. Woodbridge: James Currey, 2010.

Killingray, David, and Richard Rathbone, eds. *Africa and the Second World War*. London: Macmillan, 1986.

Kirk-Greene, A.H.M. *Lugard and the Amalgamation of Nigeria: A Documentary Record; Being a Reprint of the Report by Sir F.D. Lugard on the Amalgamation of Northern and Southern Nigeria and Administration 1912–1919; Together with Supplementary Unpublished Amalgamation Reports, and Other Relevant Documents*. London: Frank Cass, 1968.

——*Crisis and Conflict in Nigeria: A Documentary Sourcebook, 1966–1970*. Oxford: Oxford University Press, 1971.

Kirk-Greene, A.H.M., and Douglas Rimmer. *Nigeria since 1970: A Political and Economic Outline*. New York: Africana Pub. Co., 1981.

Luckham, Robin. *The Nigerian Military: A Sociological Analysis of Authority and Revolt 1960–67*. Cambridge: Cambridge University Press, 1971.

Lugard, Frederick D. *The Dual Mandate in British Tropical Africa*. London: Frank Cass, 1965.

Mark, Monica. 'High Price Paid to Stop Virus'. *The Guardian* (London), 9 October 2014.

McKinnon, Don. *In the Ring: A Commonwealth Memoir*. London: Elliot & Thompson, 2013.

Mills, Greg. *Why Africa Is Poor, and What Africans Can Do About It*. Johannesburg: Penguin Books (South Africa), 2010.

Mockler, Anthony. *Haile Selassie's War*. Oxford: Oxford University Press 1984.

Muffett, D.J.M. *Empire Builder Extraordinary, Sir George Goldie: His Philosophy of Government and Empire*. Douglas, Isle of Man: Shearwater Press, 1978.

National Bureau of Statistics. http://www.nigerianstat.gov.ng.

Nwabueze, B.O. *A Constitutional History of Nigeria*. London: C. Hurst, 1982.

Nwankwo, Arthur Agwuncha. *Nigeria: The Challenge of Biafra*. London: Rex Collings, 1972.

Nwankwo, Arthur Agwuncha, and Samuel Udochukwu Ifejika. *Biafra: The Making of a Nation*. New York: Praeger Publishers, 1970.

Nwankwo, O.B.C. *The Making of a Nation: Landmarks in Nigeria's Constitutional Development*. London: Veritas Lumen, 2006.

Obasanjo, Olusegun. *My Command: An Account of the Nigerian Civil War, 1967–1970*. London: Heinemann, 1981.

——*Nzeogwu: An Intimate Portrait of Major Chukwuma Kaduna Nzeogwu*. Ibadan: Spectrum Books, 1987.

——*Africa Embattled: Selected Essays on Contemporary African Development*. Agodi, Ibadan: Fountain Publications, 1988.

——*My Watch*. Lagos: Prestige, 2014.

——'In Nigeria, Agriculture is 'The New Oil''. *Forbes*, 14 May 2014.

Obiaga, Ndubisi. *Nigeria: The Instability of Military Governance, 1983–1998*. Bloomington, IN: AuthorHouse, 2006.

Offoara, Godson. *Zik: The LastCampaigns*. Ibadan: Spectrum Books, 1994.

Oheagbulam, Festus Ugboaja. *Nigeria and the UN Mission to the Democratic Republic of Congo: A Case Study of the Formative Stages of Nigeria's Foreign Policy*. Tampa, FL: University Presses of Florida, 1982.

Ojukwu, Chukwuemeka Odumegwu. *Biafra: Selected Speeches and Random Thoughts of C. Odumegwu Ojukwu*. New York: Harper & Row, 1969.

Okonjo-Iweala, Ngozi. *Reforming the Unreformable: Lessons from Nigeria*. Cambridge, MA: MIT Press, 2012.

Olaniyan, Richard. *Nigerian History and Culture*. Harlow: Longman, 1984.

——, ed. *The Amalgamation and its Enemies: An Interpretive History of Modern Nigeria*. Ile-Ife: Obafemi Awolowo University Press, 2003.

Olaniyan, Richard, and Akin Alo. 'The Amalgamation, Colonial Politics and Nationalism, 1914–1960'. In *The Amalgamation and Its Enemies: An Interpretive History of Modern Nigeria*, ed. Richard Olaniyan, 1–22. Ile-Ife: Obafemi Awolowo University Press, 2003.

Oliver, Brian. *The Commonwealth Games: Extraordinary Stories behind the Medals*. London: Bloomsbury, 2014.

Olorunyomi, Sola. *Afrobeat! Fela and the Imagined Continent*. Trenton, NJ: Africa World Press, 2005.

Olusanya, G.O. *The Second World War and Politics in Nigeria, 1939–1945*. Ibadan: University of Lagos and Evans Brothers, 1973.

——'Constitutional Developments in Nigeria 1861–1960'. In *Groundwork of Nigerian History*, ed. Obaro Ikime, 518–45. Ibadan: HEBN Publishers, 1980.

——'The Nationalist Movement in Nigeria'. In *Groundwork of Nigerian History*, ed. Obaro Ikime, 545–569. Ibadan: HEBN Publishers, 1980.

Osaghae, Eghosa E. *Crippled Giant: Nigeria since Independence*. London: C. Hurst & Co., 1998.

Osaghae, Eghosa E., Ebere Onwudiwe and Rotmi T. Suberu, eds. *The Nigerian Civil War and Its Aftermath*. Lagos: John Archers, 2002.

Osuntokun, Akinjide. *Nigeria in the First World War*. Atlantic Highlands, NJ: Humanities Press, 1979.

Oyediran, Oyeleye. *Nigerian Government and Politics under Military Rule, 1966– 79*. New York: St. Martin's Press, 1979.

Paden, John N. *Ahmadu Bello, Sardauna of Sokoto: Values and Leadership in Nigeria*. London: Hodder & Stoughton, 1986.

——*Faith and Politics in Nigeria: Nigeria as a Pivotal State in the Muslim World*. Washington, DC: United States Institute of Peace Press, 2008.

Pakenham, Thomas. *The Scramble for Africa, 1876–1912*. London: Abacus, 1991.

Panter-Brick, S.K. ed. *Nigerian Politics and Military Rule: Prelude to the Civil War*. London: Athlone Press, 1970.

Perham, Margery Freda. *Lugard: The Years of Adventure, 1858–1898*. London: Collins, 1956.

——*Lugard: The Years of Authority, 1898–1945*. London: Collins, 1960.

——*West African Passage: A Journey through Nigeria, Chad, and the Cameroons, 1931–1932*. Edited by A.H.M. Kirk-Greene. London: Peter Owen, 1983.

Phillips, Barnaby. Broadcast on al-Jazeera, 2 November 2011.

Porteous, Tom. *Britain in Africa*. London: Zed Books, 2008.

Robertson, James W. *Transition in Africa from Direct Rule to Independence: A Memoir*. London: C. Hurst, 1974.

The Round Table: The Commonwealth Journal of International Affairs 392 (Special Issue: Nigeria – A Commonwealth Paradox?) (October 2007).

Saint-Jorre, John de. *The Nigerian Civil War*. London: Hodder & Stoughton, 1972.

Saro-Wiwa, Ken. *On Darkling Plain: An Account of the Nigerian Civil War*. Port Harcourt: Saros International Publishers, 1989.

Saro-Wiwa, Noo. *Looking for Transwonderland: Travels in Nigeria*. London: Granta Books, 2012.

Schwarz, Walter. *Nigeria*. London: Pall Mall Press, 1968.

Sogolo, Godwin. *Nigeria Yesterday Today: An Anthology of Social Commentaries*. Ibadan: Safari Books, 2012.

Soyinka, Kayode. 'Obituary of Sir Adetokunbo Ademola'. *The Independent* (London), 12 February 1993.

———*Diplomatic Baggage – MOSSAD and Nigeria, the Dikko Story*. Lagos: Newswatch Books, 1994.

Soyinka, Wole. *A Dance of the Forests*. Oxford: Oxford University Press, 1963.

———*The Man Died: Prison Notes of Wole Soyinka*. London: Rex Collings, 1972.

———*Aké: The Years of Childhood*. (London: Rex Collings 1981).

———*The Open Sore of a Continent: A Personal Narrative of the Nigerian Crisis*. Oxford: Oxford University Press, 1996.

Suberu, Rotimi T. *Federalism and Ethnic Conflict in Nigeria*. Washington, DC: United States Institute of Peace Press, 2007.

Tamuno, Tekena N. *Herbert Macaulay: Nigerian Patriot*. London: Heinemann Educational, 1975.

———*Evolution of the Nigerian State: The Southern Phase, 1989–1914*. 2nd edn. London: Longman, 1977.

———'British Colonial Administration in the Twentieth Century'. In *Groundwork of Nigerian History*, ed. Obaro Ikime, 393–410. Ibadan: HEBN Publishers, 1980.

———*Peace and Violence in Nigeria: Conflict-Resolution in Society and the State*. Ibadan: The Panel on Nigeria since Independence History Project, 1991.

Teriba, O. 'Development Strategy, Investment Decision and Expenditure Patterns of a Public Development Institution: The Case of the Western Nigerian Development Corporation, 1949–1962'. *Nigerian Journal of Economic and Social Studies* 8/2 (1966): 253–58.

Uhomoibhi, Martin and Ehiedu Iweriebor, eds. *Effective and Affirmative Representation of Nigeria*. Ibadan: Bookbuilders, 2013.

Uwechue, Ralph. *Reflections on the Nigerian Civil War: Facing the Future*. Paris: Jeune Afrique, 1971. New, revised and expanded edition. Abuja: Africa Books Nigeria, 2004.

Veal, Michael E. *Fela: The Life and Times of an African Musical Icon*. Philadelphia: Temple University Press, 2000.

Whiteman, Kaye. *Lagos: A Cultural and Historical Companion*. Oxford: Signal Books, 2012.

Wilson, Harold. *The Labour Government, 1964–70: A Personal Record*. Harmondsworth: Penguin Books, 1974.

Woodburn Kirby, Stanley. *History of the Second World War: The War against Japan*. 5 vols. London: HMSO, 1961.

Index